MAKING A DIFFE.

The Honourable Ruth Richardson was New Zealand's first Minister of Finance in a generation to balance the books and give New Zealand the highest growth rate in the OECD.

Her Fiscal Responsibility Act, passed just before she left Parliament in mid-1994, is landmark legislation that has successfully cemented in fiscally responsible government behaviour.

Since her departure during her fifth term in Parliament, Ruth Richardson has established a private business offering strategic and economic policy advice. She travels the world meeting the extensive demand from other countries to duplicate, adapt or adopt the New Zealand model of economic and public-sector reform.

In New Zealand Ruth Richardson sits on the boards of a number of publicly listed and private companies and undertakes regular speaking engagements. Many of her presentations are to visiting government and public-sector delegations, as well as to private investors, all of whom are attracted by the New Zealand reform model and want to understand and experience its benefits first hand.

MAKING A DIFFERENCE

Ruth Richardson

SHOAL BAY PRESS

DEDICATION

To my parents, who thought mine a thankless task;
to my husband, Andrew, whom I cannot thank enough;
and to my children, who I hope will want to thank me
for helping secure their future.

First published in 1995 by
Shoal Bay Press Ltd
Box 2151, Christchurch

Cover cartoon: Tom Scott

Cartoons by Peter Bromhead, Bill Paynter and Tom Scott
are reproduced by kind permission of the cartoonists.

ISBN 0 908704 31 3

Production and design by Orca Publishing Services Ltd
Printed by GP Print Ltd
Distributed by Macmillan New Zealand Ltd, 6 Ride Way,
Albany Industrial Estate, Auckland, Fax (09) 4156 659

CONTENTS

ACKNOWLEDGMENTS

I had always vowed that I would never write a book. An activist by nature, I am much more inclined to reach for the 'fast-forward' button than I am to press the 'pause', let alone the 'rewind' button. Yet as I left Parliament in mid-1994 I felt we needed to recapture the spirit of past reform endeavours. A fresh willingness to work for new successes to match the old, it would seem, needs plenty of encouragement. And so my effort to document the recent past is intended as a spur for future action.

I could not have undertaken my past endeavours, let alone documented them, without the help of lots of people. Many feature in my book and I hope I do them justice.

First and foremost, I want to thank my husband Andrew. Without his love and understanding I could not have managed the twin demands of politics and parenthood and survived so cheerfully to tell the tale.

My publisher, David Elworthy, who has been down the road of political memoirs before, has pulled the book together in an able and amenable way. His most singular (and he would say most sensible) contribution has been to veto my working title, *The Mother of All Books*.

As ever, Anna Symmans has acted as an invaluable sounding board, moderating both the tone and the content of this book.

But there is one person to whom I owe special thanks. Throughout the critical years in Opposition and the gritty years in government he advised me, researched and drafted for me, denied himself his own time for me – all in the cause of a better New Zealand for us all. Martin Hames was that selfless soul through all those years and he has been the ideal person to help me navigate my way through this book.

Not known for my emotion in public life, I would like to finish by acknowledging a poetic influence at the private level. The *Complete Poems and Plays* of T.S. Eliot has journeyed with me throughout my political life – an election gift from my dear friend Hazel Bull in 1981. My favourite is 'The Love Song of J. Alfred Prufrock'. Lines from that poem best capture my political emotions.

My hope:

And indeed there will be time
To wonder 'Do I dare?' and 'Do I dare?' ...
'Do I dare
Disturb the universe?'

And my frustration:

And time yet for a hundred indecisions,
And for a hundred visions and revisions,
Before the taking of a toast and tea.

INTRODUCTION

There are two kinds of politician. Most politicians spend their careers largely reacting to various forces in the body politic. Their guideposts are public opinion, pressure groups and conventional wisdom. I was never that kind of politician, and never wanted to be. From the beginning I was driven by a desire to change the political landscape. Politicians like me may be right or wrong, successful or unsuccessful, but we see ourselves as agents of change. We are not content to be passive. We are unhappy with public policy as it stands, and want to improve it. We challenge conventional wisdom, take on pressure groups, advocate often unpopular policies. We do this in the belief that it is the politician's role to lead public opinion. We are confident to leave the verdict on our actions to history. Our political lives are often short, but they do not go unremembered. For good or ill, we make a difference.

This is a story about my own political career – my own attempt to make a difference. An activist by instinct, I knew when I entered politics that activism would be badly needed in the years ahead. Yet I did not know whether I would have the chance to turn my instincts into reality. I desperately wanted to put the principles I held so dearly into practice. Luck was on my side. Eventually the country was ready, and then the National Party was ready, for an agenda of economic reform.

History is often fickle. There can be long periods of little change, despite the building of subterranean forces that will eventually rock the foundations of existing structures. There can then be a short period of rapid action, where fortune favours the brave and the agents of change are given their chance. Our own time has seen such a period. Shakespeare wrote that there is a tide in the affairs of men which, taken at the flood, leads on to fortune. In my own political career I was lucky enough to catch that tide and play a major role in transforming New Zealand. That transformation has been truly remarkable. The market reforms changed New Zealand utterly, and for the better. They have captured the imagination of the world.

Yet success can breed stagnation; praise and flattery from foreigners can breed complacency. This is now happening in New Zealand, just as it happened earlier in the century. There is a lack of vision from the government today, a tendency simply to live off the dividends of the policy reforms of the past. There is an unwillingness to confront problems and devise real solutions. There is no longer a hunger to lead the world as we once did in economic policy reform. This is a great shame. New Zealand still faces many challenges. We have a poor and dependent underclass that shows little sign of being taken up into the economic recovery. We have a grossly under-performing education sector and a steeply rising crime rate. Even in the private sector there are areas where the reform programme has not yet reached.

David Lange's celebrated 'cup of tea' – let's take a break from reform – ended up hurting the people he most wished to help. In the late 1980s it was the poor who suffered because it was the poor who most felt the impact of continued economic recession. So it is today. The people most hurt by today's tea break are the poor and the marginalised. It may be politically tempting to call a halt to further major change, but to do so is to fail New Zealanders. There are too many problems remaining.

This book looks at those problems and suggests some solutions. Fundamental reform was needed in economic policy; equally fundamental reform is needed in social policy. Our economic reforms showed New Zealanders to be far more inventive, far more resourceful and far more resilient than they had often been given credit for. Our guiding principles in those reforms were the freedom and responsibility of the individual. The same principles should guide our social policy. There, too, New Zealanders could demonstrate new purpose and new confidence if only we gave them their head. We need to release New Zealanders from the cycle of dependency in which far too many are trapped. We need to rethink the welfare state, transform the education sector and ensure that all who want to participate in the workforce have the chance to do so. A failure of nerve afflicts government policy – a paralysis both of the intellect and the spirit. We can do much better. This book plots such a path.

1

FORTRESS NEW ZEALAND

To my children's generation, the pre-1984 economy will seem a museum piece of considerable curiosity. Yet its essential elements lasted for around 40 years, and seemed to have every chance of lasting a good deal longer. To most New Zealanders living in the postwar world, the structure of the economy, and the rules under which it operated, provided their only frame of reference. They saw nothing inherently absurd in having to play a game with the bureaucrats in Wellington if they wanted to bring goods into the country, or go on an overseas trip; or in the ritual confrontation between employers and unions each year. That was how the system was. We may have had the most insulated and regulated economy in the developed world, we may have had an economy approaching that state where 'everything that is not forbidden is compulsory', but to most New Zealanders it was the only regime they knew.

Looking back, it seems remarkable the system survived for so long. Perhaps it would not have done had the 1950s and early 60s not been a time of such rising prosperity. The years immediately after the war saw rapid economic growth around the world. Britain, our main export market, was sharing in the economic boom and so – by extension – was New Zealand. These were good years for the living standards of New Zealanders.

Yet by the mid-1960s there were plenty of warning signs over the performance of the New Zealand economy. In assessing economic performance, one of the key measures is labour productivity – output per person employed. Save for an increase in its terms of trade, a country can increase its wealth only by having more people working for longer hours, or by increasing labour productivity. Labour productivity is thus a crucial concept: trends in productivity say a great deal about the underlying performance of an economy. By the 1960s the news for New Zealand was not good: growth in labour productivity since the war was well behind the rates achieved by most other countries. Not surprisingly, overall economic growth had also been slower than in other countries, especially when growth was adjusted for increases in population. From being third in the world in terms of living standards in 1950, New Zealand had begun a long slide down the rankings.

For the small number of economists and commentators who bothered about such things, these were worrying trends. There was another comparison that was just as worrying: a study showed that growth in labour productivity was lower for the years 1946-64 than for the years 1926-39. In other words, productivity growth had been slower in the postwar period, with all its 'enlightened' economic policies, than in the period that had included the traumatic years of the Depression. Various explanations were given for the poor postwar productivity growth, yet few seriously questioned whether the economic policies of the day were as enlightened as widely believed, and might not lie at the heart of our flagging performance.

From our vantage point today the explanation is not so hard to find. The years just before and just after the war were a fateful period for economic policy. New Zealand turned inward, believing that the road to economic development lay in protecting domestic industry from international competition. Import licensing was introduced, along with exchange controls. New Zealand became the most heavily protected economy in the western world.

The new import barriers were perhaps the single biggest policy mistake made in New Zealand this century. Like all forms of protection, our trade barriers protected the inefficient. They gave domestic manufacturers a captive home market that could be serviced with a minimum of risk. At the same time, they loaded costs onto the back of anyone – be they farmer or manufacturer – who was attempting to export. There was no pressure for manufacturers to take steps to become internationally efficient; in fact there was every incentive for them not to do so. Not surprisingly, very few ever did become remotely competitive in an international context.

Competition is the spur to innovation. In a small country, where domestic competition may sometimes be limited, it is especially important that there be competition with foreign goods. By facing international competition, domestic industry is forced to innovate and become productive in order to survive. By contrast, the effect of New Zealand's protection policies on the general business culture was disastrous: mediocrity became the norm, risk-taking was considered not worth attempting. Nor was it only foreign competition New Zealanders seemed keen to avoid. A large range of domestic activities were restricted, licensed or in some way shielded from competition.

New Zealand manufacturing already faced some formidable handicaps. Our industrial relations system, largely designed in the late 19th century, was inefficient in the extreme. Every job in the workplace was covered by wages and conditions contained in a national award; these awards were centrally negotiated in an annual ritual between employer groups and unions. With the exception of Australia, no country in the world had an industrial relations system less flexible, less conducive to innovation, and less likely to see high-quality business decisions made at the workplace level.

In the environment of industry protection and a monolithic labour market, an unstated complicity between business and unions developed. To business it was simply not worth the effort or trouble trying to introduce more rational practices into their workplaces. They were protected from foreign competition; they could simply plug into the national award system and pass their costs on to the consumer. The government could always accommodate cost increases by creating inflation – as it increasingly did during the late 1950s and 1960s. The unions knew exactly the same thing – that their employers could buy a quiet life by putting up prices. It was the classic breeding-ground for New Zealand's poor productivity performance. Short-term and ad hoc business behaviour mirrored the policy environment that had fostered it.

A great complacency developed in New Zealand. In the 1960s, when our living standards were still improving rapidly, we were content to drift on, still in our insulated cocoon, slipping further behind the rest of the world. With hindsight we can see what we should have been doing: opening up the economy to international competition, tackling our restrictive practices, creating a society that rewarded skills and encouraged their acquisition. In the main we failed to do so. There was high resistance to any programme of strategic adjustment. We prided ourselves on the quality of our education system, and our universities offered one of the cheapest tertiary educations in the world. But most young people left school relatively early, with few going on to higher education. The reason is not hard to see. Because of the quirks of our industrial relations system, an unskilled job was often as remunerative as a professional job. With increasingly high income tax rates and the growing generosity of our social welfare system, many young people considered it simply not worthwhile to invest in skills.

The early 1970s would be the last time for two decades New Zealanders felt confident about their economic future. While the stormclouds gathered, we were putting in place important additions to our welfare state: an accident compensation scheme, a new sole-parent benefit, and an extremely generous state pension scheme paid universally at age 60 (national superannuation). National superannuation was especially scandalous: it was offered to the electorate in 1975 as an election sweetener by Prime Minister Robert Muldoon after the onset of the two events that buffeted the economy so severely in the mid-1970s: the first oil shock and Britain's entry into the European Economic Community. Muldoon talked the language of adjustment and painted National as the party of responsible economic management, but in reality he represented the electoral auction at its worst. Helped in no small measure by the promise on national superannuation, Muldoon took office in a landslide.

During the Muldoon era few New Zealanders recognised what was so fundamentally wrong with their economy. The misconceptions started with the Prime Minister himself: Muldoon either did not understand what needed to be done or shrank from doing it – perhaps a combination of both. His nine-year performance would have done honour to King Canute. Little attempt was made to liberalise the economy; instead, with constant pressure on government finances, borrowing was used to bridge the gap between expectation and reality. The man who had told New Zealanders they needed to tighten their belts ended up presiding over a huge build-up of debt.

Much of the economic debate during the Muldoon years skirted around the central issue. The balance of payments deficit was of frequent concern to politicians and commentators. It tended to be seen in isolation, however, and treated as a problem in itself rather than a symptom of underlying malaise. Muldoon was much criticised for not devaluing the (fixed) exchange rate. This criticism was perhaps valid as far as it went, yet it missed the most essential issue, which was how to improve the woeful productivity levels of New Zealand industry. Indeed, given the heavily 'cost-plus' nature of price setting at the time, it was far from clear that a devaluation would achieve even its modest objective of improving competitiveness by reducing real wages. During my time as legal adviser with Federated Farmers, which coincided with the early Muldoon years, I recall urging that devaluation not be seen as a panacea for the farming sector. Given the institutional structure of the economy, I believed devaluation would simply set off another wage-price spiral.

One of Muldoon's responses to the economic pressures was to deflate the domestic economy whenever inflation and the balance of payments looked like getting out of hand, a move that would always be reversed as recession deepened or the next election loomed. Another of his responses was to introduce incentives to exporters – tax incentives to manufacturers and direct cash handouts to farmers. At a National Party policy forum during which the introduction of supplementary minimum prices (SMPs) to farmers was being discussed, I vigorously opposed the idea on both philosophical and practical grounds. I was especially concerned that SMPs would start a habit among farmers that would be extremely painful to kick. So it proved. One thing was certain: bribing business people with their own money – be they farmers or manufacturers – was not going to bring about an improvement in New Zealand's underlying performance. Handouts to business put so much pressure on the internal deficit that their impact on the balance of payments may even have been negative.

There were other misconceived responses from the government. Diversification of New Zealand's export base – still heavily dependent on primary products and a limited range of markets – was one of the watchwords of the time. There can be no doubt New Zealand's export base was too limited and needed to become more diverse. Rather than using market forces to that end, however, the government often strove for diversification by a deliberate strategy of picking winners. Most notorious by far were the Think Big projects – an attempt to use the energy sector for a range of export- and import-competing projects, underwritten by the government, most of which turned out to be lemons.

I well remember Think Big, though not without a certain measure of embarrassment. At the 1981 general election I made my third attempt to enter Parliament. Think Big was then one of the centrepieces of National's campaign. The government's line was that it would create 410,000 new jobs – not bad in a country of just three million people! I cannot recall ever reciting this flagrant piece of flim-flammery on a platform, but we certainly did hand out material on Think Big to my electors. Few if any of the promised 'new jobs' from Think Big ever eventuated, but billions more dollars were added to our national debt.

2

THE PATH TO PARLIAMENT

For me 1981 was a make or break year. I had wanted to be an MP since my earliest years, but I had decided that my third attempt to enter Parliament would almost certainly be my last. Absorbing as politics was, trying to get elected was a hugely time-consuming process. It was especially so for a young woman intent upon breaking into the male-dominated world of parliamentary politics. Yet politics was in my blood. My great-grandfather, G.V. Pearce, had been an MP in the early years of the century. My grandmother and my father had both been political activists.

My upbringing on our Waitotara farm had been comfortable and secure, but I had showed an early tendency to independence of thought and action. My instinct was often to swim against the tide. At school, when they announced that I, among others, had been accredited University Entrance, I stood up and denounced accrediting as a capricious and flawed system. I said I was going to sit the exam. The others presumably thought I was mad. I duly sat the exam and was successful, though by a smaller margin than I had expected.

While political activism ran deep in my family's veins, two other family characteristics stood me in extremely good stead. Curiously for a conservative family, there were extremely high expectations of the women of the clan. Great-great-aunt Lucy Powdrell (after whom my daughter was named) reigned as the Australasian women's tennis champion, long skirts and all. My paternal grandmother faced life as a sole parent with two young boys, first widowed and then divorced. My father Ross, watching his mother struggling with accountants and lawyers in her determination to keep the family's farming affairs intact, was adamant that any daughter of his would be well equipped to conduct business and foot it in a man's world.

I have early recollections of accompanying my father to the lawyer's and accountant's offices to observe the exchanges in which he often seemed to have the upper hand. Then there were the sessions with bankers. Our family bank was like our politics – National. I recall my father's advice on the strategy for dealing with bankers: 'Always keep talking to your banker.' That wasn't hard. Our family are great talkers.

While my father would quickly eschew the label 'feminist', in practice that is what he is. My mother, Joan, is a very accomplished woman in her own right. To those who know her – and very many do since she is kindness and hospitality personified – she is a very strong woman. She is also blessed with considerable artistic flair. When I reflect on my rather inadequate efforts in that department I am forced to accept that artistic ability must have skipped a generation. The garden my mother has created at Waitotara is of legendary proportions. No problem was ever too big, and if it required a bulldozer to create the desired effect, then bulldozer there was. She must be responsible for my tendency to bulldoze (figuratively) in the face of seemingly intractable political and economic problems.

I have always admired my mother's extreme generosity of spirit and action. During my ministerial years, however, I was to find that she had her limits; that generosity of spirit did not extend to critics of my performance in finance. My mother found the political hostility and vicious personal attacks I often had to endure unwarranted and wounding.

My second fortunate family trait was a substantial appreciation of the value of education. The 'feminist' in my father concluded that because a woman had a harder row to hoe it was doubly important his daughter be well educated. I was actively encouraged to secure a tertiary qualification, as were my older and younger brothers. Younger brother Mark and I completed law degrees while my older farming brother Kim did the mandatory Massey University 'sentence' – or so it seemed to him at the time.

Events had conspired against my mother's education. One of 10 children, she drew the short straw when, at the age of 13, she left school to nurse her sick mother for four years until her death. It was years later before she was able to remedy her lack of secondary education, but she was determined that the unfinished business would be addressed.

Kim and I, despite being a year apart (to the day), operated very much in the manner of twins. Thanks to Kim's early efforts to ensure that his kid sister learned after school what he had been learning during the day, it took no time at all to be in his class. We 'graduated' from the primers together and proceeded through Waitotara Primary School at a similar pace. As we set off for our respective boarding schools in the third form, with the great grounding from Waitotara behind us, my mother knew that the time for her own education had come. She enrolled in the third form at Correspondence School. Early on she decided that shadowing her two older children was too hazardous a business, given the inevitable comparisons that would be made with School Certificate marks. So she went not one but two better than us. Not only did she complete the course in two years rather than three, but she rated a Certificate of Attainment, one step up from School Certificate.

My parents were an important influence on me in many ways. I inherited their strong-willed natures. My father used to tease me about my 'PH factor', where PH stood for pig-headedness. I was encouraged to believe that girls could do anything boys could do and I knew what I wanted to do. At the age of 15 I was asking Roy Jack, my local National MP, how I should prepare myself for a career in politics. He, a Victoria University graduate, suggested I acquire a law degree. His counsel was to go to Canterbury University rather than Victoria, not just because of the excellence of the law school, but because I would have my fill of Wellington in due course if I were successful in my ambition to become an MP. I duly spent the next four years at Canterbury getting a law degree as the first stage in my political apprenticeship.

Reaching for high goals seemed to be part of my make-up. The force that drove me into politics also made itself felt in my sporting endeavours, modest though my achievements were. The pinnacle of my sporting career was undoubtedly securing the highest award in lifesaving – the diploma. This demanding physical and mental exercise was undertaken by only two of us in 1969. I had just reached the qualifying age of 18 and passed the examination early in my second year at university.

My fellow successful lifesaver was to have a fateful hand in 'saving' my life. His name was Captain Pugh-Williams, and he was captain of one of the Lyttelton-Wellington inter-island ferries. My usual mode of travel from Canterbury to Waitotara for the university vacations was by air. This prompted a fair measure of teasing from my fellow North Island students, all of whom made the journey by sea. Suitably shamed, I decided to join their ranks and take the more time-consuming and arduous journey by sea and rail. Friends and I boarded the *Maori* at Lyttelton and off we set. Fatefully, we sailed into the most vicious storm since the *Wahine* disaster. For what seemed like an eternity we 'hove to' off Cape Campbell, heaving and crashing in the heavy seas.

In the depths of despair, and long after the contents had been emptied from my stomach, I remembered thinking how futile my lifesaving qualification seemed to be. Not so for the man on the bridge – none other than Captain Pugh-Williams! He was more than a match for the storm and 36 hours later we limped into port – not Wellington but Lyttelton. I promptly beat a fast path to Christchurch airport and caught the next flight home. I arrived at Waitotara full of praise for Captain Pugh-Williams, but ferry travel was off my agenda for the rest of my student days.

With my degree under my belt, I again asked Roy Jack what I should do. He suggested I gain some experience in the machinery of government.

I shifted to Wellington and began working in the law-reform section of the Department of Justice.

My first serious taste of political activism came in 1972, when Jack Marshall's National government introduced a bill to nationalise the wool clip. The bill would effectively have brought to the wool industry the highly collectivised arrangements already prevailing in the dairy industry. There was widespread opposition to the measure from the farming community and regional wool action committees were formed. I joined the committee in my region, helped prepare its written submission to the parliamentary select committee, and appeared in front of the select committee. My chairman, Donald McNab, had to display the ingenuity for which farmers were famed even to secure a select committee hearing slot, so great was the pressure of submissions. That we were even heard at all, let alone early on in the proceedings, was perhaps attributable to the committee clerk's appreciation of the side of McNab lamb he had enjoyed!

In the face of such protest from the farming community, the government backed down. The episode was an early demonstration to me that political activism can make a difference. It also demonstrated just how far the National Party was beginning to stray from its philosophical roots. I was always a market liberal in economics, and never wavered from advocating and practising private-enterprise principles. But it would be another 20 years before I could be sure the party could be similarly relied on.

I was very single-minded in those early years. During my degree days at Canterbury, law and politics were exclusive preoccupations. Though enjoyable, those years were socially abstemious – no drink, no boys. When I emerged with my law degree before I was 21, I was wholly career-driven; social life did not fit into the equation. Marriage was certainly not on the agenda, and marriage to another lawyer was the last thing I would have contemplated. How things would change!

The shift to Wellington in 1972, and the start of my job at the Justice Department, opened up a whole new world. Like every other law graduate I was forced to endure a year split between work (which I relished) and completing my university 'professionals' (which I did not). The real joy I derived from my professional year at Victoria University came with my captaincy of the mooting team (mock legal argument) that took me to Perth to participate in the Australasian law schools mooting competition. We made it all the way to the finals only to meet our match in my old alma mater, Canterbury University.

Three live wires stood out in the professionals class, all of whom were to make their mark on my life to varying degrees. These three flatted together and had lived their university years to the full. In contrast to my all-work-no-play existence they had experienced both in full measure. Peter Waugh was to become my stand-in legal replacement at Federated Farmers during my first campaign stint against Bill Rowling in 1978. Stephen Franks, with his wife Cathie Mackenzie, was to become my landlord and mentor for all my time in Parliament, except for my ministerial years when instead I occupied the house at the bottom of their garden. And Andrew Wright, who made his early mark as the best cook of date scones and treacle pudding I had encountered, was to become my husband.

Andrew joined the Justice Department the year after I did. Our boss, Patricia Webb, seemed to have a soft spot for spirited young men with long hair and Andrew was one of several who fitted the bill. For a year we sparred, each seemingly coming from a different philosophical position in politics. I was teased mercilessly by Andrew and other colleagues for my apparent innocence and sheltered existence. After one particularly ribald morning tea break I was forced to consult my dictionary to discover the meaning of the word 'wanker', which I had foolishly used without appreciating its real meaning.

Teasing melted into date scones. High tea at the flat led to frequent tramping trips and before long something more substantial and serious was afoot. By the end of 1974 Andrew and I had announced our decision to be married. Andrew knew what he was letting himself in for. Our momentous decision to marry had been preceded by a decision of some political moment. At the age of 23 I had announced that I would be challenging Roy Jack for the National candidacy of Rangitikei.

My challenge to Jack was not, however, as callously calculated as it might have seemed. By now it was 1974, and I was not the only one in the local party putting up a challenge. Jack had drifted a long way from the concerns of his electorate and was now so out of touch that he was seriously jeopardising National's support base. In the event he won re-selection, but died in office the following year. At the ensuing by-election Rangitikei was captured by Social Credit and would not return to National for another eight years.

On failing to win the Rangitikei selection, I decided I needed to gain a wider range of experience if I were to promote myself successfully to the conservative rural constituencies that were my most likely path to Parliament. Farmers did not in general relate well to bureaucrats. For this reason I left the Justice Department and became legal adviser to Federated Farmers. This position enabled me to combine my love of politics with my love of the land. Federated Farmers was also a time-honoured stepping stone for future National Party politicians. During these years, much of my energy as a political activist was going into feminist issues: family law reform, the Matrimonial Property Act and the Women's Electoral Lobby. However, I never saw women's issues in isolation. I saw them as part of a wider agenda of the empowerment of individuals.

My time at Federated Farmers saw fierce debates over the deregulation of the meat processing industry – one of the very few economic liberalisations undertaken by the Muldoon government. This episode saw both a generational and a philosophical conflict in government, as well as in the farming industry. As the law stood, the existing players in the meat industry held a right of veto over potential new entrants.

The momentum for change was greatly helped by two activists from Hawke's Bay, Graeme Lowe and John Foster, who wished to establish a meat-processing plant at Richmond. The established industry blocked their application by arguing there was no need for a new plant. The frustrated applicants issued a legal challenge – not because they expected to be successful, but because they saw it as the best means of showing that the law was an ass. This spurred the government into action: it introduced a bill to allow open entry to meat processing.

At this point all hell broke loose. Farmers were deeply divided, as was caucus. The market liberals in caucus saw the bill as a flag-bearer for their economic philosophy. They indicated to Federated Farmers that if our organisation lined up behind the bill, their hand in caucus would be considerably strengthened. In the end Federated Farmers did, but only after a tense debate in which I took a central role. The bill went through.

In 1978 I gained the National nomination for the seat of Tasman, then held by Labour leader Bill (later Sir Wallace) Rowling. Rowling had been run close by National back in 1975, admittedly in the context of a big nationwide swing against Labour. I gave myself a chance of winning Tasman. I took a year off work and spent it door-knocking throughout the electorate.

In the end Rowling retained his seat in reasonable comfort. He had a very strong local profile; I was a brash young activist from Wellington. He had a clever campaign slogan – 'Tasman is Rowling Country'. There was also a nationwide swing against National in the course of the election campaign. Muldoon's settlement with the Meatworkers' Union, just a few weeks short of the election, had gone down particularly badly in Tasman, which was an electorate with a large number of self-employed who did not appreciate public money being used to 'buy off' one of the country's most militant unions. I had not appreciated it myself.

In 1980 Colin McLauchlan announced he was stepping down from the National seat of Selwyn – a largely rural electorate just outside Christchurch. Selwyn was a blue-ribbon seat and a considerable prize for aspiring candidates. I put my name forward for the nomination and got the nod. To this day I am convinced it was the selection process and the calibre of my support team that made the difference.

Typically there are two or three 'meet the candidates' meetings in a National Party selection process. In Selwyn there were 10, spread over a two-week period. All were well attended and the candidates closely scrutinised. After the most gruelling of these in the Sheffield Hall I was doorstopped by a most impressive and articulate couple who made it clear that they were excited by my candidacy. In this way I came to meet and form a close friendship with Burton and Jenny Shipley.

I was hugely aided in my efforts by my support team. Pat Morrison, who had been the local president of Federated Farmers and who went on to become the chairman of the Wool Board, did a brave thing. He publicly backed me – the outsider, the 'carpetbagger' from Wellington. His standing clearly helped my chances. Myra Graham, an MP to her fingernails if the times had been enlightened enough to give her that opportunity, was an unstoppable force in my camp. She cooked, cajoled, pleaded and plotted for my cause.

Margaret and Arthur Baylis from Lincoln represented local community and business interests and their open support gave me an invaluable seal of approval. Chris Charles, a self-made man from Darfield, came to each and every one of the 10 meetings, pronounced himself satisfied, rolled up the sleeves of his red overalls and worked his heart out for that and every campaign we successfully ran in Selwyn. Frances and Donald Smith, she highly capable, he unassuming on the surface and dedicated totally to her cause and mine, both generous to a fault, demonstrated just what an asset good volunteers are in the business of politics.

As if that were not a formidable enough team, one that would win campaign after campaign for me, I had the ultimate good fortune to fall on my feet with the advent of Hazel Bull. Hazel was made to measure – a superb fit politically and personally. Savvy, warm, personable, a born organiser with a reputation for getting things done, Hazel was confident I would be selected and had her focus firmly on what lay ahead of me. She would prove to be my close friend, loyal and dedicated electorate agent for all of my parliamentary career, knowledgeable soul during pregnancies, shoulder to lean on during Lucy and Oliver's infancies, political sounding board and loyal and dedicated activist.

The race for selection soon turned into an endurance contest. In the environment of a political pressure-cooker, stamina and coping under pressure became most valuable attributes. By the night of the selection meeting it was clear to me that I had outlasted and out-organised my opponents. I won on the first ballot and entered Parliament the following year at the age of 30.

When I was 15 I had vowed to become an MP. It had taken me another 15 years to realise that ambition.

3

THE 'BEADY-EYED LITTLE LADY'

The morning after my win Prime Minister Robert Muldoon was thoroughly startled. It was not what he had wanted. But Colin McLauchlan, who had failed to attend the selection meeting, was his usual nonchalant self. Always one to go onto the front foot, I rang McLauchlan's office and arranged to see him. Whatever his true feelings about my selection, he was good-natured and gave me good advice. In jest he advised me to refuse to march around the ring at the local A&P shows sandwiched between the band and the prize hacks. Never a fit man and shy personally, he had found that quite an ordeal. I faithfully followed his advice at all the shows I attended in my capacity as local MP!

His second and more serious piece of advice was very sound. He warned me that if I was any good I would rise in the ranks to become a minister. When that day came I would be asked to assume responsibilities that would certainly compromise my time in the electorate and potentially compromise my standing. His advice was to build up the maximum amount of political capital I could during my time on the back bench as I would be forced to live off that capital once a minister. How right he was.

If Alliance leader Jim Anderton thinks the parliamentary debating chamber is brutalising, he should perhaps have tried a few weeks in the National caucus under Muldoon. To Muldoon I was the 'beady-eyed little lady' who at caucus meetings always sat down in the front row, straight opposite him, taking copious notes. He never quite knew how to take me. His other woman MP at that time was also to prove a handful. Marilyn Waring, despite being on the same wavelength as Muldoon on matters economic, was at obvious and very public odds with him on liberal and social issues. For my part, I was certainly not on the same wavelength on economic issues, and not swayed in the slightest by Muldoon's bullying tactics.

At our first caucus meeting after the 1981 election – won by National with a majority of just two seats – Muldoon asked all the new MPs in turn what they wanted to achieve in politics. When I told him my goal was to eliminate inflation Muldoon was very patronising, doubtless thinking me politically and economically naive in the extreme. Years later I thought of that moment when, as a new Minister of Finance, I was signing my first contract with the Governor of the Reserve Bank – a contract to eliminate inflation.

I entered Parliament a reformer by instinct, and an economic liberal. In my maiden speech in the House I made my philosophy clear. I also made it plain that the government faced difficult political choices and needed to be firm in the face of temptations to choose politically expedient policies:

> Our legacy of the past in New Zealand is the welfare state. We have created cradle-to-grave security, income transfer and pervasive regulation. By attempting to reduce the element of risk, we have unwittingly eliminated many of the incentives to create wealth. All western-style democracies will witness, during the closing stages of the 20th century, the continuous trade-offs and strains between freedom and fairness and wealth. As a nation we clearly have the resources – natural, financial, technical and intellectual – to solve our problems. It is imperative that we display political will to implement unpopular but ultimately correct policies.

In one of our earliest caucus meetings, Muldoon began referring to the Treasury's advice in its post-election briefing. 'Is that available?' I asked. 'Can I see it?' At first he just ignored me and kept on talking. When I repeated the question, however, he growled, 'Come up to my room afterwards.' So after caucus I followed Muldoon up to his room and was given the briefing. 'Can I take it away?' I asked. 'No,' he said firmly. So I read it in Muldoon's office.

Each year Muldoon invited caucus members and their spouses to a social function at his official residence, Vogel House. At the first of these that I attended, Bill Birch was assiduously doing the rounds of new members. During his conversation with my husband Andrew he explained, perhaps unwittingly but very succinctly, how he had managed to steamroll the Think Big projects through the government process. 'The way to deal with adverse Treasury reports,' he said, 'is simply to make the argument a political one at the Cabinet table rather than an economic one.' Poor Bill! Little did he know what an albatross he was fashioning for his neck in the Think Big projects. Ironically, it was Bill who in 1995 was responsible for repaying so much of the debt he happily ran up over a decade earlier on purely political grounds.

Senior ministers had a reason for indulging their bolshie young backbencher. With an effective majority of only one seat in the House, they knew they might have to rely on me for a close vote at any time. That time came soon enough with the Clyde Dam affair. The government had failed to obtain the required resource consents for the planned dam – a project that had not even been necessary for our energy requirements. Orchardists whose livelihoods were at stake took the government to court, and won. The government then introduced legislation to overturn the court decision.

I was extremely unhappy at the government's proposal. So was Simon Upton, another first-term MP. Simon and I were philosophical allies and had become good friends – even to being dubbed Hansel and Gretel by Muldoon. We both had law degrees and regarded the legislation as an attempt to overrule the due process of law. Much of my time at Federated Farmers had been spent representing litigants similar to the orchardists who had 'won' over the Clyde Dam. I would have been outraged if a successful case in law had been overturned by retrospective legislation. Simon and I commandeered the Beehive theatrette to hold a press conference, where we made our unhappiness plain.

When Muldoon raised the Clyde Dam in caucus, he played heavily on the number of jobs that would be created by its construction. 'Who's against 500 jobs?' he concluded, looking around the room. I told him that if he wanted my vote I would have to be given access to all information on the dam. 'Never been done,' he growled. I said it would have to start now.

And so it did. We did not lack information. In the end I decided not to buck the party line – a decision I regret to this day. Two factors made a crucial difference. My electorate committee, though highly sympathetic, did not believe it was an issue that warranted voting against the government. But there was another factor: the government was so contemptuous of the process of law that the dam was already being built, even as we discussed and argued the merits of the legislation. I visited the dam site and saw the concrete being poured. I was literally being bulldozed into a decision. So I voted for the legislation, along with Simon, and a hugely expensive white elephant was given retrospective legal sanction.

The Clyde Dam affair was to prove a watershed in more ways than one. The unsatisfactory side of politics was forcibly brought home to me. Compromise and second best were not what I sought or wanted in politics, yet, however unattractive I found it, that outcome would inevitably occur from time to time.

In the wake of the Clyde Dam affair, and after eight years of marriage, Andrew and I decided the time had come to have children. We were not going to place all our eggs in the one basket – politics. Within short order Lucy was conceived, and referred to throughout my pregnancy as Clyde. Appropriately, Simon and Hazel became Lucy's godparents.

My pregnancy had been smooth sailing, but Lucy's birth and early infancy produced some nasty surprises. We had timed her birth for April to coincide with a parliamentary recess so that she could be weaned before Parliament resumed. The government's one-seat working majority had severely constrained leave from the House, and we thought ourselves very clever in planning her arrival, free from parliamentary pressure. Little had we counted on Lucy having a mind of her own.

In late January and early February, with the aid of an understanding electorate organisation, I had planned to cram in some 15 branch AGMs before the birth. On 14 February 1983, at the end of the Hororata AGM, I stood debating the prospects of the agricultural sector with two amiable cockies. It was a hot Canterbury nor'west night, and had been a long day and a seemingly endless AGM. Suddenly there was water all over the floor around my feet. With ne'er a blush, a pan-faced farmer suggested that I had better be heading for the maternity home.

Fortunately my branch secretary was the husband of the local doctor and, as if all our lives depended upon it, Andrew sped us all to Christchurch. True to the classic tale, a traffic officer pulled us up for speeding, but with one look at me obligingly showed us the quickest short-cut to the home. Lucy was born a few hours later, five or six weeks premature. Like all new mothers I ran on adrenalin and emotion for the first few days and Andrew looked the most exhausted of us all. Little did we know that we needed to steel ourselves for the political and logistical nightmare that lay ahead.

Just as birth can be unpredictable, so too was the parliamentary timetable. Parliament was summoned back into session unexpectedly to cure a defect in the Transport Regulations. I heard of the recall on the radio and discounted its impact on me since Jonathan Hunt, the Chief Opposition Whip, himself a bachelor, had shown both kindness and understanding to me when I was pregnant by promising me a pair (i.e. pairing me with an absent Opposition MP on parliamentary votes) should that be necessary. But Jonathan had not counted on the cattiness of his female colleagues. Apparently I had failed the political correctness test in their eyes; failed to conform to some sisterhood code of which I knew not. Perhaps, too, political opportunism got the better of them, since they used my very public predicament to campaign for the wider availability of workplace childcare. My pair was withdrawn, much to Jonathan's abiding embarrassment. It was a formula for instant colic. Lucy was six weeks old, and there were no facilities for breastfeeding parliamentarians, let alone tiny infants who need quiet sleeping conditions. To add insult to injury, Standing Orders forbade me to take Lucy into the voting lobbies if the vote clashed with breastfeeding time. She would have been categorised as a 'stranger in the House' and presumably evicted by the Sergeant at Arms had I pushed my luck.

Those sitting weeks were a logistical nightmare. We were forced to fly our childcare worker up from Canterbury each week and book her into the nearest hotel. Andrew lectured at Lincoln during the day, caught the early evening plane to Wellington, did the evening and early morning shift and flew back to Christchurch to begin the Lincoln day and Wellington night routine all over again. Typically, the media focus was on the least important aspect – where Lucy was housed. For us the issue was the silly and unwarranted withdrawal of the voting pair. That was what caused all the drama: colic and the inevitable consequences of moving a tiny infant between our Canterbury home, Parliament and Wellington each week.

My good friend and political mentor Sue Wood confidently assured us that the colic would disappear after 12 weeks. We clung to that timetable as to a liferaft. Sue proved to be largely correct – although matters were no doubt aided by Parliament at last going into recess – and we were finally able to give Lucy some semblance of a routine.

I never again felt quite the same about that crop of Labour women MPs, even when I went on to work closely with some of them on rape law reform. Lucy, however, had the last word. On one of the frequent flights home to Christchurch at the end of one of those weeks, Labour MP Ann Hercus had the misfortune to sit in the row behind us. Colic and air pressure changes ensured that Lucy bellowed in Ann's ear for the whole flight.

Oliver's arrival two and a half years later would be a very different proposition. We were in Opposition, my own whips were very understanding (as they had been with Lucy) and I had enough sense and experience to take it easy in the few weeks before the scheduled birth. One premature baby was enough. And whether by coincidence or not, Lucy took an early dislike to politics and the demands it made on her mother, whereas Oliver tended to be far more accepting of my political career and more willing to see the positive side.

As for Andrew, there would be only one occasion when he ever exhibited resentment towards my political exploits. He frequently had cause, but his hugely tolerant and forgiving nature always prevailed. This time, however, resentment was especially well justified. During my stint as National's spokeswoman on education I was fortunate enough to be invited to visit Antarctica. Two slots are made available to MPs each summer – one Opposition and one government. It was a blatant freebie, but luckily my marble came up. Thrilled to be invited, my immediate question was: could Andrew come? During his student days Andrew had tried unsuccessfully to be selected to go to Antarctica as a field worker over the summer university vacation. He was a keen mountaineer and tramper and saw Antarctica as the ultimate experience. Friends of his had been, and that served to whet his appetite.

I was very keen to secure this long sought-after opportunity for Andrew. My political career had imposed huge demands on him. He had had to suspend his own career in the public service, assume the prime responsibility for parenting our two very young children and endure frequent absences as I assumed increasingly onerous and time-consuming political responsibilities. I hoped that fulfilling his lifelong ambition would be some small reward for his substantial sacrifices for my career. 'No,' I was told. 'Spouses are not invited, not even the Governor-General's. Space is at a premium at Scott Base.'

Unable to quarrel with precedent, I tried a different tack. Traditionally four people make each VIP trip – one from the armed services, one from the media, an MP and a private-sector notable. Keen to explore every avenue, I suggested that Andrew be put on standby just in case one of our party could not make it at the last moment. 'No' again. I packed with mixed emotions. On the morning of our departure, the private-sector notable, Julian Mounter of Television New Zealand, pulled out. My last-minute efforts to have Andrew literally stand in Mounter's shoes (they were the same height and weight so all of Julian's gear would fit) were again in vain.

Despite this, it was a truly memorable trip. The terrible Erebus tragedy was still uppermost in the mind of any New Zealander who travelled to Antarctica. But our air force pilot, who was a constituent of mine, was full of reassurance all the way down, explaining that he had made the trip over 100 times. The five days that followed had a magic all of their own. The history preserved before your very eyes, the silken penguins, the shimmering light and the sheer vastness of the place are all truly awesome.

I was game to meet my own personal challenge – to become a member of the Lake Vanda swimming club. The membership rites are in typical Antarctica style, both rigorous and invigorating. Admission to the club requires skinny-dipping in Lake Vanda, and only total immersion qualifies. The morning of our helicopter journey to Lake Vanda, located in the Dry Valleys (I was hit by a twinge of conscience when told they were called the Wright Valleys), the Lake Vanda staff had been at work drilling out a swimming hole through the substantial layer of ice. Our two helicopter pilots raced off on landing and stripped off to become the first club members of the season. The journalist (a woman) and I followed at a distance. To this day Andrew is fearful the journalist will publish the proof of my successful membership application! Hot tea and scones followed, never more gratefully devoured.

There were times in the Muldoon years when it seemed as if the whole economy – like Antarctica – was in a deep freeze. Yet it would be wrong to give the impression that everything happening in those years was bad. Some significant economic liberalisations took place, in particular the Closer Economic Relations (CER) agreement, which gradually freed up trade between New Zealand and Australia. Though it was sold to politicians as a reciprocal agreement between countries, many in the bureaucracy saw CER as a Trojan Horse for achieving their wider objective – reducing New Zealand's import protection.

Another important initiative, in which I had a more direct involvement, was the deregulation of land transport and air services. The bill sought to allow land transport to compete on a direct footing with rail, and opened up domestic air travel to competition. Muldoon had opposed these moves from the outset. However, we had an excellent Minister of Transport in

George Gair, and the select committee, of which I was a member, was very supportive. There was a great deal of debate both in caucus and in the wider party, the final decision being taken at caucus. Seeing the debate going against him, Muldoon did something quite remarkable: he absented himself from caucus. He had not wanted to be seen to lose an issue while in the chair, so the vote was taken with Duncan McIntyre chairing.

Select committee work was my greatest area of job satisfaction during my first term as an MP. I was a member of the special committee, chaired by Mike Minogue, that considered the Official Information Bill. This legislation was the first of what would prove to be a long series of important reforms to the public sector over the following 12 years. Prior to this Act, New Zealand had languished in the same information dark ages as countries such as Britain. The Official Information Act brought a radical change, introducing the basic presumption that information should be made publicly available. There were strictly limited grounds for withholding information, and any decision to withhold could be appealed to an independent Ombudsman. The Act not only made for a better-informed public and parliamentary Opposition, it improved the quality of policy advice to ministers. Policy advisers knew that any report they wrote could eventually find its way into the public arena.

Undoubtedly there were some positive initiatives in the Muldoon years. Unfortunately, they were overshadowed by the disasters. Chief among these was the freeze on prices, wages and interest rates, which came during Muldoon's final term to symbolise his whole style of economic management.

Muldoon's overnight announcement of the freeze had caught many of his Cabinet by surprise, let alone his caucus. Prices and wages were able to be frozen by order-in-council, through an Act of Parliament that has since been repealed. A freeze on interest rates, however, required new legislation. Huge pressure was put on those of us who contemplated voting against the government. For me they sent along avuncular Venn Young, MP for my native Waitotara. Psychologically it was the right approach, but Venn's fatherly talk failed to sway me. In the end three of us voted against the government: Derek Quigley, Dail Jones and myself. I had difficulty getting the call in the debate, but managed to speak during the committee stages. I labelled the move 'flawed in principle and flawed in practice'.

Despite three government members crossing the floor, the legislation – amazingly – was still passed. The two Social Credit MPs and the two deselected and disaffected Labour MPs – John Kirk and Brian McDonnell – all voted with the government. Muldoon had made it into a high-stakes issue: he had told the four privately that he would call a general election if the government were defeated on the legislation. It is entirely possible Muldoon was not bluffing; he might well have called a general election. His threat certainly concentrated the minds of the four floaters. Not wanting to sign their collective political death warrants, they voted accordingly.

Family faces: Brothers Mark and Kim, and parents Ross and Joan.

ABOVE: My parents – a marriage 46 years strong.

LEFT: My father – the farmer.

Sweet sixteen.

Campaigning 1981 (before the curls).

Andrew – happy in the hills.

Campaigning for the Selwyn seat in 1981. Keith and Daphne Stewart's magnificent Clydesdales turned all heads in Halswell that day.

Happy families – with Oliver, Andrew and Lucy.

Sprawling over the Speaker's chair – the West Melton school visits my 'school'.

Off to see the Queen. Lucy and Oliver on 'royal parade' at Parliament.

4

SNAP ELECTION 1984

Along with monetary policy, fiscal policy was growing increasingly out of control during Muldoon's final years. Government spending was rising. The top rate of personal income tax was by now 66 cents in the dollar, applying from quite moderate income levels. The income tax regime was riddled with exemptions, and there was still little reliance on indirect tax. In short, it was a shambles. The budget deficit, which had never been under control, hit 9 per cent of gross domestic product (GDP) in 1983-84, as Muldoon tried one last round of monetary and fiscal expansion in an attempt to buy his way back into office.

There was an insidious consequence of the very high marginal tax rates of Muldoon's final years: among high-income earners, tax avoidance became widespread, even commonplace. People felt that, the law being an ass, avoidance was morally justifiable. The tax planning industry grew substantially as professionals invested more effort in testing the boundaries of the tax system. Here were sown the seeds of the failures of the professional ethic that would occur in the later 1980s.

For most of the Muldoon years there was little call from business for a radical change in the conduct of economic policy. Of course there were protests at specific measures introduced by Muldoon. But there was little recognition of the type of change needed. This is hardly surprising. Forty years of 'fortress New Zealand' economic policies and an economy run from Wellington had bred a deep dependency mentality into the business world. To most New Zealand businesses the first instinct was a simple one: if you were finding it hard to compete, you travelled to Wellington and lobbied for more protection, or a subsidy, or a tax break. The game was not to improve your productivity, but to acquire resources by shifting the costs onto consumers or the taxpayer.

There was also a huge sense of defeatism in the business mentality – a feeling that, one way or another, New Zealanders could not compete against the rest of the world. We were too small as a country; we were too far away from our markets. Other countries did not play fair by their trade rules. Anyway, protected industries were saving New Zealand foreign exchange; subsidised exporters were 'earning valuable overseas funds'.

All of these arguments were economic nonsense. The purpose they served was a psychological one that cushioned industry from the reality of New Zealand's situation. The mentality of defeat probably ran deepest among our protected manufacturers. It is sobering to recall that the New Zealand Manufacturers' Federation opposed the introduction of CER. Manufacturers did not believe they could successfully compete even against Australian industry – hardly the most dynamic in the Pacific region. In the end, New Zealand was to do extremely well out of CER.

Those in the National caucus who saw the need for wholesale change were in a small minority. Straight after the 1981 election four of us – Derek Quigley, Michael Cox, Doug Kidd and myself – held an out-of-Wellington strategy meeting on how to advance the free-market agenda. Little of our agenda ever came to pass under Muldoon. The most prominent rebel of the times was Derek Quigley, who lost his Cabinet job after making a speech obliquely criticising Think Big. Energy Minister Bill Birch was a prime mover in persuading Muldoon to move against Quigley. There had been some heated discussion behind the scenes as a prelude to Quigley's ejection.

By the middle of 1984 New Zealanders had run out of excuses for their poor economic performance. Productivity growth in the years since the war had been slower in New Zealand than in any other country in the Organisation for Economic Co-operation and Development (OECD). The same was true for growth in exports and output per head. The economy had not grown at all for almost a decade, while unemployment – though still comparatively low – had been rising steadily. We had continued to slide in the OECD rankings for living standards. Meanwhile, we were running the biggest current account deficit in the OECD, as well as having the fastest rate of accumulation of both government and external debt. We were neither growing nor living within our means. Our performance could hardly have been more dismal.

In June 1984 Muldoon unexpectedly called a snap election. It was a gamble that never looked like paying off. Yet Muldoon's fate was probably sealed whatever he had chosen to do. In his final term the odour of a dying government had hung over his administration. Labour, for its part, had a new leadership team, headed by the colourful and articulate David Lange. Roger Douglas, a known free-marketeer, had been given his party's finance job. Labour looked eminently electable, and so it proved. On Bastille Day National crashed to defeat.

The arrival of Douglas as the Treasury Minister was a most fortunate meeting of minds. Douglas had clear plans to liberalise the economy, reform the tax system and bring down inflation. The Treasury, for its part, had learnt a great deal from the failures of the Muldoon years, and was more than ready to give Douglas the assistance he required.

Douglas got off to a flying start. Before the new government was even sworn in the exchange rate had been devalued on Labour's instructions. Money had been flowing out of the country for weeks in anticipation of a post-election devaluation, and the tide had increased following the election result. In the last and perhaps least edifying act of his premiership, Muldoon refused to obey the instructions of the incoming government to devalue, doing so only when his senior ministers rounded on him to insist that he observe constitutional proprieties.

Almost immediately Douglas removed the freeze on prices, wages and interest rates, and abolished exchange controls. Before his first year was up he had also floated the exchange rate. The Reserve Bank was allowed to commence a monetary policy aimed at controlling and bringing down inflation over the medium term. Legislation was soon introduced to deregulate the banking sector.

Douglas also moved almost immediately to abolish most direct assistance to the export sector. Tax incentives to manufacturing exports were rapidly phased out, as were a range of direct subsidies to farmers. Douglas was also keen to increase the relative contribution of indirect tax to revenue gathering. Marginal rates of income tax were reduced, and a flat-rate value-added tax (GST) introduced.

No-one of my philosophical persuasion could cavil at the courage, direction and purpose shown by Roger Douglas in his first term as Finance Minister. It was a remarkable performance from a man who had inherited the most badly run economy in the western world. But the Douglas economic reforms were far from flawless. Very soon into the life of the Labour government it was becoming apparent that the reform programme was seriously unbalanced.

This imbalance mainly hurt the export sector. The tight monetary policy would inevitably drive up both interest rates and the exchange rate for some period of time, no matter how well executed. That was the price we had to pay for bringing down inflation. But the pressure on interest rates and the exchange rate was compounded by the large budget deficit. The abolition of industry assistance had improved the fiscal position, but beyond those 'easy' savings Douglas had achieved little in the way of fiscal improvement. The tension between monetary policy and fiscal policy would be a constant problem for the Labour government.

Even more significantly at first, the dismantling of industry assistance was seriously unbalanced. While most assistance to exporters was removed almost immediately, import protection was on a much slower track. The previous administration's move to replace import licensing with tariffs was accelerated, and there were staged reductions in tariff rates, taking place over a number of years. But the process was too slow: exporters were having to carry a still inefficient import-competing sector, while themselves being fully exposed to international competition. It was the wrong signal to be sending.

The problem was most acute for farmers. Prices for pastoral products were dropping in foreign markets, while farmers were simultaneously having to cope with the removal of assistance to their industry and an appreciating exchange rate. Those who had borrowed were hit with interest rates at record levels and depreciating land values. No wonder Labour's first term saw a big economic crunch in the rural sector.

The final major imbalance of the Douglas reform programme was the failure of the government to tackle the chronic rigidities in our industrial relations system. Some changes were made to labour market legislation, but for every step forward there were the proverbial two steps back. In the end, almost nothing was done to bring greater flexibility and competition to labour relations. This seriously detracted from the ability of New Zealand industry to become internationally competitive, and its consequences were just as serious for unemployment. It even had substantial implications for fiscal policy: in his very first budget Douglas was having to cope with a large and quite unaffordable public-sector wage round.

International experience in implementing liberalisation programmes tends to confirm what economic theory would suggest – that whatever the best sequence for implementing labour market reform, goods market reform and government-sector reform, financial market reform should, ideally, come only after the other reforms have largely been completed. This is particularly so in the case of the removal of exchange controls. In New Zealand, financial markets – including the foreign exchange market – were deregulated at a time when reform in both the goods sector and the government sector was unbalanced, and when labour market reform had scarcely begun. The imbalance in the reform programme was reflected in interest rates and the exchange rate.

It would be unfair to point the finger at Douglas himself for the sequencing mistakes. He undoubtedly would have liked to move faster in some or all of the areas where progress was slow. Cautious colleagues and political factors had led to the imbalance at least as much as any misconceptions about sequencing. Douglas had a short time in which to gain a sense of momentum and begin the task of changing business attitudes. He struck where he could, hoping he could go on to continue the job. And by deregulating the financial markets, Douglas gave himself the best political chance of completing his programme. Whatever its purely theoretical shortcomings, immediate financial market deregulation gave Douglas an invaluable weapon to use against his colleagues. From early on, financial markets were daily sitting in judgment on the government's economic programme. The reaction of the markets backed up, in a very immediate way, his arguments to his colleagues that unbalanced policies would compromise good outcomes.

Balanced or unbalanced, 'Rogernomics' during Labour's first term had an impetus and a sense of direction that proved one of its biggest political assets. Though hugely controversial, Rogernomics came to be seen by enough people as a progressive, forward-looking programme that was taking New Zealand away from an unsatisfactory past. Douglas was helped politically by Labour having taken office in the middle of a cyclical upswing, which continued for longer than commentators had anticipated.

The Reserve Bank's attempts to dampen demand, with the aim of bringing down inflation, were not always as successful as intended. Despite high interest rates, there was a surge of new lending as a result of the removal of both interest rate controls and various quantitative controls on bank lending. In other words, microeconomic changes to the banking system compromised for a time the anti-inflation strategy – a familiar problem for central banks. The rural sector may indeed have been in crisis, but the urban economy – aided by a booming sharemarket – was surprisingly buoyant during Labour's first term.

Roger Douglas was also hugely aided by the media qualities of his leader. David Lange played 'good cop' to the 'bad cop' of Douglas, entertained the country with his elliptical wit, and – whether planned or unplanned – ran all sorts of diversions while Douglas and others were at work in the engine room. Labour's new anti-nuclear policy gave Lange an attractive new agenda of his own to run. Whether one agrees with that particular policy or not – and personally I remain opposed – it enabled Labour to capture the moral high ground and take the heat off Rogernomics at crucial moments.

The onset of Rogernomics set the terms for the policy debate within both main political parties over the next seven or eight years. Substantial but incomplete economic reforms had taken place. There were those in both parties who rejected Rogernomics and all its works, and wished to return to the more controlled economic management of the past. Equally, there were those eager to push the reform programme forward. And, human nature being what it is, there were large numbers who were in the middle, or who were not quite sure what they thought. In the National Opposition much of the debate centred on the high interest rates and high exchange rate. Many argued that the government should loosen monetary policy and/or attempt to manage the exchange rate down. Those of us in the free-market camp argued that the high interest rates and high exchange rate were symptoms of a deeper problem: unbalanced reform. The proper response, we claimed, was to push on with the reform programme.

Douglas was able to push on with some elements of his reform programme. Before Labour's first term was up he had reorganised most state trading activities into state-owned enterprises (SOEs). Previously the commercial and social functions of many state agencies had been inextricably mixed, leading to inefficiency and poor focus. SOE reform separated out the purely commercial functions. The 'SOE model' – that of the tax-and-dividend-paying company whose shares are held by government – was one of the Treasury's most technically assured and successful contributions to the reform programme. As subsequent events showed, setting up SOEs not only led to large increases in efficiency, it put state trading activities into a form easy to privatise.

While Labour was selling itself to the electorate as the government of momentum and reform, the National Opposition was cutting a far from convincing figure. National had long thought of itself as the natural party of government. By 1984 National had been in office for 28 out of the past 34 years. But having been rejected by the voters, we sulked. This feeling of rejection was combined in many quarters with an unwarranted complacency. Under Muldoon, political sustainability had been the main criterion for evaluating policy: it had kept National in office for nine years. Many in caucus now assumed the voters would inevitably return to National at the next election, simply because of the number of sector groups Labour had supposedly antagonised. They were to receive a rude surprise.

National's own attitude to Rogernomics was highly ambivalent. We had opposed the government on almost every single element of its reform programme. On the other hand, most of us knew that a return to Muldoonism was neither feasible nor desired by the electorate. Afraid to pin our colours to the cause of reform, but also afraid of being painted as Muldoonist, we chose a muddled, middle course that was full of contradictions. In the end we found that the expectations of the electorate had shifted far further than many had appreciated. We failed to meet those expectations.

There were several major personality difficulties within the party to go alongside ideological schism. Muldoon had been dumped as National leader soon after losing office, but he would cast his shadow over the whole of our first term in Opposition. The new leadership team consisted of Jim McLay and his deputy Jim Bolger ('Town Jim' and 'Jungle Jim', as some of us irreverently referred to them). Jim McLay was very much the urban liberal, and in philosophy largely supported the free-market reforms. Jim Bolger was the rural conservative, sceptical about the merits of Rogernomics.

Town Jim McLay had little more than a year as leader before succumbing to a coup organised by the supporters of Jungle Jim. His downfall was caused by a poor public image, periodic cannon fire from an embittered Muldoon, and a feeling in large parts of caucus that Town Jim was taking the party too far down the free-market path. Town Jim's end was hastened by his caucus reshuffle early in 1986. He promoted many of his supporters and dumped George Gair and Bill Birch, the latter losing his finance role after an undistinguished stint. The two former ministers soon joined the forces plotting McLay's downfall. At the crucial caucus meeting, called to vote on the leadership, the odds looked stacked very much against Town Jim. Despite that, there were some strong speeches made by his supporters. In my own contribution I focused very much on Jim Bolger. 'We have heard a great deal about the defects of our leader,' I said. 'But what about the challenger? I have seen no such equal scrutiny of him. What does this challenger stand for? What is his philosophical framework? What policies will he want to promote on behalf of the party? We have not had answers to these questions.'

A cynic might say I was just trying to keep my place on the front bench: I had been one of those supporters promoted by McLay. On the other hand, my speech would hardly have improved my standing with the incoming leader – not that it was high in any case. I had already told Bolger to his face that he was ill-equipped to lead the party. Just as for my colleagues Ian McLean and Doug Kidd, my two-month stay on the front bench came to an abrupt end. I was pushed back down the batting order, although I retained the role of education spokeswoman. Onto my vacant front-bench seat came Muldoon.

The next time I made the front bench, I was to have a very much longer innings.

McLay was to resign from Parliament at the 1987 election, just as his friend and ally Derek Quigley had done three years before, following his sacking by Muldoon. Both were major losses to the party.

5

NATIONAL'S LOSS: MY GAIN

It was probably lucky for me that I was not involved in the formulation of economic policy in the lead-up to the 1987 election. All who were involved lost ground in caucus following our thumping election loss. National's economic policy never gained coherence, and at times was a positive embarrassment. I felt sorry for Michael Cox, who often had to take the flak for mistakes made by others.

One of these mistakes was Extax, our proposed alternative to GST. As a sales tax with exemptions, Extax would need to have been struck at a higher rate than GST to raise an equivalent amount of revenue. It was less efficient than GST, and more complex to administer. Our supposedly business-friendly tax proposal was soon being slated by big business and small business alike. Even its name was an embarrassment. I remember hearing the word Extax in caucus and assuming it meant the name of the tax had not yet been decided upon. Later, when I heard the name coming over the radio, I could scarcely believe it.

There were other embarrassments. Party spokesmen were publicly at odds over how much would need to be cut from government spending, and about whether taxes might need to go up. Monetary policy was also in confusion, and further complicated by Muldoon adding his voice. And while opposing government policy where it was pointless to do so, we also failed to stake out our ground where we could genuinely make a difference. In the area of the labour market, for instance, our policy was weak and half-hearted. There were other elements of our policy that could only be described as Muldoonist, such as the pledge to give a subsidy for every new job created in the regions. The irony of this policy was that the regions were already starting to recover. Had we been elected in 1987, we would have been confronted not with a depressed rural sector but with an urban economy sliding into recession. The regional job-subsidy policy stands as a monument to the dangers of ad hoc responses to short-term trends.

While National tried to be all things to all people, Labour was making a virtue out of its boldness, consistency and sense of direction. Labour was able to boast it had taken hard decisions, stood up to special interests and put New Zealand's interests first. At election time there was no contest between the party of reform and the party of confusion. Labour performed the unusual feat of increasing its majority in Parliament. Even more tellingly, Labour's vote held up well in many of the rural marginal seats, despite the punishment taken by the farming sector.

In the National camp things were far from happy. The election loss had been a major blow to caucus morale and confidence – bigger in fact than the loss of office in 1984. Some caucus members wondered whether National would ever sit on the Treasury benches again, given the impetus Labour was now showing. There was still fierce debate within caucus about the direction of policy, but one thing looked certain: if we were to win office, we would need to formulate a much clearer, more distinctive and more coherent set of policies than we had so far managed. In my own view, party strategists had underestimated the increasing sophistication of the New Zealand electorate.

There were calls from both the caucus and the organisational wing of the party for Bolger to put a more forward-looking stamp on his team line-up. In the end, I was the one who acted as the immediate catalyst for this to occur. I decided to launch a challenge to deputy leader George Gair. George is a charming man, and had been one of the most respected ministers in the Muldoon Cabinet. But I believed the contribution he could make to the party was now largely over. I had received generally positive feedback on my performance as education spokeswoman and I assessed my chances of taking out the deputy leadership as good. But, win or lose, I was keen to galvanise the party into new directions.

It was soon apparent George would not have the numbers to win. He decided to announce publicly that he would be stepping down in favour of new blood. Jim Bolger made a hasty search for someone – anyone – whom he could stand against me. His numbers men settled on Don McKinnon, the party's popular chief whip. There was a very brief campaign, during which I told the press that mine would be 'a candidacy of ideas'. Just as the Tories in Britain prior to Margaret Thatcher had long been regarded as 'the stupid party', I wanted National to be regarded no longer as the party without ideas, without a sense of direction, without a clue.

It was a close ballot, which Don won by one vote. Though naturally disappointed, I was delighted when later that very day Jim called me into his office and offered me the job of finance spokeswoman. I did not accept his offer unconditionally, however. I demanded that Muldoon be removed from the front bench, and not be given a seat anywhere in the first two rows of parliamentary benches. I did not want Muldoon continuing to run his alternative economic policy – as he would inevitably have done had he retained a major role. I also demanded that Simon Upton be made an associate finance spokesman, with responsibility for social policy. Jim said he would think about it.

I was fairly confident he would agree – confident enough to go up to Wanganui where Raewyn, my brother Kim's wife, had just given birth to twin daughters. The next morning Jim rang to say he had agreed to all of the conditions. It turned out to be a very good week for the Richardson clan: my younger brother had the pleasure of seeing his horse come home at Awapuni. Asked by the press if he was proud of his daughter, my father – a racing man – pointed out that this week he had scored a treble.

In offering me the finance job, Jim undoubtedly placed great weight on the level of support I had received in caucus. Other factors would also have been important. I was one of the few National MPs with much support from the business community. And, as the election result showed, the tide seemed to be flowing in the direction of market liberalism.

Though I had been disappointed at missing out on the deputy leadership, in retrospect the outcome was almost certainly the right one. The deputy leader of a political party has to be the peacemaker, the healer who keeps the team together. Don has played that role well. By contrast, I was too controversial a politician to be a conciliator. I believe I made a greater contribution by taking on the finance job – a role I would never have been given had I become deputy leader.

I knew what I was letting myself in for. Finance was the most important portfolio, and usually the most difficult. I was National's fifth finance spokesperson in less than three years; many were expecting my reign to be no longer than those of my immediate predecessors. For my part, I was determined National would not make the mistakes under my stewardship that it had in the past.

There was one thing, however, that I had little inkling of, and that was just how different Labour's second term would be from its first.

6

LABOUR AT LOGGERHEADS

Roger Douglas and David Lange were almost immediately at loggerheads. Douglas wanted to press on with economic reforms, including direct tax cuts combined with reform of social policy. Lange took alarm at the direction in which his government was heading and called for his famous tea break. The debate became a bitter one that often spilled over into the public arena. The contest was doubly destabilising because it was so even; both men had powerful support within Cabinet. While Lange and Douglas were scrapping, policy was often stalled.

Despite the destabilising political battles, some significant reforms were promoted during Labour's second term. For instance, Labour passed the State Sector Act, which significantly improved accountability in the public sector. All departmental chief executives were put on five-year contracts and became directly responsible to their ministers for delivering the services of their departments. For the first time chief executives became genuinely accountable for their performance, just as their counterparts in the private sector had long been. The new legislation had major positive implications for the culture of the Wellington bureaucracy. Typically enough, National opposed the bill, arguing that it would politicise the state sector. Led by Bill Birch, we mindlessly fought the legislation at every stage of its passage through the House.

Inflation came down substantially during Labour's second term, and the Reserve Bank Bill – one of the most important of Labour's reforms – was introduced and passed into law. The Reserve Bank Act conferred day-to-day autonomy on the central bank, while giving it the clear objective of price stability. The Public Finance Act, another important initiative whose focus was long-term, changed the basis of public-sector accounting from cash to accruals, and from accounting for inputs to accounting for outputs. Public finances were required to be reported on essentially the same basis as in the private sector. A comprehensive balance sheet, featuring both assets and liabilities, whether actual or contingent, was required. Labour's second term also saw significant further reductions in import protection, and the privatisation of a number of state assets.

Still, most of these measures had been signalled or foreshadowed in Labour's first term. As the urban economy turned down, and as the fighting between Douglas and Lange intensified, it was becoming increasingly clear that key elements of the reform programme were simply not going to be tackled. Significant labour market reform remained out of bounds. Government spending was rising inexorably, leading to continued pressure on the business sector. And Labour appeared to have no answer to the huge rise in the number of people dependent on the state.

The reasons for the economic downturn were several. The worldwide sharemarket crash late in 1987 was particularly severe in New Zealand. Monetary policy was beginning to bite strongly on domestic demand. And the mixed signals coming out of the Beehive undoubtedly added to the loss of business confidence. This failure of confidence among business people and the failure of confidence within the government reinforced and fed on each other. As the recession lengthened and deepened, and unemployment continued to rise, the imbalances in the government's strategy were looking increasingly intractable.

My first outing as finance spokeswoman took me to the annual general meeting of the Institute of Economic Research. The guest lecture, delivered by Professor Conrad Blyth, was ominously titled 'The economic consequences of Mr Douglas'. Though Blyth's economic views would not always correspond with mine, on this occasion they certainly did. He hit out at the unbalanced nature of Labour's policy mix:

> Now, if the government frees up markets, in particular the capital and foreign exchange markets, it is doing this so as to ease the transfer of resources to the growth points in the economy. Very good. But, if at the same time the government creates an excess demand for resources through its budget deficit, it will drive the rate of interest and the exchange rate in the directions I have described, and in a very efficient free-market way will choke off all the growth it hoped to stimulate. Very bad.

Blyth concluded:

> The immediate economic consequences of Mr Douglas, in choosing the wrong rate of exchange, have been to make his long-term objectives difficult to achieve and greatly increase the short-term costs of his reforms.

I asked a rather innocent question: what did he think was the right rate of exchange? His answer startled me and produced substantial mirth in the audience of economists, all conscious that the first female politician to shoulder responsibility for finance sat in their midst.

'We need a feminine exchange rate,' was his reply. I must say that I had never thought of exchange rate policy in those terms. While from time to time during my tenure of finance, both in Opposition and in government, I was put under pressure to 'humanise' economics, I do not recall there ever being any pressure to feminise finance.

I was keen to bring a different style to the Opposition finance role. I did not wish to oppose the government simply for the sake of it. Political grandstanding can be tempting and has undeniable short-term benefits. For me, however, it was more important that I build up credibility within my key constituencies – business and the financial markets. To do so, I needed to pick the right issues and be more selective in my attack on the government. I am proud of the fact that as Opposition finance spokeswoman I persuaded my National colleagues to support both the Public Finance Act and the Reserve Bank Act.

This was not easy. Both Jim Bolger and Bill Birch saw the Public Finance Act, with its emphasis on outputs rather than inputs, as new-fangled stuff – Treasury-driven theory rather than the familiar system they had been used to as ministers. The Public Finance Act *was* Treasury-driven, but not necessarily the worse for that. I tried to explain how the new way of accounting would provide them, as ministers, with tools that had not been available to them in the past. Instead of their departments simply being a black box, they would be able to see how much was really being spent, and for what purpose. Residual scepticism from both men would carry over into the early stages of the Bolger administration, but would rapidly recede under the experience of working with the new system.

The Reserve Bank Act posed a considerably stiffer problem for me. The thinking behind the Act was sound. In the long run, monetary policy can only be used to influence the level of prices. Any attempt to use monetary policy to boost economic growth, or to reduce unemployment, may work in the short run, but fails in the long run. In the long run, looser monetary policy only flows through into higher inflation. That has been the experience across many countries and in many different time periods.

Given that, it makes sense that monetary policy should be aimed solely at price stability. This does not mean growth and employment are unimportant – simply that the best contribution monetary policy can make to growth and employment is to concentrate on achieving price stability. Many other policies are needed to provide the best environment for growth: a sound monetary policy is necessary but not sufficient.

Unfortunately, the fact that monetary policy can have a powerful short-term impact on growth, but no favourable long-term impact, represents a standing temptation to politicians. Relaxing monetary policy prior to an election provides a temporary boost to growth. Only afterwards, when the election had been safely won, does the growth evaporate, to be replaced by higher inflation. Muldoon was a past master at this tactic, as many politicians abroad have been.

The question, then, was how to set up an institutional arrangement so that monetary policy would be run, not for the short-term benefit of politicians seeking re-election, but for the long-term benefit of the economy as a whole.

Labour also faced a more immediate problem – how to establish the greatest degree of credibility for their own anti-inflationary policy. Their solution, enshrined in the Reserve Bank Act, was to put the Reserve Bank onto an autonomous but accountable footing. The balance struck by the Act was a good one. Price stability was specified as the primary function of the bank, with policy targets having to be agreed between the bank and the Minister of Finance for carrying out the bank's primary function. On the other hand, there was provision for the government of the day to override the bank by substituting a different economic objective to price stability. Any override was required to be done in public. Thus any government could at the end of the day have the monetary policy it wanted, but was forced to be transparent in its instructions to the Reserve Bank.

The public nature of the override, combined with the open nature of New Zealand's capital markets, made it unlikely the override would be used. A loose monetary policy only succeeded in raising output in the short term if it 'fooled' participants in the economy into thinking there had been an increase in the real demand for their services when there had in fact only been a 'paper' increase in demand. If the government's override to the Reserve Bank were made public, the 'surprise' effect would be greatly dissipated. Interest rates would rise immediately, in anticipation of the higher inflation resulting from the government's actions. This provided a built-in check against a government tempted to misuse monetary policy for short-term political ends.

The Reserve Bank Act thus represented a strong institutional commitment to price stability. By making that commitment, it added to the credibility of monetary policy and reduced the inflation risk premium built into interest rates.

My challenge was to convince enough caucus members of the Act's merits. To me it was a confidence issue; I could not have continued as finance spokeswoman had National opposed the legislation. I had little success with Bolger and Birch. Though Jim generally accepted, in theory, the economic reasoning behind the Act, he was reluctant to yield to the

Reserve Bank day-to-day operating discretion. He was concerned the Act would tie our hands as a government. Bill was similarly sceptical.

It would be unfair to suggest that the motives of the two men were entirely cynical. Both had instincts deeply rooted in the hands-on economic management of the Muldoon era and their journey away from that style of management was a slow one. Even after caucus had decided to support the legislation, Jim was still trying to persuade us to vote against the third reading of the bill. Even today, while Bill has come to accept the framework of the Reserve Bank Act, Jim in his heart of hearts would still like to run monetary policy from the Beehive.

In winning support for the Reserve Bank Act, I had greater success with other caucus members than with Jim and Bill. In the end, the numbers were extremely close. In winning the battle, the override provision in the bill proved crucial. While I personally saw no need for an override provision – and still do not – having one enabled me to argue that the bill did not preclude the government of the day from exercising sovereignty over monetary policy. Some groups – such as the Manufacturers' Federation – had campaigned against the bill by arguing it would completely tie the government's hands. That was plainly not true.

Another of my weapons in this argument was the bill's long title, which I had been involved in drafting at the select committee stage. The long title talked of 'continuing to recognise the Crown's right to determine economic policy'. The principles in the Reserve Bank Act pose no constitutional problem for any Westminster system, or any other parliamentary democracy. The accountability mechanisms of the Act within a parliamentary system are strong. At six-monthly intervals the Reserve Bank produces a monetary policy statement that is tabled in Parliament. The statement reviews recent developments and states how the bank intends to achieve its agreed policy targets. Top bank officials then appear before Parliament's Finance and Expenditure Select Committee (FEC) to be questioned on the statement. When I was the senior Opposition member on FEC, I took those sessions very seriously. Latterly, FEC has also taken to grilling the Reserve Bank on its six-monthly economic forecasts.

While always supporting the Reserve Bank's objective of price stability, I was never afraid to scrutinise the adequacy of the bank's actions in pursuit of that objective, and to criticise when I believed there were shortcomings. In 1989 I became concerned that the bank was placing such overriding weight on the trade-weighted index (TWI) of the exchange rate as an indicator of monetary policy that it was coming very close to targeting the TWI. The following year I criticised the mixed and confusing signals coming out of the bank during a period in which it tightened monetary policy. My speech, which described the bank's actions as 'daily episodes of *Fawlty Towers*', had an impact on Reserve Bank operating procedures. It would be disingenuous to deny that these attacks did not also suit me politically, in terms of my positioning among my colleagues. There was still a large anti-Reserve Bank sentiment in the National caucus. If I could with legitimacy attack the bank, in a way that did not put at risk the overall monetary policy framework, I certainly did so.

Later, when I was Minister of Finance, it was clearly important that there be no difference in public between the Beehive and the Reserve Bank. I referred any media questions regarding the implementation of monetary policy to the bank. However, I naturally had views of my own on monetary policy. If I thought the bank was doing something wrong, I told the Governor so. He was the one who took the decisions, but that did not stop me from giving him an opinion. After all, everyone else was!

In making me his finance spokeswoman Jim Bolger had taken a decision that was – for him – a major new departure. He would not have made the appointment without severe misgivings: I was seen as radical, I had not supported him for the leadership, we had little in common beyond a shared rural background, and it would be idle to pretend we were good friends. Our minds worked very differently. I tended to reason from first principles; he used a more intuitive approach. I was by instinct a reformer; he was by instinct a manager, and a man of the middle ground. I preferred to drive a tank at obstacles; he preferred to search for compromise. I was sometimes criticised for not being political enough; he was a politician to his fingertips. My opponents said I was dogmatic; his opponents that you never knew where he stood. I was praised for firmness of principle; he for flexibility and reasonableness.

In my first few months as finance spokeswoman there were also differences in public between us. There were conflicting statements over monetary policy. When Roger Douglas announced his soon-to-be-aborted flat tax rate, I publicly supported it while Jim opposed it. On one occasion Jim had reacted to a comment of mine by saying that I had been 'flying a kite'. Shortly afterwards I gave my first address as finance spokeswoman to National's annual conference and my gimmick was to bring on a large blue and white kite, declaring that from now on 'the only kite I'm flying is a National kite'. It sounds corny, but the audience loved it.

Despite our tentative start, Jim's and my working relationship soon became a great deal smoother than many had imagined possible, and infinitely smoother than the relationship between Lange and Douglas.

Gradually our trust in each other strengthened. We sorted out our lines in public and were rarely at odds. I soon made it a cardinal principle that there not be a hair's breadth between Jim and me in public. For a time this disappointed some of my philosophical allies outside Parliament. They thought I was not pushing issues hard enough, not 'leading the debate'. But I was playing a longer game.

Jim's style of decision-making is often to circle an issue, having two or three 'runs' at it and attempting to think about it from a number of different angles until he is entirely happy with the proposed course of action. He has a skill in detecting the weak points of any proposition presented to him. He also dislikes closing off options. It was a style that could sometimes be frustrating but, equally, you knew that once Jim had made up his mind he was unlikely to change it. Nor could any members of Jim's team legitimately complain that they had not been given a hearing.

Regular communication between Jim and me was, of course, crucial. I found that in attempting to get him feeling comfortable about my proposals, I needed to give him time to mull things over. I often thought of it in terms of Jim developing a 'comfort zone' around a proposal. In bringing him to such a point, I found that persistence often paid off.

Some of the less attractive aspects of Jim's management style stemmed from his sensitivity about any real or imagined challenge to his position. Like most political leaders, having got to the top of the greasy pole himself, he had a keen instinct for self-preservation. In Jim's case this translated into an unwillingness to delegate or be comfortable with a colleague's efforts to become well organised or resourced. He also tended to belittle or bury colleagues who demonstrated real leadership skills. Since for most of the time he was virtually unchallenged as leader, I always found such behaviour unwarranted and unattractive.

In those days there was very little in the way of support staff available to the Opposition. I had no formal qualifications in economics; though philosophically a committed free-marketeer I was on a steep learning curve on the detail of economic policy. Soon after taking the finance job I wrote to Roger Douglas requesting a full-time economic adviser. Douglas generously agreed and I managed to persuade my friend Charlotte Williams to take on the role. Charlotte proved to be an ideal choice. She was a breath of fresh air around the Opposition wing and helped inject a long-overdue dose of economic rigour into the Opposition's policy machine. It was a considerable contrast to our first term in Opposition, where economic policy was cast to please everybody and predictably ended up pleasing nobody.

Charlotte and I were on the same wavelength both personally and philosophically. We both had first-hand experience of juggling the demands of two very young children with the requirements of demanding careers. While we were both equally persuaded of the merits of a market-based framework, Charlotte was a great economic foil for me, and no pushover in an argument – of which there were many. With Charlotte's professional flair went a wicked sense of fun. Jim did a distinct double-take on his first meeting with her: Charlotte had quite deliberately decked herself out for the occasion with a graphic Che Guevara T-shirt very evident beneath her elegant linen jacket.

My first year or so in the finance job was the toughest of my period in Opposition. I failed to get the agreement of caucus on an economic principles paper. I also suffered the frustration of being in Australia when a paper went through caucus limiting the overseas ownership of certain designated 'strategic SOEs'. While not emerging with much visible success, during this period I was putting a lot of time into meeting and networking with the business sector. I also met regularly with participants in the financial markets. The Opposition's reputation with both audiences was still low and I was well aware that the first step towards business and financial markets gaining confidence in the party was their gaining confidence in me personally.

I also managed to persuade Jim to institute regular weekly meetings of his front bench. Prior to that, most decisions on strategy had been taken by the Jim and Bill team, with little conspicuous success. I was keen to break up that duopoly and obtain a wider involvement for myself and other members of the front bench. I said to Jim that if we wanted to be a successful government we needed to practise being a Cabinet. After some initial resistance, he agreed. So on Friday mornings the eight members of the front bench talked strategy – minus Winston Peters, who could rarely be bothered to turn up.

Labour's first major initiative after the 1987 election was the so-called December 17 Statement, hurriedly brought together to counter deteriorating business confidence in the wake of the sharemarket crash. The statement contained important announcements on reducing import protection and on privatisation. But by far the most controversial elements were the proposed flat tax rate and the associated guaranteed minimum family income (GMFI) for those in work. As we now know, the flat tax rate-GMFI proposals were to be unilaterally reversed in the new year by David Lange.

I had a great deal of sympathy with what Roger Douglas had been attempting to do. To me, a progressive tax structure is a concession to the politics of envy and a drag on our most skilled, enterprising and hard-working citizens. A progressive tax artificially discourages savings. It leads to fiscal drag – that insidious practice whereby inflation pushes people into higher tax brackets. A flat tax rate would be administratively simpler and it would eliminate a number of anomalies. Those whose income varied from year to year would no longer be taxed differently from those whose incomes followed a stable path. A flat tax rate would simplify questions about the definition of the family unit; income splitting would effectively become automatic. And a flat rate would eliminate the tax-avoidance practice of shifting income between family members. For all of those reasons, I have long supported a flat rate.

I was also sympathetic to the intent behind the GMFI proposal in the package. That intent was to encourage workforce participation by establishing a gap between low-income families in the workforce and those on a benefit. For me, the big question mark hung over the cost of the package. There was little evidence the fiscal arithmetic had been done in a rigorous fashion, or even done at all. To me the package looked unaffordable: we were awarding ourselves a fiscal dividend that had not been earned. Three years later National would take a more hard-headed route to establishing the differential between welfare and work.

We shall never know how the package would have worked out in practice. While Lange's scrapping of the GMFI-flat tax rate undoubtedly detracted from business confidence in Labour, my own view is that Douglas had overestimated in his own mind the dynamic effects of that part of the package. It would not have solved – indeed may well have exacerbated – Labour's fiscal problems, and its impact on job creation would have been limited in the absence of serious reforms to the labour market.

The warfare between Lange and Douglas went on all through 1988, during which domestic demand was contracting sharply. The resignation of Douglas at year's end left David Caygill as the new Finance Minister, with the difficult task of establishing credibility with the financial markets. In order to achieve greater credibility in monetary policy, Douglas had set the target of 0-2 per cent inflation by the early 1990s. For similar reasons of credibility, Caygill added the target of a balanced budget by 1990-91. Despite increasing GST in 1989, Caygill would not come near to achieving his fiscal target.

7

NATIONAL'S TRANSFORMATION ... AND MINE

Early in 1989, at the annual retreat of National's caucus at Waipuna Lodge, I at last succeeded in getting an economic position paper agreed with my colleagues. It was a bland document, but considerably better than not having anything. The document did not seriously tackle monetary policy, saying merely that National's monetary policy would be 'appropriate'. The treatment of fiscal policy was stronger, though not yet strong enough. The document committed National to 'diminish the demands of the state on the economic resources of the nation'. It also committed National to balancing the budget and 'reining in' government spending. The document contained a reasonably strong statement on National's intentions for labour market reform. On the negative side, the document committed National to introducing a tax incentive for retirement savings. I supported such a policy at the time, seeing it as a means of counterbalancing the many negative signals sent by government to private savers. However, I later came to regard a tax incentive as unfeasible.

The Waipuna document was a little over-reliant on what I sometimes used to call 'puberty economics' – the assumption that growth will solve all of one's fiscal problems. Puberty economics was a tempting mirage for politicians on both sides of the House. The skilled exponent of puberty economics often combined it with a specious form of circular reasoning. Asked by an interviewer how they would achieve economic growth, they would reply 'by reducing the deficit'. Asked how they would reduce the deficit, they would say 'by getting growth'. It could often sound plausible, if the questions were sufficiently far apart. This technique is far from confined to New Zealand: I recently heard it performed by a member of the British Labour Party. When a politician uses this technique, it generally indicates they have nothing useful to say about either growth or the deficit.

Besides the Waipuna document, I had other reasons for starting 1989 in good heart. Early in the year I secured Jim's agreement to hire a press secretary. It was not done without difficulty: Jim never took readily to institutional innovations. Earlier I had encountered resistance to my idea that we should hold front-bench meetings. Now I was at him again, this time with the perfectly sensible idea that I should have media as well as economic expertise on board. Tense scenes and manoeuvring followed. For the only time in the whole of our working relationship Jim took me to dinner so that we could work the issue through on a more informal basis.

I was very pleased to be able to tempt former Press Gallery journalist Anna Symmans to take up the new media position. Anna stayed with me for the next five years, became a very close friend, and was invaluable throughout that time. She had a keen political nose, took little nonsense from anyone and was especially good in a crisis. She revelled in her job. Her father before her had been another Finance Minister's 'minder': to Gerry Symmans often fell the task of knocking the rough edges off Muldoon. I like to think that Gerry faced a more demanding task than his daughter did.

Prior to Anna's arrival I had paid very little attention to questions of image. To me it had always been the policy debate that mattered. In the end, however, no politician can afford to ignore image, and I was no different – even if I was often a reluctant pupil.

The first step of my image overhaul had already taken place the previous year: I had returned from Australia with my hair permed. The dramatic transformation from straight hair to curly had happened on a whim. No image consultants had been involved, though my protestations to that effect were believed by no-one. More systematic and serious efforts were initiated by two very successful Wellington businesswomen, Sally Logan and Tina Symmans. Public relations was their game and they correctly concluded that I was in dire need of their expertise. With one hand they extended friendship and the other pearl earrings and lipstick! It was Anna's responsibility to follow through. In the months leading up to the general election, Anna ran what she dubbed a 'value-added' campaign for me. It included a range of image-transforming exercises from media training to eyebrow-plucking. My wardrobe was completely overhauled. Dresses were out, smart business suits were in. No longer would Lange taunt me in the House about my 'fruit salad' dress: I was now a power dresser. I even came to enjoy it. Anna was both impressed and amused by my new-found ability to select the most expensive suits. Andrew, always the more frugal member of the family, was less impressed.

I launched the 'new me' at the National Party conference in Wanganui, wearing a new suit and sporting a softer hairstyle. I spoke about the benefits of a reformed economy for women. Political commentator Colin James knew me too well. He sidled up to Anna after the speech and asked her where the party had buried Ruth.

For a short time my image change was a media talking point. I remember the frustration I felt the day an important speech of mine in the House was ignored by the media, who instead focused on my new dark green double-breasted suit. Later, when I was in Cabinet and my suits were still a topic of media discussion, John Banks assured me of my sartorial status. He sent me a note: 'You are looking very cool today, Ruth. I really do like your suit'!

But the transformation went beyond just the exterior. Anna articulated the concerns of many of my supporters in both politics and business about my political style. Logic and reason were my principal tools for decision-making. While they were obviously essential, Anna believed I needed to present myself as more warm and approachable and less abrasive. 'People respect you, Ruth, but we need people to like you more,' she would say.

As well as logic and reason I needed to be seen to be affected by emotion and feeling. To help me achieve this new 'softer' persona I was sent to 'charm' school under the guidance of former United States image-maker Jack Byrum – the man who had reputedly turned Richard Nixon from losing presidential candidate into president. Jack, Anna and I met a number of times over the years and his task was always the same – to help me to create simultaneously the perceptions of intellect, ability and toughness alongside inspiration, warmth and understanding.

When I first took up the 'value-added' campaign my objective was to secure the finance portfolio in government. I have little doubt my efforts to be more presentable to the business community and the media helped me to win some of Jim's confidence. Whether the public really saw a new Ruth Richardson is debatable. A joke about me that did the rounds perhaps summed up the public's cynicism of the image changes:

> Question: What's the difference between Ruth Richardson and a rottweiler?
> Answer: Lip gloss.

Late in 1989 I had an intensive two-day session with Jack Byrum. He analysed me relentlessly, stripping me down and gradually building me up again, making some extremely acute points along the way. Towards the end, thoroughly brainwashed, I was ready to do almost anything he asked. Unfortunately, at that point Jack got his hands on the speech I was due to deliver the next day. The speech was to the Mont Pelerin Society – a prestigious worldwide association of market liberals which was having its first ever conference in New Zealand. It was one of the most intellectually high-powered audiences I would ever address – precisely the wrong audience on which to try out Jack's touchy-feely approach. However, by this stage I was past resistance. My speech was completely rewritten. Out went all the boring economics and in went some heart and soul.

The next day I stood up before an audience that included a Nobel Prize-winner and other luminaries, treated them to my coquettish new smile, and delivered a speech of numbing emptiness. Still under the influence, so to speak, I thought I had gone down rather well. I little knew that over morning tea a dozen conversations were going on to the effect of: 'What has got into Ruth?' My philosophical allies had intended the conference to be a symbolic handing over of the torch from Roger Douglas to me. Over subsequent days, as I gradually became myself again, various people quietly broke the news to me that my speech had in fact been less than a roaring success. The moral of this story is not that I should have made no attempt to soften my image – only that I should have picked the right audience.

At the same time Anna came on board, I also finally managed to persuade Jim to have a Treasury economist seconded to his office – something he had always been entitled to do. The economist who came, Iain Rennie, would do an outstanding job in helping to educate Jim, and steadying him at crucial times. Jim even became considerably attached to Iain, who, when we eventually took office, for a time went into the Prime Minister's Department. Those of a paranoid disposition, who believe Treasury has its tentacles everywhere and secretly runs the country, would have had their theories further reinforced had they observed Iain Rennie's influence on Jim.

In a further staff change at this time, Martin Hames took over from Charlotte Williams as my economist. Martin came to the job with impeccable economic credentials: he had been working for a major bank and had earlier done a stint with the Reserve Bank, so he had an excellent theoretical and practical understanding of the world of finance. But Martin was much more than a mere economist. While personally reserved, he would become fiercely assertive across the whole spectrum of economic and social policy. Politically he was no shrinking violet either, and had much to say about and to contribute towards political strategy and day-to-day tactics.

Martin, like Anna, ended up staying with me until the end of my time as a minister. Like me, he was insistent and persistent about the need for high-quality labour market reform. Like Anna, he lectured me about style. His memoranda were often laced with dry humour. On one occasion, teeing me up for a forthcoming meeting with market economists, his memo began:

Tone:
- realistic
- determined
- confident
- relaxed

Charm optional

According to my handlers, market economists were the only audience for whom charm was optional.

Despite having the surface appearance of being anything but lonely, politics is in reality a very lonely job. A politician's personal staff can prove to be important figures. They may be his or her only source of entirely disinterested advice, the only people with whom the politician can completely relax and let down his or her guard – even a substitute family away from home. Strong loyalties develop on both sides. I like to think politicians get the personal staff they deserve; whether true or not, I was extremely pleased with the quality of people making themselves available to work for me. This would carry over to when I was minister. When I arrived in the Beehive, Treasury economist David Hunt would join Anna and Martin as a key member of my team. He would prove to be as efficient as he was unfailingly patient and considerate. David could fit an elliptical analogy to any predicament, from the most humorous to the most dire. Journalist Suzanne Smith would prove another valued addition to my Beehive team.

8

THE POLITICS OF IDEAS

By the time of the Waipuna document in early 1989 I had a strong strategic view of what I wanted in National's fiscal policy. Labour's fiscal policy was seriously compromising the growth prospects for the economy. Steadily rising government spending was leading to an increase in the tax burden, pressure on interest rates, and an alarming increase in the already high levels of government debt. To ease the burden on the private sector, government spending needed to be substantially reduced, and deficits turned into surpluses. Such an outcome would take more than just cosmetic changes and the occasional freeze on departmental expenditure. It would require major structural changes that reduced spending pressures over time.

That clearly meant tackling social spending, which made up almost three-quarters of the government's discretionary budget. It meant changing bureaucratic systems in health and education to make them more efficient, and more responsive to the needs of their users. And in social welfare it meant restructuring a system that was unwieldy and unaffordable and that sent the wrong signals to New Zealanders about the choice between work and welfare. In preparing us for this task, I was pleased to have the skills of Simon Upton as my associate spokesman with responsibility for social policy.

The biggest area of social spending was, of course, national superannuation. National already had a standing commitment to abolish the superannuation surcharge imposed by Labour. This was an expensive commitment and it did not provide a good starting point in developing a fair and affordable superannuation policy. There were already major questions over the long-term sustainability of national superannuation. With an ageing population, it could only survive in its current form for long into the next century by placing an intolerable burden on the working-age population.

Both Simon and I firmly believed national superannuation needed to be unhooked from its automatic indexation with wages. The wage linkage meant economic growth would never solve the affordability problem; if real wages increased so would the real cost of superannuation. Our proposed solution was to index superannuation to the consumers price index

(CPI). That would guarantee the standard of living of those already receiving superannuation. But it would also mean that, given reasonable economic growth, superannuation would constitute a smaller and smaller burden on the working-age population over time. Simon and I eventually gained the agreement of caucus to this proposal. Jim was attracted to the idea that he could give a 'cast-iron guarantee' that the living standards of superannuitants would not fall (something Labour could not do). However, he was never entirely comfortable with not having an explicit 'floor' to the relationship between superannuation and wages, as Labour had. Simon and I were content with the line that it was far too early to say anything about the relationship between superannuation and wages next century. Jim, however, felt uncomfortable with that degree of uncertainty, which is one reason the indexation mechanism ended up being revisited in government.

Simon and I were also influential in the adoption by National of the proposal to split the funding of hospitals from the provision of hospital services. That proposal had been put forward by the hospitals taskforce, whose advice Labour had ignored.

There was promising work done in the housing area by spokesman Jim Gerard, encouraged by Simon and myself. Instead of the current uneven and anomalous provision of rental units and subsidised lending, National would develop a policy of empowering the low-income user of housing services through an accommodation supplement. Simon also did good work on restructuring accident compensation so that individuals took more responsibility for their short-term risks. Sadly for a rational accident compensation scheme, that work was discarded when we took office.

As guardian of National's fiscal policy, my most immediate concern was to prevent too many spending commitments by my colleagues. There is a perennial temptation for an Opposition to run up a fiscal wish-list. Promising to spend money is one of the easiest ways of buying popularity – in the short term. In the medium term the bills all have to be paid. All spokespeople with proposals involving new spending came before the Caucus Economic Committee, chaired by my other associate finance spokesman, Doug Kidd. The committee had little formal power but it did provide us with a forum for scrutinising new initiatives. I kept a running tally of National's spending commitments, which I would periodically run past my colleagues, especially in front-bench meetings where confidentiality was greater than at full caucus. On one occasion I wrote a letter in which I warned of the $1 billion gap between our spending commitments and the savings options we had identified. Several months later Bill Birch's copy of the letter accidentally found its way to the media, providing an embarrassing moment for Jim and me.

To my colleagues it doubtless seemed I was playing the Jeremiah ad nauseam. The fiscal situation we eventually inherited, however, would end up much worse than even my own gloomiest prophesies.

In the end National's new spending proposals would be fairly limited. I was helped by the demotion late in 1989 of high-flying populist Winston Peters for bucking the party line once too often. He lost his employment responsibility. Peters had pledged to put all the unemployed on make-work schemes – a proposal both expensive and pointless. New employment spokesman John Banks had a much more realistic grasp of how new jobs are really created, and in consequence the employment policy was significantly modified.

National was committing new spending on extra police and on tertiary education. There were also tax reductions, which I was happy to promote: the abolition of land tax, diesel tax and estate and gift duties. The biggest and least justifiable of our fiscal commitments was the abolition of the superannuation surcharge.

Along with monetary and fiscal policy, labour market reform was a third area I saw as crucial to our economic strategy. Though I did not have direct responsibility for labour policy, I was intent on using my influence as finance spokeswoman to the greatest extent possible. There were two camps in the National caucus. One camp was content to make marginal alterations to the existing Labour Relations Act, keeping national awards in place but allowing more flexibility under some limited conditions. The favoured mechanism of this group was the balloting-out option: a workplace could opt out of the national award system into a site agreement by a majority vote of the workers on that site. The type of new bargaining structures under this approach would be very limited, and there would be a heavy built-in advantage for the status quo. The limited nature of the reform envisaged by this group in caucus is illustrated by the fact that many of them saw no contradiction in supporting Labour's pay equity – a policy utterly incompatible with greater flexibility in the labour market. Jim, in particular, was extremely nervous about being seen to oppose pay equity. Though caucus decided to oppose it, Jim would be still trying to persuade us to vote in favour of the pay equity legislation right up to its third reading in the House.

Those of us in the opposite camp on labour market reform were thinking through the issues from first principles. Maurice Williamson deserves praise for being an enthusiastic advocate of fundamental reform. Maurice and I and others like us wanted a radically new regime where there was genuine freedom to contract. As I put it in a paper to colleagues:

> The starting point for successful labour market reform must be a recognition that in any employment relationship, there is a common interest between employer and employee. As in any transaction, both parties must stand to gain something or the exchange would not take place at all. We must assume that people themselves are the best judges as to the merits or otherwise of any labour market contract they enter into.
>
> Labour market reform should be about giving people the freedom to make employment contracts on the terms they think fit. Of course the freedom to make contracts must be backed up by adequate legal safeguards against fraud, duress, misrepresentation and so on. But what the legal framework should not do is arbitrarily restrict the type of contracts people can enter into. That should be up to the individuals concerned.
>
> This applies to both sides of the labour market. The employer is the best person to handle industrial relations with their own workforce, or – at the very least – determine to whom the task should be delegated. The employer has more of the relevant facts than any outsider, and has the greatest incentive to get things right. The employee, on their part, deserves the chance to sell their labour services on terms and conditions they think fit, not on terms and conditions imposed by a third party. Much of our current unemployment – much of the marginalisation of the young,

the unskilled, those wanting to work a particular pattern of hours, and so on – comes from the arbitrary imposition of terms on others by third parties.

I argued that a labour market based on a common-law freedom to contract would lead to major improvements in work practices. It would result in higher productivity and much higher employment. Because employment contracts would now be based on the mutual interests of employer and employee, the new system would be far more stable, with fewer strikes and less industrial disruption. It would revolutionise the business culture, with firms taking a fresh look at how they utilised their human capital. I also argued that signals sent by the government would be important:

> The more quickly and clearly the shift to an open labour market is signalled to the business community, the more quickly the benefits from reform will begin to flow. The best employers are in a position to take immediate advantage of a completely new labour relations environment. Many others, not surprisingly, are still trapped in the thought habits of the only system they know. For this reason, it is important that labour market reform not only change the legal environment substantially, but be seen to do so. If we succumb to giving mixed signals, this will delay the adjustment process and the benefits that flow from it.

Progress within caucus on shifting to an open labour market policy was slow. Bill Birch, our labour spokesman, at first had reason to thank the fact that he also controlled the caucus agenda. His first attempt to get his position paper through caucus was unsuccessful. That morning I had learned, an hour before caucus, that labour market reform had been placed on the agenda. Bill's position paper was essentially a re-run of his 1987 policy. I hurriedly had an alternative version drafted. I distributed and spoke to the alternative version, gaining plenty of support from other speakers. Seeing that Bill would lose, Jim allowed him to withdraw his paper. Bill did so, then waited until I missed a caucus meeting through illness. This time Bill was successful.

But the battle was far from over. It was only a position paper and had yet to be approved by the policy committee. Early the next year, 1990, I launched National's principal economic policy paper, National's Economic Vision. In it I had drafted some strong words on the reform of the labour market:

> National will provide all employers and employees with the freedom of choice to negotiate contracts determining wages and conditions of

> employment. This will result in a range of agreements being developed, including workplace, industry and individual forms of contracting.

Surprisingly, Bill did not object to this passage, despite its being very similar to the words we had argued over in caucus just a few months previously. Following this success in the Vision document, I upped the rhetoric on labour market reform in my own speeches. Perhaps riskily, I told the Business Networking Society:

> Under National the only parties to labour contracts will be the employer and the employees. The government's role will be restricted to enforcing the standard rules of contract.

Bill, however, soon tried to release his earlier position paper as a final policy paper, but he made the serious tactical mistake of being overseas at the time of the launch. I found out about it at the very last minute, got hold of the paper, and managed to persuade Jim that it was inconsistent with the Vision document. Jim altered the paper, fudging the crucial passages.

The ups and downs of this saga stand as a good example of the capriciousness, the zig-zags, the manoeuvring, the tricks, the blind chance and the sheer confusion that constitutes so much of policymaking within a political party.

Later Bill developed his own re-interpretation of the words in the Vision document, judging by his public statements. He still wanted only a balloting-out mechanism for those in existing awards, but was prepared to allow individual contracts for new entrants into the labour market. This was a significant improvement, though it was clumsy and did not go far enough. The Business Roundtable put a great deal of effort into trying to educate Bill on the concept of free contracting, with some limited success. But right up until the time we took office, Bill was still thinking in terms of simply amending the Labour Relations Act. I knew there would still be a contest ahead of me.

Early in 1990, when National had no settled policy on inflation, Jim gave an interview to AP Dow Jones that would have deep repercussions. Jim had recently come under pressure from Labour on the cost of our election promises and appeared to be taking refuge in puberty economics. He said growth would replace low inflation as the principal economic goal under a National government, and that National would aim for growth of at least 3 per cent. According to Jim, Labour's target of 0-2 per cent inflation by 1992 would be abandoned. National would aim first for inflation below that of our trading partners, then for a rate of 2 per cent.

Jim's comments came as a complete surprise to me. The interview had an immediate impact on financial markets, which saw a weakened inflation commitment from the political party likely soon to become the government. Bond rates rose. Jim was both surprised and rattled at the market reaction; he did not want to be blamed for adverse movements in interest rates. It was a most valuable lesson.

Jim and I had a meeting on damage control. We agreed that National's target would be 0-2 per cent inflation by 1993, i.e. one year later than Labour's target. From my point of view, getting Jim settled on the 0-2 per cent target was a major advance; our one-year extension to the target was relatively minor by comparison. To 'clarify' National's position, I issued a statement announcing the new inflation target, and repeating the growth target.

The incident illustrated how much of an ally the financial markets would prove to be for me. It also convinced Jim that the time was now right to produce a formal economic policy document, to improve market confidence in the party. I got to work with enthusiasm, and National's Economic Vision rapidly came together. I was careful to get as wide an agreement as possible among key colleagues on the contents of the document.

The relevant sections were run past each spokesperson, the document went twice to the front bench, Jim had a significant input, and finally the document went through caucus. I wanted to gain the maximum possible sign-up on the strategy and did not want to be perceived by colleagues as ramming things through. In the event, the process went extremely smoothly and I was delighted at the quality of the end product.

National's Economic Vision presented an integrated – if broad-brush – economic strategy. Our commitment to price stability was reconfirmed. Labour market reform provided one of the themes of the document, as did education and training; both were seen as keys to assisting the shift from welfare to work. And there was a strong section on fiscal policy, emphasising redesign of the welfare state:

> National believes better economic performance requires not just a halt to the increase in the state's taxing and spending, but a sustained reduction ... Real progress can be made in turning back the negative tide of government taxes and spending to release resources for productive investment. National's industrial relations reforms and careful adjustments to the eligibility criteria for key welfare benefits will improve the opportunity and incentive to work.
>
> Redesigning the welfare state is at the heart of any serious attempt to rescue New Zealand from economic decline. Work must be rewarded

more highly than continuing dependence on benefits intended to provide temporary assistance.

One of the most important sentences in the Vision document came almost at the end. After a section listing the things National would do for business, came the words:

> In parallel with our strategy for economic excellence to improve the climate for industry, National will move to reduce the level of import protection provided to business.

No weasel words, no qualifications – just a straight statement. My reason for placing the sentence almost at the end was to have reductions in import protection seen as a quid pro quo for National's other policy changes. Once we had delivered on labour market reform, price stability, lower interest rates and lower taxes, protected manufacturers could not legitimately claim National was denying them the chance to become internationally competitive.

Import protection was another of those areas where Jim had come quite some distance over the previous 12 months. In 1989 he had been angry at a speech I made to farmers, where I had attacked the slow pace at which import protection was being taken down, relative to the cold-turkey treatment already given farmers. Now Jim was signing up to further reductions in import protection.

The Vision document contained a large number of goals that National committed itself to achieving in its first term:

- growth of at least 3 per cent per annum
- a halving of unemployment levels
- inflation of 0-2 per cent
- single-digit business and mortgage interest rates
- a balanced budget
- a fall in the share of government expenditure and taxation as a percentage of gross domestic product

At the time of the Vision document these goals already looked to be stiff targets. Growth had been near zero, unemployment was still rising, inflation was over 7 per cent and primary lending rates over 15 per cent. By election time the goals would be looking even more difficult. The economy we inherited would be contracting, and government spending out of control. In the end, though, all but one of the goals – that of halving unemployment – would be achieved within the timeframe we set for ourselves.

To me the goals were a calculated risk. The only way to achieve all or most of them would be through implementing the strategy in the Vision document. By raising the stakes, I raised my chances of success, though I also raised the costs of failure. For instance, some thought that the commitment not to put up taxes was making us a hostage to fortune. As it turned out, making that pledge was probably crucial to holding the line on tax increases. If we had not taken a firm position on taxes, spending ministers would have been in a very much stronger position once National had taken office.

I had originally presented an even stronger version of the document, which had commitments in place of goals. My front-bench colleagues softened it, which was undoubtedly the safer political option. There was then a lengthy debate in caucus over the goals. Some did not want them in the document at all. Others suggested there should be no timeframe for achieving them. Making the goals timeless would have seriously weakened the document and I was pleased when caucus decided to run with first-term targets.

Another of my debates with colleagues concerned the merits of putting numbers to National's planned expenditure-saving initiatives. I wanted numbers to be in the document because I thought it important to establish our fiscal credibility, but I received little support from other members of the front bench. This was another area where my colleagues proved politically wiser. Including numbers in a document may raise more questions that it answers, and the numbers themselves may become the focus of debate, rather than the key themes in the document. The Opposition inevitably has an information disadvantage compared with the government. Rightly or wrongly, experience suggests that it is better politically for Oppositions to run with a degree of fudge regarding their budgetary intentions. What Oppositions must do is spell out their general framework. This the Vision document certainly did. Once in government we acted on that framework.

National's Economic Vision was launched jointly by Jim and me and was a considerable success. The feedback was extremely positive. It was the first occasion I had used the slide show 'Economic Excellence', which I had developed as a means of presenting the key ideas in the Vision document. It was also the first time Jim and I had shared a platform in front of the business community. Disillusioned with Labour, the business community was curious not just about our policy but about the developing chemistry between Jim and me. It was years since business had been represented in such numbers at a National Party function. Most were impressed, as was

the National Party hierarchy. Our natural philosophical allies in the business community, who had left us in droves for Labour, were showing every sign of returning to the fold.

Muldoon also attended the Vision launch. Standing alone, he appeared agitated after the event, which had been marred only by one technical slip-up – the screen for the slide show had not been high enough for some at the back of the room to see. Muldoon, perhaps sensing and smarting at the success of the event, bawled out my press secretary for his failure to see. Anna, fearing a scene in front of the cameras, grabbed hold of his hand and massaged it. 'Sir Robert, I really think you should calm down,' she said, and he did!

Muldoon was not the only one to play the Economic Vision spoiler. Fatefully, Jim phoned me in high dudgeon the following day to demand that the Economic Vision's commitment to repeal the superannuation surtax in the first *term* be strengthened to read the first *budget*. Apparently he had been got at by the media overnight. Not content with ignoring my advice to avoid promising what we could not deliver, Jim compounded the error with his unilateral demand that we engage in fiscal folly sooner rather than later. History will record the unhappy chapter of broken promises to superannuitants that followed this episode.

Jim's new-year reshuffle of his line-up in 1990 reinforced the message sent out by the Vision document. First-term MP Jenny Shipley was given a big promotion to take on the social welfare role, replacing the retiring Venn Young. Jenny was to prove a key appointment. She possessed undoubted ability, drive, a clear sense of focus and considerable political courage. The pressure on her to rule out cuts in benefit levels prior to the election was intense but she withstood it and went on to play a crucial role in the Bolger Cabinet. If there was one minister whose absence in government would have made my task of driving through the economic strategy doubly difficult, it was Jenny.

Despite the success of the Vision document, there was continued speculation over whether Jim would appoint me as his Finance Minister. In April a caucus opponent of mine told the press that a National government would curtail the role of its Finance Minister by splitting the finance portfolio.

Jim was abroad and Don McKinnon was not in a position to deny the suggestion. The media seized on the idea that splitting the finance job would be the ideal way to sideline me in government. Television New Zealand's Richard Harman reported caucus concern that I was too hardline and too dogmatic on economic issues. Harman said it was probable National would opt to split the Treasury. I would become the Budget Minister, while another minister, presumably less dogmatic, would be responsible for overall government economic policy. I would merely be the bean-counter while the other minister held the real power. The media were picking Bill Birch and Philip Burdon as candidates for the real job.

I rang Jim and told him he needed publicly to rule out splitting the portfolio. He said he would do so on his return to New Zealand, but by the time Jim was back in the country the issue had reached fever pitch. There was huge unhappiness in the business sector and in large areas of caucus about any suggestion of split responsibility. Jim was true to his word: he publicly denied that he had any plans along those lines. But it was not an issue that would ever go away completely. When we were in government, the concept of splitting the Treasury would periodically resurface when Jim was reportedly unhappy with me.

As 1990 went on, the economic news became worse and worse for Labour. Both external and internal shocks hit the economy. We suffered a serious weakening in the prices of many of our pastoral products, plus rising oil prices as the conflict in the Gulf got under way. New Zealand's current account deficit deteriorated substantially. That year also saw a weak budget, with a paper 'surplus' achieved only by including asset sales. Many spending decisions had not even been included in the budget numbers. The budget led to a rise in interest rates and further eroded business confidence. Between the budget and the election Labour continued to make new spending commitments in a raft of promises up and down the country. It was apparent National would be inheriting an expenditure blowout of major proportions.

A National win at the election had long looked inevitable. What most concerned me was the extreme business pessimism that had developed in the course of the year. Some businesses were quietly getting on with things and making the best of an often difficult environment, but elsewhere many of the old attitudes seemed still to be flourishing: we can't compete; things are too hard. In too many business people there was a fatalism that New Zealand was doomed to a declining economic performance. While not eschewing party political rhetoric, in my message to business I was just as concerned to fire a shot across the bows of defeatist attitudes. For instance, I told students on an advanced Institute of Management course:

> Too many excuses are made on behalf of the New Zealand economy, and for the most part they are quack excuses.
>
> For instance, it is said that New Zealand must always be at a big disadvantage because we are a small country. Yet Switzerland, too, is a small country. The Swiss have the highest standard of living in the world. So much for that argument.
>
> It is argued that our geographical isolation puts us at a disadvantage. Clearly that is true, to a degree. Yet we have made the problem of transport costs much worse for ourselves by grossly inefficient practices on our wharves and on our ships. These can and will be rectified under National.
>
> Again, it is argued that New Zealand has only a narrow base of natural resources. True again, but again misleading. Countries with far fewer natural resources have done, and are doing, far better than New Zealand. Whatever has been the secret of South-east Asian success, it has not been natural resources. If they can succeed with so little, surely we can succeed with more.
>
> Still others argue that our land-based products are doomed to a long-term relative decline in prices on world markets, and to permanent market access problems. Since our competitive advantage is in land-based and not other products, it is claimed, we are doomed to long-term mediocrity.
>
> That argument is nonsense, and would remain nonsense even if I believed the future for agriculture and forestry were gloomy (which I do not). Competitive advantages are not fixed for all time; they are created

> by entrepreneurs. Because New Zealanders are good at agriculture, it does not mean that they cannot be good at other things as well ...
>
> There is no reason why New Zealanders cannot have a wealthy, self-reliant society. New Zealanders can innovate. New Zealanders can upgrade capital equipment, organise the workplace in new ways, develop new products. New Zealanders can seek out developing markets, respond to change, lead consumer tastes. If others can, we can.
>
> It is a question of attitude. The right attitude is crucial.

As part of that right attitude, I was keen to see as many business people as possible keying into the new possibilities opening up under National's labour market reform. Many business people were looking forward with anticipation to the changes. Many others, however, were slow to appreciate the significance of labour market reform; they had known the national award system all their lives and were happy enough simply to take it as given. I saw it as my task to play the evangelist – to 'talk up' the possibilities I saw opening up.

As the 1990 election neared we undertook planning in the National camp for our first days in office. I saw the two months prior to Christmas as critical. If we could not get away to a running start before Christmas, our momentum as a government would be severely compromised. We had to demonstrate early to the financial markets and the business community that we meant business. The sooner we did this, the sooner we could start to bank the upside that would be flowing from our strategy. There would be plenty of short-term downside. I was acutely conscious of the shortness of our three-year electoral cycle. I was well aware that, if I were lucky, there would be one year of radical reform. After that it would be consolidation, and nerving ourselves for the next election.

We agreed that we would aim to have legislation reforming the labour market in the House by Christmas. By then we would also have opened the books and made a start on – to use Jim's words – controlling, reducing and eliminating the budget deficit. I was keen to sign a new contract with the Governor of the Reserve Bank before Christmas. Also by then I would have liked to have a statement, if only of general principle, about the shape of the post-1992 tariff regime. National's watchword on tariffs, however, was 'consultation', which ruled out an early resolution by the government.

By now I had also discussed with Treasury Secretary Graham Scott how I wanted my office to run in the event of my becoming Minister of Finance. The discussion had been initiated by Graham at the request of David Caygill – a generous gesture on Caygill's part.

The election campaign itself had few memorable moments. It was all but inevitable National would win; the main question was the size of our majority. Privately I feared too large a caucus. A large caucus inevitably meant a large number of new members, most of whom would not be as keyed into National's economic strategy as existing members. Too big a swing would also bring elements into caucus from some of the more 'unwinnable' seats: many of these MPs would not have expected to get into Parliament at all. On election night, the swing turned out to be of monster size: National would have a caucus of 67. It was the most overwhelming victory in New Zealand's political history.

That night I was not worrying too much about the size of caucus. I was on my Selwyn farm, where my party workers had gathered in a marquee. On every side were the people who had helped me so much in my campaign in Selwyn, and it was a special moment when I was able to thank them for their efforts.

Party activists are a rare and very special breed. As my father, himself an electorate chairman and long-time office-holder in the National Party, would say: 'The difference between a politician and party official is this. When the campaign is over the politician goes on to a paid job in Wellington and the party official goes back to dagging old ewes!'

An MP's electorate organisation is in very substantial measure a reflection of the MP him- or herself. Activist MPs tend to gather around them an activist organisation. As the MP's political fortunes wax and wane, so too does the strength of the organisation. While party activity obviously peaks only at election time, there is a detectable difference in the behaviour of the organisation during Opposition and government years.

The party gets a better run and certainly more say during the Opposition years. Stripped of office the politicians are readier to listen – there is no competition from the bureaucracy. The drive to return the party to the Treasury benches fires up the organisation while the politicians, unburdened by office, are consequently more available and less likely to be in the line of fire. In government the organisation switches to more of a defensive position. Whatever their private misgivings, party people are expected to bat for government policy. While typically accessories after the fact, party officials are held to account in their communities for the actions of the government. This is a tough, demanding proposition, as my loyal electorate workforce was soon to find out. I was extraordinarily well served throughout my tenure as Selwyn's MP.

When I first won the Selwyn nomination they had not had a contested selection for over 30 years. The high-profile contest to succeed Colin

McLauchlan ignited the electorate and brought in a wave of new members. The selection process was presided over by an extremely able party man with a wonderful sense of humour. In Bill Johnston I could not have wished for a better electorate chairman to manage the transition from super-conservative Colin McLauchlan to radical conservative me.

Bill, an exacting grammarian, bridled at the somewhat colloquial language we chose for our first campaign advertisement. 'This is where it's at' the headline proclaimed in an ad designed to draw attention to the fact that Andrew and I had bought a property in Selwyn and had made our home here. Very unsubtly, we were seeking to counter the carpetbagger flak. Bill had no quarrel with the intent, just the execution.

I continued to be blessed with able and exacting chairpeople throughout my parliamentary career. Jeanette Miller followed, a veteran of Colleen Dewe's successful quest for the Lyttelton seat in 1975. Jim Sunckell succeeded her and proved to be a great political and personal help to me. Talking the Representation Commission out of some of its sillier ideas was Jim's speciality. Off duty, Jim and his wife Bettye became close friends and surrogate grandparents to Lucy and Oliver. Both of the children's sets of grandparents were 'from the North Island' (a very South Island expression) so we were grateful for a local set of on-course substitutes.

Bernard Duncan, who went on to become chairman of the Canterbury-Westland Division of the National Party, took over the reins from Jim and sharpened the policy focus in the electorate. My most able policy officer, Jenny Shipley, proved to be an inspired choice. Once recruited it was clear she was destined for higher things – it was a matter of when, rather than if.

When Bernard stepped up to the divisional job my campaign chairman the previous year, Bill Studholme, was made to measure for the electorate chairmanship. A man of irrepressible wit, personal dynamism and lots of political savvy, Bill would be a tower of strength to me during the turbulent years in finance that were to follow. While many around me were wavering, Bill would be absolutely rock solid on the merit of the policies I was promoting. He conducted the electorate meetings like none other I had encountered: they were a riot. Bill reckoned that politics was to be enjoyed to the full and with much gusto he led from the chair.

Throughout my ministerial career I would take my electorate committee into my absolute confidence and never once did they let me down. They gave me wise counsel and never broke a confidence.

The gem of the electorate was undoubtedly Frances Smith. Frances has baked more scones, cakes and biscuits in the National Party's cause than anyone I know. Oliver, in particular, looked forward to the monthly electorate meetings. Invariably I would return with a back seat full of Frances's cooking, including Oliver's favourite chocolate chippie biscuits. Frances's great personal kindness was matched by a sharp political sense. She could and would speak her mind at political meetings, sometimes withering in her attack but always winning in her ways. Frances and her wonderful husband Donald supported me through every branch AGM, every campaign, every crisis. There was so little I could do to repay their numerous kindnesses save press on with the job they expected me to do – and on the odd occasion cut Donald's hair!

Accompanied by people such as these, I savoured that October evening in the Selwyn marquee. I had a great deal to celebrate. I had been in Parliament for nine years, and National had come a huge distance over that time. But now, and only now, would I be in a position to make a real difference. The preparation was over. Now would come the opportunity of a lifetime.

Jim had talked about the '56 action-packed days' National would have before Christmas. Little did we know that in the first few days following the election we would be working, not on our own agenda, but on a rescue package of the utmost urgency.

9

FIFTY-SIX ACTION-PACKED DAYS

The day after the election, when Prime Minister-elect Jim Bolger arrived back in Wellington from Te Kuiti, he received news that was as unexpected as it was unpleasant. The Bank of New Zealand (BNZ), in which the government was majority shareholder, was in a parlous financial state so serious that unless the government produced a rescue package the bank would almost certainly collapse.

We had all been aware that recent years had been difficult for the BNZ. A number of banks had over-extended themselves during the sharemarket boom and the BNZ had become more carried away, and more divorced from reality, than almost any other. Slack lending criteria and a gung-ho corporate culture, not least in its Australian operations, had left the BNZ seriously exposed when the loans began to turn bad. In 1989 the bank declared a huge loss. As a means of injecting capital, the Labour government had allowed investment company Fay Richwhite to buy a substantial minority holding in the bank.

Everyone was assured at that time that the BNZ was putting its losses behind it. That impression was strengthened when, the following year, the bank brought down an upbeat annual result. But unbeknown to the public, the bank's position worsened further in the second half of the year as the New Zealand and Australian economies both deteriorated. It was becoming apparent that a massive write-down of nonperforming loans would be needed, and officials began preparing rescue contingencies. Labour, however, had no desire to do anything on the eve of an election. Their political cravenness did not save them from electoral annihilation, but it did increase the urgency with which the new government needed to act. The bank would shortly be announcing its half-yearly result, and a rescue package was needed by then – at the latest. Every day that passed increased the risk of news of the financial state of the BNZ leaking and starting a run on the bank.

On learning the news, Jim immediately brought me, and his ever-present comfort-blanket Bill, into the circle of those dealing with the issue. We had extensive discussions with officials. In theory we could simply let our largest bank go into liquidation. But this would have had such serious flow-on effects to other companies, and to general economic and financial confidence, that we did not even contemplate it. The real question was how to inject funds into the bank in a way that minimised the inevitable loss of confidence and gave the clearest possible signal that the bank had put its troubles behind it. We also wanted Fay Richwhite to contribute to the rescue package. Involving the smaller shareholders was, of course, totally impractical.

The favoured option of officials, which the three of us accepted, involved isolating the BNZ's bad loans into a separate 'bad bank'. This had the presentational advantage of allowing most of the losses associated with the write-down of the past bad loans to be absorbed in the accounts of the 'bad bank', rather than through the profit and loss statement of the BNZ. The details of the rescue package were extremely complex, but involved the government injecting over $600 million into the bank.

During one of my meetings with Jim, Bill and the officials, Jim indicated, obliquely, that I would be his Finance Minister. He did so simply by referring to me as the Minister of Finance. It was the first time he had given me a firm indication of his intentions, and it was a strange way in which to do it. I had been fairly confident of securing the job ever since the publication of the Vision document, despite periodic speculation to the contrary. But Jim had played his cards very close to his chest. I had never been 100 per cent confident; with Jim, you never could be.

Because of the need to act urgently, I strongly advised Jim to bring forward the naming and swearing in of the new Cabinet. He had planned to wait until the following Monday but I did not want other ministers to have any perception that Jim, Bill and I were ramming the BNZ issue through without reference to Cabinet. On my urging, the new Cabinet was sworn in and held its first meeting on Friday. There we agreed to the broad outlines of the rescue package, and to negotiations between the government, the bank and Fay Richwhite. The only minister who objected to the package was Winston Peters. In his view, we should have let the bank fall over – a huge irony, given that Peters would later set himself up as the champion of the BNZ's small shareholders.

Over the weekend there was a great deal of work to do. There were the final details of the transaction to strap down. I also had to work on the release of an updated fiscal forecast for 1990-91, which would need to be released at the same time as the announcement of the rescue package. The injection of funds to the BNZ was significantly worsening the fiscal deficit and it would also mean an addition to the government's debt programme. The previous government had planned no new net borrowing on the domestic market in 1990-91. I was faced with the choice of undertaking new domestic borrowing (which might put pressure on interest rates), or adding to our offshore debt. I had no hesitation in choosing new domestic borrowing. I wanted to signal to the financial markets that, unlike my predecessor, I was not a Minister of Finance for the soft option. The full BNZ package went through Cabinet on the Monday and was duly announced later that day.

Though I chafed at having to spend my first few days following the election hunkered down on the BNZ issue, in a strange way the episode had its advantages. It had Jim and I working closely together right from the start. And it added to the sense of fiscal crisis that enveloped the early weeks of our government, which could only add impetus to my agenda. The episode was also excellent propaganda value for the government. As Roger Douglas knew only too well, a crisis inherited from your predecessor can give you a flying start in terms of impetus and goodwill. Jim, in particular, enjoyed using the line: 'We had to pay out $640 million on the BNZ' as a means of helping justify National's fiscal stringency. He liked the line so much that, when I first seriously raised the question of privatising the bank, Jim opposed it ostensibly on the grounds that he would no longer be able to use that line!

Politically useful it may have been, but the BNZ crisis was also thoroughly unsettling. Despite protestations from the bank that the bad news was behind it, I was acutely aware that the same assurances had been made the last time the bank had been bailed out by the government. I did not want it happening a third time. I invited myself to the next board meeting and acted suitably appalled: I was at my most intimidating. I asked the bank to undertake a wide-ranging operational review of its policies and procedures regarding credit management, information and reporting systems, and nonperforming loans. The board agreed and the review was subsequently undertaken. The following year I also moved to strengthen the board of the bank, bringing in economist Kerry MacDonald and banker Sandy Maier. Both men would do an excellent job.

Over that first BNZ weekend I had shifted across from the old Parliament Buildings to the Beehive – the government's executive wing. Like my two predecessors in office, Roger Douglas and David Caygill, I chose to occupy the 6.3 suite of offices in the Beehive. This suite was wired up for a Minister of Finance with financial market screens, several individual staff offices, and a big ministerial office to accommodate the huge traffic of officials in and out.

Nestled in behind each ministerial office in the Beehive is a dinky little bathroom and changing room. Mine had a very masculine look about it, so I proceeded at once to tear down all the shaving clutter and install a hair dryer and ironing gear. When I turned my attention to the cupboard beneath the basin my gales of laughter prompted by what I had discovered were loud enough to be heard through the thick concrete walls, and curious staff poked their noses around the door. Sitting on the shelves were David Caygill's abandoned goods: one container of Joe Weider's Dynamic Bodybuilding Blocks, one container of 300 Carbo Energisers, and one bottle of Dynamic Deep Relief! We sometimes wondered whether David had turned to Joe's potent remedies as his stewardship of finance became progressively unstuck.

David is the most decent of politicians, who studied law at Canterbury University just ahead of me. He took over the finance portfolio in difficult circumstanccs and peppered his early speeches with dynamic bodybuilding language. Then came his attempts to rev up the economy. We reckoned the Carbo Energisers must have come into their own at that point, but it was only after the failure of his 1990 budget, with its transparent myth of a claimed $89 million surplus, that David must have turned to Dynamic Deep Relief.

To be fair to Caygill, he cemented in the legacy of Roger Douglas in two key respects. He saw into law both the Public Finance Act and the Reserve Bank Act, the latter in the face of considerable opposition from within his own ranks. Though these were Douglas initiatives, it was Caygill who had to see them through. Caygill and Richard Prebble had also been outstanding 'outriders' for Roger Douglas in Labour's final term. They were his highly effective associate ministers who 'front footed' the case for reform tirelessly, and 'mixed it' for Douglas when he wished to stand above the fray. (I would not be lucky enough to have such a consistent run with my own various associates.) In his own right, Caygill was also Minister for Trade and Industry, and obviously relished that role.

As Minister of Finance, Caygill had one special responsibility that did not end happily – the Development Finance Corporation. He had travelled to Hong Kong to launch a lavish publication by the DFC. His speech, which I am told was written almost entirely in his office, betrayed his strong personal commitment to the DFC: it was little short of a ministerial advertisement for the DFC delivered to an audience of Asian investors. Days later the DFC crashed, leaving not just David's reputation the poorer but, more damaging, New Zealand's. The DFC by that stage had no government backing or guarantee, but that was not the impression the DFC staffers had given or Japanese investors had received. It took over $100 million of taxpayers' money, and prolonged and very professional efforts by Sandy Maier and the Debt Management Office, to put New Zealand's relationship with the Japanese financial market back on a normal footing.

The Beehive receives a very bad press – not just the occupants but the building itself. In my earlier political career Parliament had proved a hostile place for families. Now as a minister I discovered that the Beehive was hostile to my health. It was not just the typically long hours a minister works. Most often I would run from my ministerial house at 6.30am and not set foot back there until after midnight. The Beehive was a health risk in its own right. It had no windows that could be opened. Jim McLay contracted legionnaire's disease from the air conditioning; blocked sinuses and bad headaches were frequent afflictions suffered by previously healthy ministers. I made up my mind early on in the piece to rectify matters. Often criticised for sloganeering, I had a ready slogan for what would happen. I announced to my staff – equally complaining about the foul Beehive air – that I would not just 'open the books', I would open the windows. The former would prove easier to accomplish than the latter.

There followed endless confrontations with engineers. Doug Kidd, in the suite next to me, a heavy smoker, joined the cause and gave considerable moral support. Tests were done, the spirit of the architect Sir Basil Spence was invoked to say that nothing must change and, predictably, I was given the big guilt trip on the public-expenditure consequences of my demands for fresh air. Not easily thwarted, I persisted. It was not until my third and final year in the Beehive that I prevailed. Opening windows were installed not just in my office but in all my staff offices as well.

The BNZ had not been the only shock awaiting the new government. The first document I received on becoming minister was the Treasury's post-election briefing (PEB), which showed an alarming fiscal picture. In the absence of changes to government policy, deficits were projected of $3.7 billion in 1991-92, $4.5 billion in 1992-93 and $5.2 billion (6.3 per cent of GDP) in 1993-94. The projected deficits had a large structural, as well as cyclical, component. The outlook in the PEB was worse than my own most gloomy predictions. If I was surprised, Jim was appalled. Our manifesto policy was to balance the budget in three years without raising taxes. Clearly we had a huge amount of work to do.

We were caught in a double bind. We had been surprised at the size of the deficits we had inherited. At the same time, our manifesto contained commitments – particularly on superannuation – that should not have been made. Keeping our promises would make our fiscal task even harder. Failing to keep our promises would cause huge political fallout. The scene was set for the loss of moral authority that would dog the government for the whole of its first term in office.

As Minister of Finance I generally had a practice of maximum frankness with financial markets. On this occasion, however, I did not believe it responsible to release the fiscal projections until we were in a position to disclose simultaneously the government's initial policy response to those projections. Jim was of the same view.

Major cuts in government spending would be needed at a time when the economy was already in a fragile state. The latest deficit projections had come at the end of two decades of steadily rising government spending, taxation, deficits and debt. I had no truck with the view that the economy was too weak to sustain spending cuts. Constant deficit spending had not brought growth; it had led to excessive interest rates, a huge build-up of debt, and a gradual erosion of foreign confidence in our fiscal policy. We had to break out of the vicious circle of debt, high interest rates and falling confidence. As for raising taxes, I dismissed without qualification any such idea. Besides being contrary to our policy, tax increases would send quite the wrong signal to New Zealanders about work, savings, investment and the acquisition of skills. The tax burden was already too high and I was not about to make it higher. Even moderate tax increases, besides being wrong in principle, would substantially weaken my bargaining hand against other ministers in any attempt to find expenditure reductions. As far as I was concerned, there was only one feasible strategy: to prepare a sustained assault on government spending.

Very early on Jim decided to invite business and sector leaders to a growth summit at the Beehive. To me the conference was, frankly, a distraction. I had been listening to business for three years; the time had come for action. Jim saw the conference as a public relations exercise. It was memorable chiefly for an intemperate attack by Fletcher Challenge chief executive Hugh Fletcher on Treasury Secretary Graham Scott and Reserve Bank Governor Don Brash – both of whom were present. Fletcher called for the two men to be sacked, and for the Reserve Bank's price stability goal to be abandoned. Graham replied that if he gave advice of the sort Fletcher was advocating, he would deserve to be sacked. Jim defended Graham and Don, as did I – stoutly.

Though Jim's public reaction on that occasion was entirely proper, in private it would take a long time before he was entirely comfortable in dealing with the Treasury. To Jim the Treasury staff were ideologues whom he instinctively mistrusted. I would regularly arrange meetings between Jim, myself, Graham and Don, seeking to provide Jim with that 'comfort zone' around macroeconomic policy that I knew would be vital. I thought it important that Jim be exposed regularly to Don Brash's thinking. I also thought it important that the Treasury re-establish contact with the ninth floor of the Beehive – a region they had rarely seen in the latter years of the Labour government. These meetings often started with a Jim grizzle about how the Treasury's advice to the last government had not worked. The Treasury's forecasting performance was another sensitive area. The frequency and scale of their revisions often left Jim unsettled. Over time, however, he gradually became more and more comfortable with their advice, and with the uncertainty associated with fiscal forecasting.

The Treasury would qualify as New Zealand's best-known but not best-loved bureaucracy. Theirs is the tough patch. Curiously, the Treasury became the media's and the politicians' favourite whipping boy, but so often it was a case of visiting the sins of their masters on them. Lange became most vitriolic about the Treasury when the relationship between him and Douglas had irretrievably broken down. Muldoon became most dismissive about 'Treasury theory' as the practical failure of his own policy prescriptions became most evident. And even Jim, with his periodic musings (sometimes out loud) about splitting the Treasury, was reflecting a latent suspicion about the Treasury position.

If you were to listen to the Treasury's critics, and there were many, you would be forgiven for thinking they were a bunch of pimply-faced, scarcely-shaving, economic eggheads who had done their very best to wreck the New Zealand economy. One had to assume when the catchcry went up – 'What about the human face of the economy?' – that their designs were inhuman. Nothing could be further from the truth. They have played a major role in transforming the New Zealand economy from an object of national shame to a source of national pride. Their economic and policy skills put them at the forefront of best international practice. With a little licence to boast, their ambition to be 'the best little Treasury in the world' has largely been fulfilled.

Admittedly, the Treasury tend not to have sophisticated political antennae, but that constitutionally is not their job. I recall running into Roger Douglas soon after I became minister and we compared notes on the Treasury. 'There is only one thing wrong with them,' said Douglas. 'They are hopeless at anything political,' a verdict with which I readily concurred. Yet even that, in a backhanded way, is a tribute to their integrity as public servants.

I had had little contact with the Treasury in Opposition save for the ritual grilling before the Finance and Expenditure Select Committee. The politics of the occasion meant these sessions were always conducted in an adversarial atmosphere and, unhappily, the sum of human wisdom was rarely advanced.

My first real introduction to the Treasury came with a more pleasant ritual – the formal tour by the new minister of the Treasury offices. With an eye to the media entourage in tow, I shook Graham Scott's hand of welcome and produced two stamps. One read 'Just Dreadful' and the other 'Just Excellent'. These stamps had been given to me as a swearing-in present by my office staff, capturing in print two of my favourite but much overworked expressions. With tongue in cheek I challenged the Treasury to earn my liberal use of the 'Just Excellent' stamp, although I warned that I would not hesitate to apply the 'Just Dreadful' label if it were warranted.

Three years later, in my farewell visit to the Treasury, I would formally present them with the 'Just Excellent' stamp. The Treasury had collected numerous brickbats in their time – I wanted to leave them with a well-deserved bouquet.

Dr Graham Scott was the Secretary of the Treasury for all but the last few months of my tenure as Minister of Finance. Highly experienced and possessing a considerable intellect, Graham led the Treasury for the bulk of the decade of reform. He was fortunately better at economics than he was at picking who would be his minister on the change of government. Once he got to know me, Graham confessed he had been far from convinced that Jim would take the plunge and make me his Finance Minister in preference to his old friend Bill Birch, and had bet accordingly. Graham had retired by the time his Birch bet came good three years later. His replacement was Murray Horn. Youthful, buoyant and talented, Murray will be a highly influential figure in public policy for as long as he chooses to stay in the ranks of the public service.

Graham was quick to redeem himself after his initial lack of faith. His Treasury was teeming with talent and he gave them inspired leadership. While it was up to me and the government to set the policy agenda, much of the horsepower to translate those ideas into practice came from the Treasury. The very excellence of their expertise would often set up resistance, which the Treasury – and therefore I – experienced from many quarters, particularly fellow ministers and the senior bureaucracy. At these times, often while I was away overseas, dumping on the Treasury became a favourite Cabinet sport. When all else fails, or in the absence of a better argument, berating the Treasury for some sin – sometimes real but most often imagined – seems to be standard practice. Likewise, other senior departments would cover their own inadequacies with a collective or individual whinge about Treasury interference or influence.

Treasury people, to their credit, wear such criticism as a badge of honour. They have much to be proud about. They emerged from the long trauma of the Muldoon years with their economic powder and shot dry. Their advice to the incoming government in 1984 was a legendary piece of work. During Labour's years the Treasury's public-policy influence came to be matched by their private-sector presence. A wave of key Treasury thinkers migrated from the public to the private sector, taking with them an analytical quality that was to become such an asset to private enterprise.

The most influential migrant was Roger Kerr, who became the brains behind the New Zealand Business Roundtable. Roger is a market missionary. Unfailingly courteous, unflinchingly principled and unceasing in his advocacy, Roger was to acquire somewhat of a Treasury-in-exile reputation. His contribution to the quality of public policy, while often pivotal, is generally unacknowledged. Indeed, when praise should be his due, scorn is heaped upon his head. I was less than impressed, for example, when Jim chose to employ that tactic midway through our first term. We had started to make some headway with the fiscal position, but it was still early days and New Zealand remained substantially afflicted by the twin scourge of debt and deficits. Helpfully, I thought, the Business Roundtable issued a study entitled Budgetary Stress, advocating a substantial fall in public expenditure levels to between 25 per cent and 30 per cent of gross domestic product. Jim immediately, and without any reference to me, dismissed the target out of hand as 'too ambitious'. The rich irony is that getting public expenditure levels below 30 per cent of GDP is now official government policy. Persistence pays off.

While the Treasury is expected to be a source of robust economic advice, New Zealand is virtually alone in enjoying similar leadership from the private sector. With Roger Kerr as anchorman and a parade of prominent private business people, the Business Roundtable has made a major contribution to the quality of public policy in New Zealand. What distinguishes that contribution is that the advice tendered is often against the immediate self-interest of the businesses that back that advice. The New Zealand experience is very atypical. Generally businesses are complicitous with governments in advocating the maintenance of poor-quality public policy. One only has to look at the behaviour of subsidised industries in Europe and the protectionists in the 'free-market' United States to know that economic virtue in the private sector is the exception rather than the rule. It is a bit like asking the voters to give up their gravy. Generally they won't and they don't.

Whatever his own private doubts about the Treasury, Jim Bolger was never more solidly behind me than during the government's pre-Christmas period. One of my first actions as minister was to prepare a strategy paper to Cabinet stressing three key planks of our economic policy: fiscal consolidation, price stability and labour market reform. I was pleased – and not a little surprised – when Jim offered to sign it onto the Cabinet agenda himself. At an early stage Jim also gave the assembled Cabinet a strong message on the importance of all ministers cooperating with the fiscal strategy. Jim gave a similar message at a gathering of departmental chief executives. Bill Birch was fully behind the fiscal strategy, which was extremely valuable given his role as unofficial deputy leader. All three of the ministers in the biggest-spending departments – Jenny Shipley in social welfare, Simon Upton in health and Lockwood Smith in education – also lent their support to the government's wider fiscal policy. This too was of considerable importance. Though over the coming months I would inevitably have arguments with Simon and Lockwood over their own votes, they – along with Jenny – always took a responsible line on the need for the government to hold to its economic strategy. Roger Douglas had received a far lower degree of co-operation from his big-spending ministers.

It is never easy for ministers with large and vocal constituencies to accept spending restraint in their portfolios. Lining Cabinet up behind the fiscal strategy was largely a matter of making ministers claim ownership of the economic outcomes we sought. All ministers wanted to associate themselves with an economic recovery. By accepting spending restraint, they would at least be able to say that they were contributing to that recovery. In obtaining leverage over my colleagues, there was also a potent and far more immediate weapon available to me – the financial markets. The threat of interest rates going up always concentrated the minds of my colleagues.

In our search for savings before Christmas I was well aware of the need to balance two key objectives. We needed to find immediate savings that made a demonstrable inroad into our fiscal problem. But we needed to take this short-term action in a way that did not compromise our ability to make savings over the long term. For we needed to begin the task of making long-term structural change to the delivery of social services.

The biggest potential source of both short- and long-term savings was undoubtedly social welfare spending. My discussions with Jenny were extremely fruitful; not only did she fully support the fiscal strategy, she also shared my philosophy on the need to make inroads into state dependency. Neither of us saw the exercise simply as one of budget-cutting. We saw it as restoring integrity to our social welfare system. We believed independence and self-reliance needed to be encouraged; that low-income workers should not be penalised compared with those on benefits; and that state assistance should be directed to people in genuine need.

We had three broad ways in which we could make savings:

- reduction in the levels of some benefits;
- complete abolition of some benefits; and
- tightening the eligibility requirements.

Both of us saw scope for reducing benefit levels. At that time, an unemployed married couple with three children received $341 net per week from the unemployment benefit and family assistance. A household earning the wage of the lowest quintile of full-time wage and salary earners had, after state assistance, almost the same income: $363 per week. Once transport and other work-related costs were taken into account, the difference was even narrower. This was clearly unsatisfactory. Similarly, a sole parent with two children would gain just $49 per week if he or she moved off state assistance and into a job earning in the lowest quintile of incomes. With transport and childcare costs, there was little if any incentive for a sole parent to take that job. Not surprisingly, our ratio of benefits to wages was higher than in many other countries, such as Australia.

Jenny and I agreed on a schedule of new benefit levels to take to Cabinet. The reductions to the unemployment benefit rates for single adults and for those with children, and to domestic purposes benefit rates, were generally in the region of 10 per cent. The sickness benefit was also being cut because, like the unemployment benefit, it was intended as short-term assistance. The invalid's benefit, designed for those who needed long-term assistance, would not be cut. Cabinet made few modifications to our proposals, but accepted the further suggestion by Lockwood that the under-20 rate of unemployment benefit be extended to all those under 25 without dependants. This category of people are flexible, mobile and often short on work experience. It was reasonable to set their benefit at a level that strongly encouraged workforce participation.

The universal family benefit cost the taxpayer a considerable sum of money, yet was very poorly targeted expenditure. Many households receiving this benefit had no need for it. For instance, despite earning the salaries of Cabinet ministers, Jenny and I both received family benefit – and at the same rate as someone on one-fifth of our income. This was nonsensical. We believed the time had come for its abolition. However, to fully protect those on the lowest incomes, we proposed that some of the savings be reinvested in enhanced family support. That was consistent with our policy of directing assistance to those in genuine need.

Changes to benefit eligibility went hand in hand with adjustments to benefit levels. These included a 26-week stand-down for those who left their last job voluntarily, who had been dismissed for misconduct, or who had refused a suitable offer of work or training; and a stand-down of up to 26 weeks for those receiving sufficiently large redundancy payments. Further savings were made by not inflation-adjusting any social welfare benefits for the 1990-91 year – including national superannuation. The full-year savings from all of these welfare measures together totalled well over $1 billion.

My colleagues and I also reached agreement on immediate savings in the areas of health, education and housing. In health we modified the over-generous subsidies for medical prescriptions and doctors' visits brought in by Labour in their last budget, but in a way that protected high users and the chronically ill. In education we reversed Labour's scandalous decision to dedicate some of the proceeds from the sale of Telecom to the maintenance of school buildings, and scrapped Labour's May employment package. In housing we shifted the Housing Corporation's higher-income clients to market rates for both rent and mortgages, and scaled back both new lending and the acquisition of new rental units.

The concentration of resources on those in real need was as much a theme of these changes as it had been with the social welfare initiatives.

While we were taking these decisions on social policy, those of us on the Cabinet Committee on Expenditure Control (chaired by Doug Kidd) were reviewing all of Labour's spending initiatives that had not been in the 1990 budget. Some of these initiatives were cancelled, while others were put on hold pending further review.

In all, we identified immediate savings of over $2 billion – an excellent effort from a few short weeks' work. Because we had set our strategic goals and had a clear set of priorities, we were able to make rapid progress. Looking back, the quality of the expenditure decisions prior to Christmas was extremely high. While we did not expect expenditure cutting to be popular with the public, few if any of the decisions made before Christmas would rebound in an unforeseen way. The Labour Opposition would noisily oppose the benefit cuts, but they conspicuously refrained from pledging to restore the old benefit levels – a tacit recognition that benefits had been too high relative to wages.

I was delighted at our progress in finding immediate savings. However, I was keen to ensure that the momentum of reform continued over into the new year. In controlling expenditure, if you are not going forwards you are usually going backwards. The key to continued progress would be the structural reforms to social expenditure National had planned, and I wanted these signalled to the financial markets before Christmas.

Luckily, Jim had the bit between his teeth. He decided that he himself would be chairing the key Cabinet Committee on Social Policy Reform. Cabinet reached agreement on the composition and terms of reference of a series of taskforces that would be reporting to the government in time for decisions in the 1991 budget. Just as important, Cabinet agreed to think the previously unthinkable – that we might need to take a fresh look at our commitments on national superannuation. Two considerations drove Jim to that conclusion. Our commitment to repeal the surcharge was expensive. But just as important in Jim's mind was the 'fairness' question. The government was cutting the incomes of many of the poorest in our society. Economic conditions had already cut the incomes of many others. To boost simultaneously the position of wealthy superannuitants seemed incongruous in the extreme. I, who had never wanted the surcharge repealed, was happy to add leverage to this line of thinking.

Jim's initial idea was to hold a multi-party conference on national superannuation in an attempt to reach cross-party agreement. I was personally sceptical that we would be able to reach a satisfactory agreement with Labour. National had been offered just such a chance of all-party talks when in Opposition; we had preferred to stand back, let Labour take the flak for imposing the surcharge, and outbid them at the electoral auction. Labour now had precisely the same incentive: to excoriate the government from the sideline for broken promises. However, it was probably good public relations for National to be seen at this stage to be at least attempting to forge a bipartisan agreement. Whatever the merits of bipartisanship, by Christmas it was clear that rethinking national superannuation was on our agenda for 1991.

A similar unease with the degree of pain National was inflicting on low-income earners led Jim and others in Cabinet to favour doing work on charging high-income earners more for their social services. This was an initiative I also favoured, but for a different reason. Philosophically, Jim and I were poles apart on social policy, but in practice we had ended up at the same destination. For Jim it was a 'fairness' issue; he favoured charging high-income earners more for social services for the same reason that he favoured a progressive income tax. To Jim, as to most of his colleagues, one of the roles of government was to redistribute income. Jim's instinct would probably have been to put up income tax, had that route not been blocked by our pre-election commitment. To me, the role of government was not to redistribute income, but to provide a guaranteed minimum of income and services for those unable to look after themselves. For that you needed targeting.

One of the inevitable problems of targeting is that, because the targeted assistance is phased out as income rises, high effective marginal tax rates (EMTRs) can arise. If targeting were introduced over a range of government services, there would need to be co-ordination to ensure that EMTRs did not become cripplingly high at certain income levels. For this reason the Treasury proposed that a global exercise be undertaken to co-ordinate targeting across different social services. This led ministers to set up the management team on targeting social assistance.

Fiscal policy was taking up a large amount of my time in the weeks prior to Christmas. But I was very conscious of another issue that could not be neglected: labour market reform. Late on the Friday, in our first full week as a government, I received a paper on labour market reform that Bill Birch had succeeded in getting accepted for Monday's Cabinet. In theory all Cabinet papers with 'economic, financial or revenue' implications required a Treasury report. Bill had signed his paper up with a declaration that it had no such implications. Since Bill's was a 'late' paper he must also have obtained the Prime Minister's authority for it to go on the agenda. Bill's paper was short on detail and lacked a clear framework. It was not clear how far Bill was intending to go on labour market reform, but it was clear that he was proposing only to amend the existing legislation. He envisaged a two-tier process: before Christmas he wanted legislation introduced on voluntary unionism and bargaining reform; after Christmas he wanted to examine second-order issues such as labour market institutions and the minimum wage.

By the time Cabinet came around on Monday I had an alternative paper prepared, much fuller than Bill's. Mine argued for a clean break from the industrial relations regime of the past. I recommended that the government adopt a regime of complete freedom to contract in the labour market. In my paper, the government's role would be confined essentially to enforcing the rules of contract.

My paper even had a draft labour market statute attached to it. It spelt out the rules of free contracting and contained a set of 'default conditions' that would apply to a contract if, and only if, certain elements had not been specified by the parties to the contract. The default conditions were a means of protecting the unsophisticated, while at the same time not limiting in any way the types of deals that could be entered into by freely contracting parties. I did not expect – though I hoped – that my own statute would win acceptance by Cabinet. My motivation had been partly to counter Bill, who was arguing we did not have time before Christmas to draft a completely new labour statute. But as my own statute showed, it was a relatively simple exercise to encapsulate free contracting in labour legislation.

I had circulated my paper just prior to Cabinet. When Cabinet came to consider Bill's paper, ministers also had mine. The outcome of the discussion was perhaps a draw, but my aggressive approach had paid off, at least in shifting the balance of the debate within Cabinet. Bill was given the pen to prepare draft legislation, but the instructions minuted by Cabinet were for as 'comprehensive' a reform of the labour market as possible.

Over the next three or four weeks the Employment Contracts Bill gradually came together. The issues in the bill received remarkably little Cabinet attention in total. I managed to get Treasury and the Prime Minister's

Department involved in the drafting of the new legislation, along with the Labour Department. This was extremely important: my own officials were firmly on my wavelength, whereas the Labour Department was still trapped in the old way of thinking. At the Cabinet level I continued to do all I could to push the legislation towards the free-contracting model. Bill himself seemed to have moved some distance towards me, though at no stage did he fully sign up to the essence of free contracting.

The draft bill was verbose, contained anomalies, and in places lacked focus. It reflected Bill's concern – which to my mind was peripheral – about representation and the actual process of negotiation. But the draft bill was still a very major advance. Though never explicitly couched in terms of free contracting, that is what the various elements in the bill mostly amounted to. We had brought Bill a huge distance from the positions he had taken in Opposition.

The bill provided for both collective contracts and individual contracts. Some elements in the bill were inconsistent with free contracting. The personal grievance provisions for collective contracts imposed potentially costly rules that should really have been up to the parties to negotiate. Similarly, the clauses on strikes and lockouts were unnecessary and excessively prescriptive. Even the exclusive concept of voluntary unionism in the bill arguably did not fit with the free-contracting model: in a free-contracting world there is no reason why union membership could not itself be subject to negotiation between employer and employee.

Other battles had been lost. The bill contained no commitment to abolish the specialist Labour Court, whose brand of judicial activism had been such an unwelcome feature of the existing labour relations regime. Bill's position was that we should keep the Labour Court (renamed the Employment Court) for political reasons, but revisit the issue down the track if the institution was not working. I think Bill overrated the political difficulties of that issue. And we never did revisit it, even after Judge Goddard continued to read his unique interpretations into employment contracts, injecting considerable uncertainty into the business sector, raising the costs of hiring, and hampering job creation.

Another battle was lost over the minimum wage, which I had wanted abolished. Most of my colleagues – even Bill – accepted the argument that a minimum wage costs jobs. But here, too, the perceived politics were the determining factor. The needs of young and low-skilled job-seekers lost out to the need for the government not to seem heartless. The minimum wage stayed.

A potentially important clause stated that nothing in the legislation limited the right of any person 'to negotiate for an employment contract in a manner other than that provided by this Act'. This 'opt-out' clause, though ambiguous in wording, seemed to open a window onto a regime of truly free contracting that could be chosen by the parties to any contract. Unfortunately, the following year this clause would become one of the casualties of the select committee process. Instead of the wording being clarified and strengthened, the clause was dropped. Another casualty of the select committee process would be the exemption of individual contracts from the compulsory personal grievance provisions.

For all the bill's defects, it represented a huge advance for industrial relations in New Zealand. As it came together I was both excited and proud. From having one of the most regulated and distorted labour markets in the western world, we would now have one of the most free and flexible. The legislation was one of the most significant initiatives in New Zealand's reform programme. In my own view, it was second to none in importance. And in Bill Birch we had the ideal person to push the legislation through, over the inevitable protests from the union movement. There was no minister better at flattening or out-foxing opponents than Bill.

My final pre-Christmas task was to renegotiate the policy targets agreement (PTA) between the government and the Reserve Bank. Despite our manifesto commitment, and Jim's reiteration of that commitment throughout the election campaign, there was still a degree of scepticism about National's intentions, especially among the media. This reflected partly Jim's and Bill's past, and partly the huge personal popularity of Winston Peters, who had publicly opposed the price stability target. I had private bets with more than one journalist over whether National would really endorse price stability. I will not embarrass the gentlemen by naming them, but all stumped up with their champagne with commendable grace.

The renegotiation of the PTA did not take up a great deal of time. In considering the new agreement my main focus was on the clarity of language in the document, and on giving monetary policy maximum credibility. Though in no way bad, the existing PTA struck me as too wordy. I stripped back some of the language. One substantive change, of course, was the pushing out of the inflation target from 1992 to 1993, in accordance with our manifesto policy.

Another change to the agreement related to how the Reserve Bank would deal with shocks – such as a change in the terms of trade or in government charges – which temporarily pushed the inflation rate outside its target band. The existing PTA required a renegotiation of the agreement whenever any such shock had a sufficiently strong influence on the inflation rate. However, the Reserve Bank now believed this provision created more uncertainty than it was worth. It was very difficult to specify both clearly and sensibly in advance the type and magnitude of shocks that would justify a complete renegotiation. The trigger point for a renegotiation would inevitably be arbitrary. In the Reserve Bank's view, the key requirements should instead be that the bank publish its own estimate of the price effects of a significant shock, and that it detail the action it is taking to ensure the effects of the shock on inflation are transitory. I accepted this reasoning and the new PTA was drafted accordingly.

The government had taken a very substantive body of decisions prior to Christmas. I believed all the measures should be announced as one package, despite big packages having had a rather mixed history under Labour. A coherent package helps business and the wider public to understand the strategy behind the government's individual decisions. It gives the government the best opportunity to bring out the links between policies. In our case there was a clear link between our fiscal measures and monetary policy: spending cuts would mean lower interest rates.

Similarly with our social welfare changes and the Employment Contracts Bill: there was a clear theme of workforce participation and greater opportunity. Combining a large number of controversial measures into one package is also good politics: if you are bound to raise a storm anyway, you may as well put as many controversial measures together as possible. The most controversial tend to drown out the less controversial. We knew what we were getting into. Business and financial markets would like the initiatives, but there would be howls of outrage from the interest groups affected.

Jim was also in favour of a large package. It was agreed that there would be three speeches in the House. Jim would open up, I would detail the fiscal measures, then Bill would talk about the Employment Contracts Bill. The bill would be introduced to the House later that day. The package, to be called the Economic and Social Initiative, was rapidly drafted. Looking back, I sometimes wonder how in just six weeks we had managed to do everything. I had put huge pressure on the Treasury and they had responded in the way that they usually did when the pressure was on – outstandingly well.

For weeks there had been very few announcements from the Beehive. One journalist talked about National's '56 vacuum-packed days'. But 19 December was to change that perception. There was an air of real excitement in the Beehive and in the Press Gallery. It was the day New Zealanders would for the first time see the stripe of their new government. We knew what that stripe would be.

Jim was his usual phlegmatic self. He had led the country outstandingly well during his baptism of fire as Prime Minister, even if much of what he had done was against his natural instincts. As Jim and I made our way across to the debating chamber I said to him, 'This is my proudest moment in politics.'

'Don't say that to anyone,' he replied.

In my own address I launched straight in to the key reason for my announcements:

> The Prime Minister has outlined the scale and nature of the problems confronting this new government. At the heart of these problems is the crushing burden of government spending. The continuing increase in the size of the state has resulted in growing debt, punitive tax levels and intolerable pressure on interest rates.
>
> These burdens have sapped the initiative and the energy of New Zealand's wealth-creators. We cannot prosper as a nation if we put spending ahead of earning.

After the announcements in the House, I joined in a press conference with other ministers. Then it was time for the signing of the new policy targets agreement with Don Brash – a moment of huge personal satisfaction for me. This, too, was held in front of the media.

There were the expected reactions to the package from the expected quarters. The trade union movement was up in arms over the Employment Contracts Bill. The Beneficiaries Movement proposed to fight the benefit cuts. Some of National's back bench protested loudly. Various social commentators chided the government for its alleged heartlessness. All of this reaction was expected. So too was the positive response from the business sector. Bank lending rates came down – the first of many such falls.

I went to Christmas content enough. But I was far from complacent about the year ahead. Though I was utterly confident the government was following the right strategy, I was well aware I would have to wait for months – perhaps years – before the upturn in the economy took place. I knew 1991 would be a war of attrition, which would sorely test the political nerves of the Cabinet and caucus. I also knew there was a great deal more work to be done in bringing the budget under control. We had made a start. But the battle had only just been joined.

Little did I know just how early in the year the first battle would start. When Pat Duignan, the head of the Treasury's Debt Management Office, rang me at my Selwyn home one day in January to say that he had 'very bad news' for me, I imagined from his tone of voice that someone had died.

10

IN JEOPARDY

Actually, New Zealand was facing a double downgrade from Standard and Poors, the highly influential international rating agency. A single downgrade, from a rating of AA to AA-, though far from welcome, had been half-expected. But no-one had been expecting a double downgrade to A+. It would have placed New Zealand in the same category as countries such as Iceland. It was a sobering verdict on the fiscal policy of the Labour administration, and of the Muldoon administration before that. Any downgrade increases the cost of borrowing, not just to the government, but right throughout the economy. It increases not just the government's debt-servicing bill, but also those of the corporate sector.

The verdict from Standard and Poors was not yet finalised; they were asking for our comment. Standard and Poors had visited New Zealand in 1990, when they had been sweet-talked by David Caygill into believing fiscal policy would come right. They had since been watching the deteriorating fiscal position and widening balance of payments deficit with growing alarm. Standard and Poors had come to the view that New Zealand had run out of chances and run out of excuses. They had not been personally briefed on the December Initiative, though they had seen it reported. They had concerns about the political sustainability of the measures in the Initiative.

The odds seemed to be against our being able to persuade Standard and Poors to alter their verdict. Nevertheless, my own instinct was that anything I might do to help change their minds was worth attempting – even if it meant flying to New York. Some in Treasury were gloomy about the prospects of such a mission. Jim, too, had his doubts. He saw there would be a high risk of failure and did not want to expose me, as a new minister, to the political damage associated with that failure. Standard and Poors, however, had been sounded out, and indicated that they would welcome a direct approach from the New Zealand minister. I decided I could not live with myself if I did not give it my best shot.

A case needed to be prepared. We also discussed how my office would handle the media, who knew nothing of the pending double downgrade. Ideally I would have liked to go to New York incognito, but slipping out of New Zealand unnoticed when you are Minister of Finance is no easy task.

At that time Briscoes was running a series of humorous advertisements in which I was being impersonated by an actress. David Hunt of my office waggishly suggested we get 'the Briscoes lady' to sit at my desk while I was away! In the end we put out a statement simply saying I would be visiting New York to acquaint the rating agencies with the contents of the December Initiative.

I flew off as the first shots were being fired in the Gulf War. Accompanying me were three senior Treasury officers: Graham Scott, Pat Duignan and Graeme Wheeler. In New York they soon experienced the ways of their new minister. Me being me, I wanted my usual run in the morning. Graham felt he could not leave me to the wilds of Central Park alone, so gallantly offered to come with me. Not wanting to be upstaged, so did Pat. The only sensible one was Graeme. The three of us must have made a strange sight as we ploughed through the snow.

The presentation to Standard and Poors went extremely well. My Treasury team performed admirably and deserve a large share of the credit for the eventual outcome. Standard and Poors were impressed by an opinion poll Treasury had commissioned, which showed a high degree of public support for the economic strategy, and by much else in the presentation. I also shamelessly 'worked on' the women on the panel during a break in proceedings. Women are still few and far between in finance, and in the interests of swinging a crucial vote I was prepared to play the sisterhood card. At a pivotal point in the proceedings, when the panel's attitude appeared to be hardening against us, I recall passing Graham a note saying, 'How frontal should I be?' He scrawled back 'very', so I weighed in with guns blazing.

Though the presentation had been encouraging, we did not know Standard and Poors' verdict until after we had arrived home. Then I was elated to receive the news – a single downgrade.

The trip to Standard and Poors had been as unplanned as it had been unexpected. Soon afterwards I was off on the first of my 'normal' overseas trips as Minister of Finance. Over the next three years I would do five of these trips, each of about two weeks' duration. The key destinations, to which I would repeatedly return, were the financial centres of Tokyo, Zurich, Frankfurt, London and New York. I would also visit at various times Osaka and Kyoto in Japan, Seoul, Singapore, Hong Kong, Milan, Geneva, Bonn, Amsterdam, Washington, Boston and Chicago. Though the schedule was usually extremely heavy, I greatly enjoyed these trips.

A New Zealand Minister of Finance naturally gets to meet his or her counterparts in the foreign countries he or she visits. These meetings can be interesting, but are not in themselves of much serious value. A New Zealand Minister of Finance rarely undertakes genuine negotiations in the way that, say, the Minister of Foreign Affairs might do. My meetings were mostly courtesy calls. Not that I always stuck to platitudes; I tended to be direct, perhaps more so than our embassy people hovering at my elbow might have wished. I would never have made a diplomat. On my first major overseas trip I visited the British Chancellor of the Exchequer, Norman Lamont. I must have let him know that I was not very impressed with British fiscal policy. Months later, Jim himself met Lamont. 'I believe you met my Minister of Finance', he said. 'Yes, she gave me quite a lecture,' Lamont joked.

By far the most memorable of my meetings with foreign politicians was the hour or so spent with Lee Kwan Yew, the beautifully spoken architect of modern Singapore's economic growth. Lee Kwan Yew, by then installed in the side palace in Singapore as the Senior Minister, and very much the power beside the throne, was in reflective form. The New Zealand politician he knew best was Muldoon. Together they had met at many Commonwealth Finance Ministers' meetings and, as their careers progressed, at the Commonwealth Heads of Government meetings. The way Muldoon used to tell it to the caucus, he and Harry Lee were bosom buddies sharing not just similar aspirations but similar policy approaches.

From the man himself I heard a rather different story. He told me how impressed he was by the efforts of the new National government to come to grips with the economic and social malaise that had been afflicting New Zealand for too long. He acknowledged how difficult it was to slaughter the sacred cows of social welfare and union dominance in a democracy where attitudes and expectations were very entrenched. He then contrasted for me the respective situations of New Zealand and Singapore in a way I will never forget. He said that when Singapore possessed nothing but its people and their hunger to better themselves, New Zealand had everything. We were a resource-rich country with one of the highest standards of living in the world. While we went about sowing the seeds of our own decline in the form of protectionism, debt and welfare dependency, Singapore was totally focused on pulling itself up by its bootstraps.

How much easier it was, he said, to call for sacrifice and effort from a nation willing to better itself than to impose similar demands on a nation unwilling to face up to the causes of its decline. Moving up the rungs of the ladder was a far easier proposition than halting the slide. He lamented that it was only when New Zealand's problems were of crisis proportions that we summoned up the will to act. My thoughts entirely.

Her Majesty's Loyal Opposition 1987–90, at last serious about our claims to be an alternative government.

1990-93 Cabinet at the mid-point – the difficult decisions behind us, the economic recovery in front of us.

DOMINION

Eager beaver Finance Minister – just sworn in and keen to get on with the job.

EVENING POST

Presenting my credentials to the Treasury – Dr Graham Scott, Secretary to the Treasury, hoping for the 'Just Excellent' stamp of approval.

Centenary of the vote for women, 1993. Celebrating with Jenny Shipley at the Malvern A&P Show. Displayed is the Parliamentary Bill Book of Sir John Hall, my predecessor, the MP for Selwyn 100 years ago, who successfully moved that New Zealand women be the first in the world to exercise the right to vote.

The main value of my overseas trips, and where most of my effort was concentrated, was in the meetings with overseas investors. New Zealand was a heavy sovereign borrower, and a country wishing to attract as much high-quality overseas direct investment as possible. It was – and remains – highly important that the New Zealand Minister of Finance puts across a strong and convincing case for the New Zealand economy. The greater the confidence foreign investors have in government policy, the lower will be interest rates and the stronger will be the flow of foreign investment.

Besides smaller meetings, on each trip I would typically give a number of investor presentations to large audiences. In these presentations I used slides to present trends in our economy and the government's economic strategy. I would typically give my standard presentation six or seven times in the course of a trip. Having a travelling roadshow was a relatively new departure for a New Zealand Finance Minister, and was unusual for any Minister of Finance. However, I always received extremely good feedback on my investor presentations. We had a good story to tell, and as time went on the story became even better. The economic reforms begun by Douglas and recommenced under my stewardship were widely admired by my business and financial audiences. Though a small country, we had attracted a degree of interest quite out of proportion to our size. On our travels I, and the Treasury officers with me, received a gratifying amount of praise, flattery and encouragement.

Like any traveller, I had my share of comic incidents. On my first trip, at a formal dinner in London, a banker came up to me to introduce himself. Thinking he was the waiter (since both bankers and waiters were in long tails) I handed him my plate to take away. Doubtless completely taken aback, he obliged! It was only later that I learnt of my faux pas.

On that trip I made another mistake that I was never to make again – one that haunted me and dogged my efforts to sell the government's need to cut costs. Our party flew by Concorde from Britain to the United States. It saved time and, ironically, money, because a Concorde flight for the party was cheaper than all staying another night in London. But the up-front cost was high and was noticed back home. The press like nothing better than to run stories about politicians living the high life at public expense. At a time when the government was cutting benefits, such stories met an especially receptive audience.

Already I had been criticised for accepting a large and grand ministerial house, the rent on which was $900 a week. I was conscious the rent was high – higher than that of any of my Cabinet colleagues, although nowhere near as high as the $1687 a week rental the Labour government had stumped up for Bob Tizard when he was a minister. I had decided to forfeit my right to a self-drive car in Wellington in an effort to keep my personal costs down. I ran to work every morning in any case, and a car in Wellington was an unnecessary perk for me.

The Concorde and the house rental were two incidents that plagued my time as Minister of Finance. While personally I have little truck with small-mindedness and envy, so often massaged by the press, I have to admit with hindsight that both those decisions were public relations blunders. They were particularly so given the fact that I was the minister most identified with cutting government expenditure.

In the opening months of 1991 not everyone in New Zealand was welcoming the government's policies with open arms. I returned to face the year's challenges unaware of precisely the strength of feeling the cutbacks had generated. There were a number of demonstrations against the benefit cuts, and against the Employment Contracts Bill. Public meetings could be turbulent: I was burnt in effigy at least once.

Soon after arriving back from my first overseas trip I was given a boisterous reception in Titirangi, Auckland. It was one of my first public meetings after the Christmas break. With two press staff, I arrived at

Titirangi's Lopdell House in a ministerial car for an evening speech. As soon as we saw the fire engines outside the hall we knew we had trouble. Before our arrival a hoax call to the Fire Service had forced the evacuation of the building. Outside on the pavement were about 25 protesters, irate at the social welfare cuts and ready to have a piece of me. I stepped out of the car and was immediately splattered with a blue paint bomb. My way was blocked and the scene was turning seriously ugly. Frank, my driver, luckily a huge man, lifted me up under his arm and, almost using my head as a ramrod, pushed his way through the protesters. My staff say they saw my shoe-clad feet waving momentarily as I disappeared into the hall. It was a most splendid piece of work on Frank's part. After delivering my speech in a paint-spattered suit I left by the back door to have my last ride in a marked ministerial car: from then on I travelled less conspicuously. The incident must have made a considerable impression on Frank because shortly afterwards he named his daughter after me.

On another turbulent occasion, trying to enter a building past a hail of missiles, I donned my driver's raincoat. It looked as though I was wearing a tent but it did the job.

The practice of politics in New Zealand is distinguished by two freedoms – freedom from corruption and freedom of movement. Never once did I encounter any compromise of the former. After the Titirangi incident, however, I experienced significant compromise of the latter freedom, for the first half of my ministerial career. Titirangi had alarmed the powers that be. I, along with Jenny Shipley, was considered a security risk. I suspect our respective husbands and private secretaries knew more about the nature of the threats than we did and, frankly, I wanted it to stay that way. Protest and placards were never going to deflect us from our policy course, but I owed it to my family to take sensible precautions in the interests of personal safety.

The men and women of the Diplomatic Protection Squad (DPS) became my constant companions during my working day. At times it must have been as trying for them as it was for me. First there was the business of getting to work in the morning. I always ran, and that meant they did too. With mixed alarm and amusement I was told by a neighbour that she suspected we had an early-morning prowler in our safe and secluded street. She had seen him every weekday morning, standing outside my house in running gear at about 6.30 in the morning and had always wondered what was in the bag strung around his waist. I had to confess that this was an exercise in protection, not prowling!

My fitness level rose measurably over the next 18 months, as typically long-legged policemen and women took one stride to my two. One seasoned DPS member suffered from shin-splints after a three-week roster with me but soldiered on, too proud to tell his superiors that the not very fast Finance Minister was running him into the ground.

DPS presence was not just the order of the day for public functions. It was part and parcel of semi-public and even private events. Our attending the children's concerts and musicals with two incredible hulks in tow appealed to the macho in Oliver, but for Lucy it simply meant mortification. And I do not know who was more embarrassed by the necessity for me to be escorted on a quick shopping trip down Lambton Quay to buy a new set of knickers. The poor cop was distinctly out of place in the ladies' lingerie department.

Midway through 1992, with the economy clearly recovering, I called for a review of the security situation. The powers that be were persuaded that any threat had largely disappeared, and for the rest of my term as minister I again roamed free.

The period of protest had not, in fact, lasted too long. I had been confident that as a government we would ride it out. Indeed, the union demonstrations against the Employment Contracts Bill had an almost perfunctory quality about them. There was no attempt, for instance, by the union movement to engineer a substantial nationwide strike. Partly this was due to the government's very large recent mandate in the polls, and partly – no doubt – to the weak state of the economy. But a third factor, I feel sure, was the absolute commitment shown by key members of the government to the Employment Contracts Bill. The unions could see we were not a government for turning. So it proved: the bill was passed into law and became operative in May. By then the new benefit rates were already in force and the world had not come to an end as many had predicted.

The fiscal and economic news in the opening months of 1991 was not encouraging. Domestic demand seemed, if anything, to be weakening further, while unemployment was showing no sign of levelling out and business confidence remained low. The only good news was that the long fall in interest rates was already well under way. It would continue for the entire year.

Early in the year the Treasury advised me that they were substantially revising upward their forecast fiscal deficit for 1990-91. All the numbers seemed to be going in the wrong direction: pharmaceutical expenditure was blowing out, we had to revise rubbery education numbers (an almost constant problem with Lockwood's department) and so on. But the most serious news was on the revenue side. A major shortfall in tax revenue was becoming apparent – particularly in company tax. This was partly due to a previous underestimation by the Treasury of the extent of weakness in the economy but, in the case of company tax, it was mainly due to growing use of tax-avoidance mechanisms.

Many of these avoidance mechanisms involved the use of the inter-corporate dividend exemption. This exemption had become an historical anomaly in the New Zealand tax system. Originally designed to prevent the multiple taxation of dividends flowing through a chain of companies, it became redundant for this purpose once the imputation regime was introduced. The exemption did, however, provide a crucial element in many complex tax-avoidance schemes involving the transferring of tax losses between companies. One technique growing in popularity involved the issue of redeemable preference shares.

I had no intention of seeing the company tax base eroded through substantial tax planning techniques – least of all when many of the poorest in society were seeing a cut in their incomes. The Treasury believed the most effective way to counter the avoidance activity was:

- to remove the inter-corporate dividend exemption;
- to move directly against redeemable preference share schemes; and
- to tighten the rules relating to the ability of companies to carry forward losses and offset losses against the income of another company.

I accepted that analysis, and the measures that were to be announced in the 1991 budget were gradually developed.

In the meantime it gave me no great pleasure to announce a revised estimate of the deficit for 1990-91. The new figure was $1.4 billion, up from the $0.7 billion published at the time of the December Initiative. The underlying deficit was considerably higher again, as the financial markets well knew.

11

THE MOTHER OF ALL BUDGETS

A great many processes led up to the 1991 budget. It was the biggest and most complex budget produced in New Zealand within recent memory, if not ever. My description of it as 'the mother of all budgets', though certainly not wise, was undoubtedly apt.

One stream of work leading up to the budget was the expenditure review process, outside of the longer-term social policy reviews. The expenditure review work resumed in February, when we identified savings in 11 'second-tier' departments that we had not had time to examine before Christmas. In March I obtained Cabinet's agreement to the ground rules by which departments would prepare their draft budgets for 1991-92. We agreed that departments would receive no compensation for any increases in their input costs; any such increases were to be absorbed through productivity gains. Cabinet also agreed that any new policy initiatives would have to be funded by reallocating resources from within budgets.

In April I received a fresh set of three-year fiscal projections, using the new draft departmental budgets. The outlook was by now substantially worse than in the December Initiative, mainly owing to the weakness in tax revenue and an upward revision to expected benefit numbers, both reflections of the weaker than expected economy. It was clear that if I were to be able to bring down satisfactory fiscal projections in the budget, considerably more work would be needed on departmental expenditure. Fortunately, I was able to secure Cabinet's agreement that departments be asked to offer up new savings options.

It was at this stage that the Officials Committee on Expenditure Control (OCEC) was formed, to assist the work of the Expenditure Control Committee. OCEC did its work superbly. It was chaired by the Treasury and had representatives from both the Prime Minister's Department and the State Services Commission. OCEC worked through the savings options with each department, presenting them in a form that made it easy for ministers to digest. Each departmental minister then had his or her day in court at the Expenditure Control Committee, as we went through the options. These sessions were always chaired by an associate minister of mine – first Doug Kidd and later Maurice McTigue. It was a 'good cop, bad

cop' routine from the finance team. In the chair, Doug and Maurice were unfailingly courteous; always firm but fair. I was free as a member of the committee to drive some of the harder bargains.

It was at this point, above all, that the value of the Public Finance Act became especially apparent. The new focus on outputs brought about by the Act meant ministers had genuinely meaningful information about the services produced by their departments and were in a position to make informed trade-offs between competing priorities. Our exercise was the first genuine yield from the Public Finance Act. Progress would have proved far more difficult to make under the old public accounting system.

During these weeks I sometimes thought back to Muldoon's '3 per cent cuts' exercise, which had taken place in the face of considerable public unease when I was a backbencher. The call for 3 per cent cuts had brought a variety of responses from ministers and departments – few of them constructive. Some ministers had sold departmental assets to come up with a paper '3 per cent cut'. Some had deliberately put up as offered 'savings' something they knew Cabinet would not accept. Others had come up with almost nothing, pleading the inability of their extremely efficient department to part with any of its functions. Despite generating considerable bad publicity for the government, the whole exercise was largely a failure.

By contrast, the expenditure review process between the December

Initiative and the 1991 budget generated around $600 million. We managed to do it with very little in the way of histrionics from either ministers or departments. While no-one pretended it was enjoyable having their budget cut, most of my ministerial colleagues submitted to the process with good grace.

There were other major contrasts with the Muldoon era. Ours was a much more collegiate budget process. Four ministers in Cabinet had learnt their ministerial craft under Muldoon – Bolger himself, Birch, John Falloon and Warren Cooper. They had only ever known budgets Muldoon-style. Apparently a budget 'round' under Muldoon was more like a one-man play. There was an initial numbers exercise involving Cabinet. Thereafter, virtually solo, Muldoon picked his way through the numbers, determined the priorities, made the trade-offs, and then served it up to Cabinet as a fait accompli. When the ink was dry on the budget documents Muldoon would then 'bring' the budget to Cabinet.

This meaningless ritual, I am told, involved whipping out of his bag 20 copies of screeds of unintelligible numbers, circulating these papers around the Cabinet table, then calling them in after allowing an opportunity for only the most cursory glance.

It was Warren Cooper who drew the comparison with my budget style. Under me, every minister had the chance to be heard on his or her own vote. Every minister could contribute to the overall budget strategy. The budget documentation was copious. It was a highly transparent process with the Cabinet very much an accessory before, rather than after, the fact.

Not everything in the expenditure review process proceeded smoothly. Some spending items slipped through the net, most notably the hugely expensive Museum of New Zealand.

Typecasting, slagging and stereotyping politicians is both national and international sport. Typically, 'popularity' polls will reveal that politicians, along with used car salesmen, are regarded as the lowest form of animal life. The odium is generally undeserved and is often a function of the difficult and demanding business of governing. The adage is generally true that Oppositions do not get elected – governments lose office. Ever conscious of their political mortality, it is not therefore surprising that some politicians should succumb to the monument syndrome – not the monument of successful policy but the monument of tangible bricks and mortar. The decision to go ahead with building the Museum of New Zealand at the height of the public expenditure cuts was solely attributable to the monument mentality.

The whole process of approving the building was rich with political theatre bordering on farce. Sir Wallace Rowling, chair of the establishment board, came to the Cabinet committee room to make the pivotal presentation armed with all the same arguments he had previously employed as Minister of Finance, and then Prime Minister, to spend money we did not have.

The Cabinet committee room, the most architecturally awkward you could ever encounter, became a potential heart-attack zone as unfit politicians and their advisers pushed and heaved the huge scale model of this strikingly ugly building over the ringed tables and into the central well. Sir Wallace then proceeded to employ the monument arguments with a skill I had to secretly admire. 'Of course, there is never a right time to build a building of such importance,' he said. 'Of course the government is responsibly reigning in public expenditure [pity he had not done the same in his day], but think of the economic activity and jobs that will flow from this decision.' Doug Graham made his 'men of vision' speech and the boys fell for it all – and only the boys, since Jenny Shipley and I vehemently opposed the project. The two hair-shirts were at work again. We called for shared sacrifice and a sense of proportion. I recall saying that while a decision to build could be countenanced, even celebrated, when the economy was in recovery, now was a totally inappropriate time. I asked that my vote be specifically recorded against the decision, knowing full well that under Cabinet convention that was not possible.

While the expenditure review process was going on, the tax policy announcements in the budget were also being developed. These included the measures to clamp down on tax planning by corporates. They also included an initiative to extend tax on gambling activities to cover gaming machines. Wyatt Creech, the Revenue Minister, had no major disagreement with me over these measures. However, there was one budget tax initiative Wyatt was extremely sceptical about: the near-abolition of non-resident withholding tax (NRWT) on interest. I saw this as an important initiative for lowering the cost of capital. Treasury's proposal was to allow an exemption from paying NRWT, on payment by issuers of a levy equal to 2 per cent of interest paid. The proposal was designed to maximise the positive impact on domestic interest rates, while minimising its negative impact on the New Zealand tax base. It was targeted at those fixed-interest investors who received no tax credit in their own country for NRWT paid in New Zealand. These investors would now be able largely to escape paying NRWT, with positive implications for New Zealand interest rates.

Investors who did receive a tax credit, and who were thus not being deterred by NRWT from investing here, would be deterred by the 2 per cent levy from claiming an exemption. Accordingly, these investors would not be a loss to the New Zealand tax base. The policy was a shrewdly targeted measure.

Wyatt opposed this initiative. He realised, as I did, that the less we taxed non-residents, the stronger our rules would need to be for taxing residents on their worldwide incomes. Though the major debates on international tax still lay in front of us, already it was clear that Wyatt and I had fundamentally different views. Wyatt favoured a soft regime for taxing residents on their worldwide income, and a harder regime for taxing non-residents on their New Zealand income. I favoured the opposite.

The third stream of work feeding into the 1991 budget was the medium-term reviews of social policy. These varied considerably in quality. The Accident Compensation Corporation review achieved little, despite accident compensation being a prime candidate for a major overhaul. ACC costs had risen enormously since the scheme had been introduced in the mid-1970s. There was also widespread anecdotal evidence of people ripping off the system. Unfortunately, National's review did little to tackle the underlying pressures driving costs up; ours was an exercise in cost-shuffling. We reduced the direct costs to employers, but only by imposing an 'earner premium' on those in the workforce – the next worst thing to a tax.

The housing reforms were more successful. They were one of the best-conceived reforms undertaken by the National government. The existing system of housing assistance had essentially been one of rationing. Not only did assistance bear only the roughest correspondence with genuine housing need, but the system failed to make good use of housing resources. As such it was both unfair and inefficient. Assistance was partly through state rental units, for which there was a long waiting list, and partly through concessionary lending for those low-income earners able to buy a house. There was also assistance available from the Social Welfare Department.

The system was unco-ordinated and ad hoc. Many low-income earners were not assisted at all, while many who were could scarcely be described as having a pressing housing need. Often people would stay on in a state house, despite long having had the ability and means to go elsewhere. Many people were also in larger state houses than they needed to be, while others waited in the queue. Meanwhile, the private rental market was languishing because low-income people could not access their Housing

Corporation assistance in a way that enabled them to rent private properties.

The National government's policy was to give the housing assistance directly to low-income families in the form of a cash subsidy, targeted by income. That subsidy could then be spent on rental or mortgage payments, in either the public or private sector. The Housing Corporation would be split into two organisations. One organisation would hold the state rental units and charge market rents. The other would hold the mortgage portfolio. For me it was philosophically a very attractive policy: maximise competition, empower the consumer. It also made sound practical sense. Low-income families in similar circumstances would be treated equally, while the new regime would encourage a much more efficient use of the country's housing stock. There was a clear gain in both efficiency and equity.

A similar concern to separate the funding of services from their provision drove the government's health reforms. The health reforms were the largest and by far the most complex of our social policy initiatives. Our starting point was a hospital sector in which funding and provision were largely wrapped into one in the form of area health boards. These boards were government-funded and were meant to reflect the health needs of the areas they served. But they were unwieldy institutions, with little incentive to seek out cheaper or more innovative ways of providing care. We were well behind the rest of the world in such practices as greater use of day surgery, shorter hospital stays and community treatment alternatives. Legislative constraints on area health boards were also a problem. It was difficult for area health boards to rationalise their resources by entering joint ventures with the private sector, leasing out capital or otherwise raising revenue.

There was little focus on outputs in the health sector. The Minister of Health was not in a position to contract easily for services or to be assured about certain outcomes. In most cases accounting systems were so rudimentary that area health boards did not even know the costs they faced. As businessman Peter Troughton said: 'If you cannot measure it, how can you manage it?' Capital spending was haphazard and often poorly planned. There were grossly under-utilised buildings – whole wards that had never seen a single patient.

Resources were often captured by the special interests of those working in the health sector, rather than going to meet the needs of users. Health services that made a good tabloid news story often won out in the battle for funding over less glamorous but equally deserving areas. When hospital boards did attempt strategic change, they often ran into a wall of public and professional opposition. Thus, a heavy tyranny of the status quo prevailed, with very poor integration between the hospital sector and the primary health sector, and between the public and private sectors. Procedures and facilities were often unco-ordinated and often duplicated.

The government's health reforms were designed to get maximum value for every health dollar spent. That clearly meant setting up hospitals on a more businesslike basis. They would become Crown health enterprises (CHEs). It also meant giving to a different agency of government the role of 'purchasing' health services for communities. Four regional health authorities (RHAs) would undertake this function. It also meant setting priorities for public health, so that resources could go to meeting those priorities. A major consultative exercise would be undertaken to identify the 'core' health services funded by government.

RHAs would be charged with funding the total health services for their region, in both primary and secondary care. For the first time there would be genuine co-ordination between the various branches of health care. RHAs would not themselves own any hospital facilities, so would face no conflict of interest. Their sole incentive would be to contract for the provision of health care in the way that made the health dollar go furthest. That obviously involved contracting with the most efficient providers.

In undertaking such major reform, we knew as a government we would be doing battle with highly articulate interest groups working in the health sector. These groups would fight the changes with considerable tenacity. We also knew that the implementation period for the health reforms would be long and drawn out. This would give the forces opposed to the reforms a great deal of time to mobilise their forces, but we were prepared to do battle. One of the first shots we would fire was the sacking on budget night of area health boards, and their replacement by appointed commissioners. Interim agencies would be set up to manage the transition to the new system.

One aspect of the health policy developed for the budget held considerable significance for me – the commitment to allow individuals and groups to opt out of their local RHA. Individuals and groups would be able to take their share of government funding and purchase alternative health-care plans in the private sector, which would manage the total health-care needs of their clients. New Zealanders would be empowered to make their own choices as consumers of health, providing greater competition and an added customer focus to the whole health sector. Sadly, this aspect of the health reforms was not to be realised. Though the policy would be announced in the budget, it would later fall casualty to a failure of nerve on the part of the government.

Health may have been the most technically difficult of the social policy reforms, but the most politically difficult was undoubtedly national superannuation. As expected, the discussions with the other political parties early in the new year did not make progress. The government was on its own, needing to break an election promise if it were to make savings from superannuation – at least in the short term. But in the end the figures meant we could not pass up superannuation as a source of savings.

Probably in no other area of policy did ministers examine a more bewildering variety of options. Cutting the level of superannuation was not seriously considered, but there were many possible variations of the income test, involving both the free zone before the surcharge applied and the abatement rate of the surcharge itself. There were questions about the age of eligibility: should we accelerate the planned shift from 60 to 65? And should we – as I favoured – aim eventually for an even higher age of eligibility, such as 68 or 70? There was also the question of whether at some age superannuation should become universal.

The combinations and permutations were endless. As the budget approached, ministers settled on the broad outline of the favoured option: an accelerated shift to 65; CPI adjustment of superannuation from 1 April 1993; a stiffer income test, to be administered by Social Welfare rather than Inland Revenue; and superannuation to be universal at age 70 to the level of 50 per cent of the married rate. This last was an idea promoted by Bill Birch, who argued that it would enable us to say National had retained at least an element of universality in superannuation. Very late in the day, we settled on the final form of the income test: a free zone of $50 per week before the income test applied, followed by an Effective Marginal Tax Rate of 68 per cent. I was at that time giving briefings to trusted backbenchers on some of the social policy measures in the budget. I naturally included the chosen superannuation option in these briefings.

Unfortunately, from my point of view, the chosen option was to change: Wyatt Creech came up with a new scenario over the weekend, which he tabled at Cabinet on Monday. This option had a free zone of $80 per week and an EMTR of 93 per cent. Wyatt argued that his option had political advantages: fewer people would be affected by the income test, and those who were affected could scarcely be more alienated than they would already be under the alternative option.

Wyatt's option was examined and costed by officials: it yielded more fiscal savings than the alternative. Cabinet took the final decision to run with Wyatt's option. I did not believe Jim should have allowed this relitigation by Wyatt: it set a bad precedent in terms of Cabinet process. However, since Wyatt's option had been put on the table, I supported it on fiscal grounds. Jim himself was against it.

The untidiness of the process meant backbenchers had been briefed on the wrong superannuation option. Not only were we poised for an inevitable loss of moral authority with the general public over superannuation, but Cabinet members would also lose moral authority with their own back bench.

As the budget neared, a new source of concern had arisen for me: a growing sentiment within Cabinet favouring an increase in taxes. In part this was because we had made little real progress in charging high-income earners more for their social services. We had, admittedly, taken the decision to means-test student allowances more strongly on parents' income. But we had not come near to achieving the benchmark set out in the December Initiative, where we had suggested that the top third of all income-earners might pay for most or all of their social services. Because of our slow

progress, the 'fairness' issue looked increasingly like coming onto the agenda again as we finalised the budget.

I was as adamantly opposed to tax increases as I had been on first taking office. I asked the Treasury to come up, if they could, with a social policy initiative where higher-income earners were charged more for social services. The Treasury suggested targeting health charges by employing the categories already used for family support. This was the genesis of the interim targeting regime. As a targeting mechanism it was far from perfect; however, it did embody the important principle that those who could afford to pay more for their health services should be required to. It also enabled us to reduce the health costs of working families on the lowest incomes substantially, without costing the government any money. Previously, beneficiaries had been treated more favourably than low-income working families. That had clearly been perverse.

The main weakness of the interim targeting regime was the wide scope of the third, 'high-income' category. This category included the higher-income elderly and all those who did not qualify for family support. This meant middle-income earners paid the same health charges as genuinely high-income earners such as myself. It would have been desirable to introduce a fourth category covering perhaps the top 20 per cent of income-earners. However, there turned out to be no administratively feasible way that this could be done.

I did not have great difficulty obtaining my colleagues' agreement on the principle of the interim targeting regime. The new initiative served its ulterior purpose for me extremely well: there was little pressure from colleagues for general tax increases in the budget. Increases in excise on alcohol and tobacco constituted the only changes to tax rates.

By the time the final budget numbers came together, the fiscal track looked extremely encouraging – at least in comparison to where we had been. Government spending as a percentage of gross domestic product (GDP) was projected to fall markedly, taxation as a percentage of GDP less markedly, and the financial deficit was to be $1.7 billion in 1991-92 (compared with $3.7 billion in the Treasury's post-election briefing or PEB), falling to $0.5 billion in 1993-94 (compared with $5.2 billion in the PEB). There was no significant sign of an upturn in the economy, but we had a very good fiscal story to tell on budget night.

Naturally, there was a huge media build-up to the budget. It was the first of the new administration, and it was widely known that it would be a blockbuster. I had made no secret of that fact. For the first time the budget would be telecast live. It was also the first budget anywhere in the western world to be delivered by a woman. Days before the budget my office was receiving queries from the press – not the usual 'What's in the budget?' but 'What will the minister be wearing?' That, like the contents of the budget itself, was always a secret.

As part of the build-up, television's current affairs programme *Frontline* wanted to film me during the budget preparations. Among other things, they filmed me having breakfast with my staff. Two things went wrong. First of all, I failed to keep out of the sight of the cameras the name of my breakfast cereal, aptly labelled Just Right. Naturally, *Frontline* reporter Ross Stevens could not resist highlighting the name. More seriously, it was at this time that the phrase 'the mother of all budgets' was born.

The phrase was not originally mine. Stevens was filming me as I gave a phone interview to talkback host Robin Harrison of 3ZB in Christchurch. Robin was a thorough professional and not of the hectoring kind. I felt at home with him, and the more relaxed I was the more I tended to let my guard down. Robin was his usual chatty self and could not resist some pre-budget baiting. He asked me if I had a name for the budget. I threw the question open to the room and Stevens offered up 'the mother of all budgets'. The phrase alluded, of course, to 'the mother of all battles' Saddam Hussein had just lost spectacularly to end the Gulf War. Stupidly, in the full glare of the cameras, I did not equivocate but said yes, this could be considered to be the mother of all budgets.

The rest, as they say, is history. The name stuck. I well remember the panic in my office and upstairs on the ninth floor when they heard on the radio news what I had dubbed the budget. Shortly afterwards the phones in our office were hot – many from supportive people and organisations who suggested that our marketing of this budget was somewhat over-aggressive!

The budget documentation in 1991 was immense. In addition to the two documents containing the speech, accompanying economic and fiscal analysis, and the standard budget 'estimates', there were two documents on tax policy, five on social policy, one on education, one on employment, and a schedule of expenditure decisions. Plus press releases galore. It put very heavy pressure on the Treasury, on other departments and on ministerial offices, but nothing fell down in the rush.

By tradition the budget is very much the Minister of Finance's occasion. As the person delivering the budget speech, I was enabled each year to set out what was primarily my vision of the government's economic strategy. Jim always saw a copy of the speech in advance and had a significant input. These could be tense occasions, as Jim would sometimes try to change the speech substantially. Often I would run past a trusted colleague a passage relevant to his or her portfolio, but I showed the speech as a whole to no other minister. While Jim obviously needed to be happy with the speech, most of the initiative still lay with me. I also had the opportunity to shape strongly the accompanying Treasury-written material in the first two budget documents.

Among the documentation was an important paper describing for the first time the government's entire economic strategy. I had long thought it important that my colleagues see the government's policies in a strategic framework, and that they appreciate where initiatives in their own portfolio areas fitted into the government's wider strategy. I was particularly concerned to dispel the notion that everything we were doing was fiscally driven; our economic strategy was much wider than the elimination of the deficit. With this in mind, earlier in the year I had presented a strategy document to the Cabinet Strategy Committee. It turned out to be a less than successful occasion. Colleagues saw my initiative as Treasury-driven, which caused them to become defensive. Having been repulsed in this quarter, my next logical step was to use the budget as a vehicle for articulating an economic strategy.

The budget strategy document presented the strategy under a number of key headings. Stable and balanced macroeconomic policies set out the government's fiscal and monetary policy. There was a section on fair and affordable social policies – an important theme of the budget. Investing in people took in a wide range of policies, including the new national curriculum in schools, a revamped immigration policy, various training initiatives and the Employment Contracts Act. The section on enterprise and innovation described policies that were improving the environment for enterprise, such as privatisation, tax measures, changes to public-sector science, and the refocusing of business assistance schemes. Under the heading Strengthening International Relationships we discussed the importance of reducing border protection and the government's encouragement of foreign investment in New Zealand.

By the morning of budget day an eerie calm usually prevailed in my office. All the work had been done, the documents had been printed and it was mostly a matter of waiting. I used to spend much of the morning boning up on the contents of the budget one final time. The previous night had been spent practising the presentation of my speech. For that I received professional coaching; reading the budget live on television for 90 minutes is no easy task.

In the afternoon the budget lock-ups would begin. In these lock-ups media and market analysts are shown the budget documents in advance, but are held inside the lock-up until after the minister has finished reading the speech. This allows a much more informed reaction by the media and financial markets to the budget, while preserving budget secrecy.

The lock-ups were my first major event of the day. I would visit each lock-up, give a short address and field questions. The atmosphere in these lock-ups was often a good guide to how the budget would be taken by the various audiences. Before they were over I would brief the full caucus on the contents of the budget. Cabinet ministers already knew the numbers; in contrast to Muldoon, I always kept Cabinet well informed on budgetary matters. But because of the market sensitivity of the information, caucus received the details only shortly before the speech was due to be delivered.

I then changed into my budget outfit. On the night of the mother of all budgets I wore a flame-coloured suit and cream blouse. Thus attired, it was time to meet Jim for the walk to the debating chamber. It was always good symbolism for Jim and me to be seen walking down together. The chamber was soon packed, the public galleries overflowing, the television crew ready to film.

On this, the first of my budget nights, I held a huge speech in my hand – the product of the very large number of announcements. I had also wanted my speech to constitute an overview of the government's entire economic strategy. It took me over one and a half hours to get through it. Technically a budget speech is supposed to be heard in silence, but it is usual for there to be murmurs of shock – real or feigned – from the Opposition, and periodic applause from government members. As the speech went on there was an increasing amount of both. And though Labour members had been under strict instructions not to interject, David Lange – master of the one-liner – became increasingly playful.

> Richardson: Our target for unemployment clearly stands as the toughest of all our targets.
> Lange: The mother of all targets.

The Minister of Finance, however, gets the last word. Though the budget had contained very stiff medicine, it finished on a rousing, upbeat note:

> In times of change and transformation, the progress of a nation depends on the strength of its leadership and the will of its people. Tonight's announcements have shown the resolve of our leadership. We inherited a nation adrift. We have arrested the drift of decades, looked out over the

> span of a generation and charted the path for the future. Now it is time for all of us, as New Zealanders, to begin building that future. I am confident we have the guts and the spirit to meet that challenge.
>
> I believe the 1990s will be New Zealand's decade. The decade in which we rediscover the energy and self-confidence we had of old. The decade in which we become a true enterprise society. The decade in which our business people discover they can take on and beat the rest of the world. The decade in which we cease to think of ourselves as a poor, struggling country and begin to think of ourselves once more as winners.
>
> We are still a young country. We were born out of an optimism and a hope for the future. The future is ours to make. It is in our hands.

The standing ovation from colleagues may have had a fair amount to do with the length of time they had been sitting. Still, I can't pretend I didn't enjoy it. Peer pressure even caused Winston Peters to put down his newspaper and half-rise to his feet, though he refrained from clapping.

Once out of the debating chamber I made a quick check on the immediate financial market reaction to the budget before heading into the television studio for my interview. After a few more media events I was ready to join the traditional budget-night party in the Minister of Finance's office, which was already well under way. The next day, of course, there would be many more interviews.

That night I could reflect with satisfaction over the distance the government had come since taking office. But the hardest period was not over for the government, or for me personally. The hardest period still lay ahead.

12

KEEPING OUR NERVE

There had been numerous calls for the government to change course. Many had argued that the government's strategy of cutting the deficit in the middle of a recession would inhibit growth. Some even argued that it would make the deficit worse. The dissenters came from within the government's ranks, from the parliamentary Opposition, from some in business, and from many in the academic world. Our economic strategy was criticised by the churches for its alleged heartlessness, by others for its alleged obtuseness.

Typical of much of the comment was the circular letter sent to the *New Zealand Herald* by 15 members of the Auckland University economics department. The letter condemned the 'overriding priority' it claimed the government was placing on eliminating the budget deficit:

> We wish to state in the strongest possible terms our view that in the present state of the economy, and in the midst of an international recession, the deficit-cutting strategy is fatally flawed. It can only depress the economy further and because of this it will be to a considerable extent self-defeating; a lower level of economic activity means less tax revenue for the government and more demands for expenditure in areas such as unemployment relief. How long is it proposed to continue with this vicious circle?

The academics argued that lower interest rates would not give the necessary stimulation to recovery so long as 'demand continues to be squeezed out of our economy'. They argued that our exchange rate was overvalued, and that we needed 'an adjustment to exchange rate policy, with the aim of enhancing the profitability of exporters and import-competing manufacturers'. By this the academics presumably meant a loosening in monetary policy. They argued that, under such a strategy of stimulating the export-sector, 'the government's deficit cures itself as unemployment falls and as tax revenue rises with rising incomes'.

The letter concluded by saying that the sacrifices being demanded of New Zealanders 'are at best unnecessary, and at worst will turn out to be counterproductive'.

The academics' letter certainly showed one thing: that Keynesian economics still flourished in New Zealand universities. In my public reply to the academics I labelled the letter 'shallow and unscholarly'. I pointed out that the government had a balanced economic strategy and was not seeking deficit elimination in isolation from other policies. I also criticised the vagueness of the academics' prescription to adjust exchange rate policy:

> It says nothing about how such an adjustment is to be brought about and, even more importantly, how it can be sustained ... The whole of the government's economic strategy is about achieving a permanent shift in resources to the traded goods sector, not by attempting to wave a magic wand, but by policies that prove sustainable because they tackle our underlying problems.
>
> Having offered us their instant prescription, the academics go on to make the extraordinary statement that the deficit problem would then 'cure itself'. It is precisely this sort of wishful thinking that has led to decades of government overspending and the huge build-up of debt that all of us now face.

I could not resist ending my response with a reference to one of my favourite incidents in the career of one of my favourite politicians:

> Open letters from academics have a chequered history. Early in Margaret Thatcher's premiership, 364 prominent economists wrote a now notorious letter to the London *Times* urging the government to abandon its economic policy. No U-turn was forthcoming from the British government, and almost from that moment the British economy began to recover. It went on to record its longest postwar expansion. The contribution from the Auckland academics deserves no better a fate.

Deserved or undeserved, the contribution from the Auckland academics received precisely that fate. In the very next quarter, the New Zealand economy began its recovery – an expansion that after four years shows no sign of coming to an end.

Economics is not a laboratory science, where controlled experiments can be performed. It takes its observations from the real world, in which many influences are interacting simultaneously. In economics, a single incident in history does not in itself 'prove' one side of an argument to be right or wrong. But this much is undeniable: the direction of the economy since the middle of 1991 has in no way added lustre to the arguments of those such as the Auckland academics.

There can be real debate about the short-term impact on the economy of cutting government spending. It is entirely possible – though in my view by no means certain – that the government's fiscal policy depressed overall economic activity in the first two quarters of 1991. Thus, technically, the Keynesians may be right, if just the very short term is considered. Keynes may have said, in a much overrated aphorism, that in the long run we are all dead. But it is the long run that still matters most for government policy, tempting though it is for politicians to be diverted by short-term expediency. If short-term policy is not consistent with the best outcomes over the medium term, that policy is almost certainly misconceived. We did not make that mistake in 1991. I am confident that our expenditure-cutting strategy brought a recovery that was stronger, more soundly based, and more sustainable than the absence of such a strategy.

In talking the language of recovery, however, I am getting ahead of my story. The statistics were to show that the economic upturn began in the third quarter of 1991. But between the budget and the end of the year there was no general feeling that the economy was beginning to recover, either in the business community or among the public. Economic statistics come out only after a lag, and during this period the published news on domestic spending, on output and on unemployment was heavily depressing. Gloom was the predominant mood.

I have rarely been one to shoot the messenger. I did, however, come perilously close to knuckling a few of the political media during this time. There seemed no way of convincing many of them that the statistics we were being confronted with largely represented a past picture of the economy. In their defence, the media were being fed by some of my own colleagues, who also remained unconvinced an economic recovery was on the horizon.

Overall, I believe I had a good working relationship with most of the media. There were a few with whom I struggled to remain civil, such as Pam Corkery, then of Radio Pacific talkback. Still, I was not alone on that score; even Jim ceased interviews with her. But journalists such as Pattrick Smellie, then of the Christchurch *Press*, and Jane Clifton and Mike Munro of the *Dominion*, were fair and courteous. Simon Collins, then of the *New Zealand Herald*, was tenacious and often frighteningly correct in his analysis.

Despite the efforts of my staff I did not socialise much with the media. Unlike many of my male colleagues I never paid impromptu visits to the Press Bar on a Friday night. I was always on a plane to Canterbury to be with my family. In an attempt to make up for this my staff did organise the occasional media dinner. One such enjoyable occasion was with a group of media my staff nicknamed the Three Dicks – Richard Long from the *Dominion*, Richard Harman from Television New Zealand and Richard Griffin from Radio New Zealand. Long was a valued supporter of my policies and I was delighted when later he was promoted into the editor's chair of his newspaper. Harman and Griffin had no particular love for me, tending rather to hunt with the Press Gallery pack. I had crossed swords with each of them more than once. However, it is a truism that media and politicians need each other. In a relaxed atmosphere, mutual grudges could give way to friendlier fire – which certainly happened that evening with the Three Dicks.

The economic news after the budget was not all bad. The gloom was lightened by some strongly improving economic fundamentals. Inflation was falling rapidly, as were interest rates, suggesting the economy might be almost through its period of disinflation. In fact, inflation pressures were dropping so rapidly that the Reserve Bank was, in my view and in the view of a good many others, overcautious in its stance following the budget, particularly in its August monetary policy statement. Given the rate at which inflation expectations were falling, the softness of domestic demand and the minimal wage pressures, I believed an explicit easing at the time of the August monetary policy statement was both warranted and entirely consistent with reaching the 0-2 per cent inflation target well ahead of time. In the event, the easing took place late in September.

Alongside the very positive inflation trends, the real exchange rate had fallen significantly since the government had taken office. Our export performance had been highly encouraging and exporters were feeling increasingly confident. The balance of payments was improving. To me these were all signs that the economy was on the right track and the strategy was beginning to work. But to the person in the street, or to the business serving the domestic market, it was far less obvious.

With the economy seemingly stuck in the doldrums, and after a very tough budget, it was no surprise to see the government's popularity falling substantially. The months between the budget and the end of the year were the toughest period, politically, for the government. Some in our ranks were asking not whether the government would be re-elected, but whether we could be re-elected. The atmosphere in Cabinet was at its most difficult.

We all know what happens when a government gets nervous: compromises occur, supposedly firm policies fray at the edges, outright U-turns take place. It our case the outright U-turns were relatively few. But there was slippage in some areas as ministers reacted to what they saw as an unfavourable political environment. It became clear to me that the next two years would primarily be ones of consolidating and entrenching the gains already made – an important task, and one no less challenging than the reforms of the government's first nine months.

My relationship with Jim waxed and waned considerably in the course of my term as Finance Minister. Our closeness was strongly related to how well Jim perceived the government to be doing at the time. In his mind, I was closely identified with the government's overall economic strategy. When he was having doubts about the strategy, or when the news was bad, he tended to drift away from me, and I often found him unreceptive to my ideas. When the news was favourable, or when the government was going through a good patch, Jim was a far more receptive audience. Not surprisingly, over the four or five months following the 1991 budget, he was to drift some distance away.

In attempting to maintain control over the economic strategy, I had a number of important audiences. The most crucial was Jim. Next in importance came my other Cabinet colleagues. Another audience I could not afford to neglect were the government members of the Finance and Expenditure Select Committee (FEC). And, in view of its size, the wider caucus was also an important forum. On taking office, it had quickly become apparent to me that there was a huge gulf between Cabinet and the rest of caucus in their understanding of the economic strategy. Cabinet was exposed repeatedly to information and arguments that caucus received far less frequently. Yet ordinary caucus members were required to go back to their electorates and defend some very tough policies that they had played little part in formulating. This inevitably made the relationship between Cabinet and caucus a difficult one.

Of all my target audiences, it was FEC that would most often disappoint me. In considering legislation, they tended to view issues in isolation, without appreciating their place in the wider economic strategy. My attempts to bind FEC into that wider strategy were often unsuccessful. A more successful forum for me was the Caucus Economic Committee, in general a supportive group. In the early stages Muldoon was a highly disruptive influence on the occasions that he turned up to this committee. Though by then very frail, he was still able to make strong men quake in their size elevens. On Muldoon's resignation from Parliament the committee gained cohesion and operated with a positive atmosphere. I tried, where possible, to expose ideas to the caucus committee before raising them in full caucus, and this proved to be a useful tactic.

Given the prevailing nervousness in Cabinet and the recessed state of the domestic economy, the outcome of the government's deliberations on the post-1992 tariff regime, a lynch-pin of our economic policy, was reasonable enough. The government's decision was portrayed in the media as a 'defeat' for me. However, since I quite properly did not make my position publicly known, the media reports must have resulted from a Cabinet opponent putting that spin around the Press Gallery. It is true that the government's tariff-reduction schedule was slightly slower than Labour's own schedule announced the previous year. However, from my point of view the outcome could have been a great deal worse.

Certainly, I wanted a faster rate of tariff reduction than Cabinet decided upon. National had more than met its side of the bargain with New Zealand's protected manufacturers. The government was fast bringing about price stability, lowering the tax burden, reducing interest rates, and had passed into law the Employment Contracts Act. The government had even undertaken its period of consultation with manufacturers, which Commerce Minister Philip Burdon had insisted on. The conditions were daily improving for exporting and import-competing manufacturers. The overall economic liberalisation programme was seven years old – more than fair warning for protected manufacturers. The quid pro quo for all of these considerations was continued significant reductions in tariffs.

An officials committee had looked at the question of tariff reductions after 1992, and had come up with a generally sensible recommended schedule. In it, most tariffs would fall to 10 per cent by 1996, while a small number would fall to 5 per cent. Philip Burdon published the officials' report, perhaps so he could portray himself to manufacturers as 'less extreme' than the officials. We had preliminary discussions in Cabinet on the issue, where I made my views plain. However, Philip did not promote his own paper to Cabinet until I was out of the country. It was a measure of my waning influence with Jim during these months that he did not hold Philip's paper over until I came back. Though my deputy, Maurice McTigue, fought my corner in Cabinet, Philip's proposals were largely accepted. They entailed a generally slower reduction in tariff rates to an average of around 12 per cent. Even Philip's schedule, however, represented a reduction by around one-third in the course of four years. All tariffs for items on the global programme remained on a firm downward trend. As far as I was concerned, that was the key signal needed from the exercise.

During these months Jim was increasingly coming to feel that a more 'hands-on' economic approach might be needed from the government. Our existing strategy of controlling inflation and government spending, and deregulating the labour market, seemed to Jim to be a leap of faith whose merits had not yet been demonstrated. Jim wanted to do something more 'positive', to actively 'encourage' growth and development. Such instincts, unless channelled in relatively harmless directions, could become positively dangerous. There was a range of proposals that might potentially appeal to Jim. I asked the Treasury to consider which of these might be the least harmful; I called it the Prime Minister's 'rabbit'. The Treasury suggested that a small venture capital fund might do the trick and this became the proposal I supported at Cabinet level. Undeterred by the fate of the Development Finance Corporation we eventually did, after long delay, put in place a small venture capital fund.

Post-budget nerves had perhaps the greatest impact in the area of social policy. Political nervousness certainly impeded the development of the interim targeting regime. Ministers made a series of ad hoc changes, few of which had any consistency. The interim targeting regime had never been expected to be a big revenue-earner for the government. With the added anomalies, it ended up earning the government even less.

Far more spectacular, however, was the climb-down on superannuation. The post-budget reaction to the 93 per cent EMTR faced by some superannuitants had been fierce. Many in the organisational wing of the National Party, and much of the National back bench, were among those most opposed to the high abatement rate. The debate became highly emotional. It became even more heated, and even more emotional, when an unknown official leaked a draft form for means-testing superannuitants. As fate would have it, Jim, Jenny and I were all overseas when the leak occurred and the public furore that ensued was handled weakly by ministers. Given the stiff income test announced in the budget, rigorous means-testing of superannuitants was always going to be crucial to achieving the savings from superannuation projected in the budget. That had been one of the rationales for integrating superannuation into the benefit system, rather than continuing with the surcharge administered by Inland Revenue. With the government now back-peddling over the leaked form, those savings already looked difficult to achieve.

Matters then took a turn even more definitely for the worse. By now the pressure on Jim from the back bench over the abatement rate had intensified. Jim did not seek a solution through Cabinet. He called a press conference and unilaterally announced that the government was abandoning the income test for superannuation announced in the budget. He said that the government would look again at the parameters for superannuation.

And look again we did. It took several more weeks of work, and consideration of new combinations of (mostly old) parameters, before we finally settled on the details of the national superannuation scheme that would operate from April 1992. The accelerated shift to age 65 remained, as did the CPI indexation. The 50 per cent universality from age 70 was dropped. But the income test was substantially relaxed, taking the form of a modified surcharge to be administered by Inland Revenue. The income test was now similar to the one we had inherited from Labour; though slightly tougher than Labour's regime, it represented a big loss of revenue compared with the budget scheme. On all the changes combined, we were down by around $400 million on a full-year basis.

I was not only having to fight battles on the spending side of the ledger. The closing months of 1991 saw two major tax issues contested within Cabinet, in which Wyatt Creech and I were on opposite sides.

My working relationship with Wyatt was one of the less attractive aspects of my job as Minister of Finance. I had partly myself to blame. In Opposition I had gained a wholly mistaken impression of Wyatt's abilities and approach. Wyatt was then associate revenue spokesman and an MP in his first term. I had told Jim, shortly before the election, that I wanted Wyatt in Cabinet as Minister of Revenue. Wyatt may already have been such a favourite with Jim that he would have gained that position anyway, but my urgings probably did make a difference. It was a bad judgment call that I lived to regret.

Far from Wyatt being a philosophical ally, he turned out to be an opponent on most of the contentious issues in Cabinet, and we were never further apart than on revenue policy, for which we had shared responsibility. I wanted a tax system that in general was as neutral as possible between different activities. I wanted to be active in countering tax avoidance – I sought a pre-emptive base-maintenance strategy. The cost of capital was also a consideration that weighed heavily with me. Wyatt did not accept the concept of tax neutrality, and placed much higher weight on reducing compliance costs than on plugging loopholes in the tax system. We were bound to be at loggerheads. Wyatt and I did have one thing in common, however – a mutual doggedness: we were probably the two most stubborn people in Cabinet. No wonder Richardson-Creech ding-dongs became such a frequent feature of Cabinet. One day, seeing a big tax agenda, Warren Cooper jested: 'Why don't we just leave you and Wyatt to fight it out together?'

I can hardly blame Wyatt for being stubborn, or for having different views from me. But what I frankly did resent was his attitude to Cabinet collective responsibility. I was no angel when doing Cabinet battle. An encounter with me was not invariably a pleasant experience. Often the unpleasantness was not intended; it was a fault in me that I sometimes treated people more abrasively than I realised I was doing. But at the end of the day I was a team player. Once Cabinet had made a final decision, I defended it in public and did not attempt to overturn it. Wyatt, when he lost a decision in Cabinet, turned to Plan B. Plan B was to stir up caucus, or to ask outside organisations to renew their lobbying. Once or twice he was caught out in Cabinet having done precisely that. But by letting relitigation occur, Jim implicitly encouraged Wyatt in this behaviour. It was a weakness in Jim's Cabinet management that in allowing relitigation by ministers he encouraged untidy processes.

Personalities, however, were not the root of the problem. I soon came to learn a lesson that I had failed to learn prior to the election – that having a Minister of Finance sharing responsiblity for revenue with a Minister of Revenue is the wrong institutional arrangement. It is wrong because budget-making intimately involves both expenditure decisions and revenue decisions, and trade-offs are inevitable. If you want the best co-ordinated budget policy, one minister must be in charge of both sides of the ledger. Only then will there be the incentive to make the best possible trade-offs.

A stand-alone Minister of Revenue faces quite different incentives to the minister whose name goes on the budget deficit. The Revenue Minister's constituency is groups such as tax practitioners and large corporates. The Revenue Minister's political incentive is to run as soft a revenue policy as possible, because another minister wears the fiscal and wider economic consequences of that stance. This was an institutional weakness in having a stand-alone Revenue Minister quite apart from any personality difference between Wyatt and me.

There were other tax lessons I learned in government that I had not learned in Opposition. In retrospect, tax policy was the one area where I could clearly have done a better job in preparing myself for office. For instance, I had wrongly opposed Labour's international regime. I had never knowingly advocated policies that departed significantly from the principle of tax neutrality. However, I had sometimes given insufficient weight to the need for a government to maintain its tax base. When I was Minister of Finance, that need very quickly came home to me.

As Jim drifted away from me in the latter part of 1991, he saw Wyatt increasingly as a counterweight to his Minister of Finance. In Jim's October reshuffle Doug Kidd lost his associate finance and SOE responsibilities, instead replacing the dumped Winston Peters in Maori Affairs. Joining Maurice McTigue as an Associate Finance Minister was Wyatt. My two associates could hardly have been in greater contrast. The undemonstrative Maurice McTigue, whose low public profile belied his true quality, was level-headed, conscientious and loyal. Wyatt did not support the fiscal strategy and I found it wise to send him as little information as possible. Wyatt was also one of the few ministers who both wanted my job and believed he had a reasonable chance of getting it. Though he was a favourite of Jim's, Wyatt was probably wrong in that calculation. If I was to be dumped, Bill Birch always had the inside running as my replacement.

The inter-corporate dividend exemption had been removed by budget-night legislation. However, a related tax bill was in the House. Private-sector groups had begun a heavy lobbying campaign to have the exemption reinstated. They were encouraged in this campaign by the Finance and Expenditure Select Committee (FEC), which called for submissions on the inter-corporate dividend exemption. Wyatt changed his mind on the issue and the members of the committee also became convinced that we needed to restore the exemption. I can recall few of the arguments that were used – either by colleagues or by tax practitioners. However, they had the apocalyptic flavour often apparent when measures to combat tax avoidance are being countered by government action.

Riding on the outcome of this debate was around $150 million of revenue and the integrity of the tax system. We had more than one meeting between government members of FEC, Wyatt and the Treasury, on both the technical aspects and the estimated revenue from abolishing the exemption. My officials answered all questions with ease. If ever there seemed an open-and-shut case, this was it, but I had to battle hard. Luckily I managed to keep Jim on my side, so that when Wyatt brought up the subject in Cabinet he was unsuccessful. FEC members then raised the same issue in caucus, handing out a paper bearing the unmistakable font of Wyatt's computer, and Wyatt spoke against the Cabinet-agreed position. The vote, however, went in my favour.

Wyatt was in agony afterwards, telling me how much this would destroy his credibility with the Society of Accountants. I can only speculate on what he might have said to them to get himself into that pickle. Wyatt was extremely unhappy at losing the issue. He would try another rearguard action in the new year, and would again be unsuccessful.

I had less success in the other major tax debate before Christmas: depreciation. This issue was always going to be difficult: Jim, Bill and Wyatt all saw the setting of depreciation rates as a means by which we could stimulate business investment. The budget had signalled that we would be reviewing the depreciation regime. In the existing regime the rates of depreciation for various classes of assets bore little relation to economic rates.

The positive step we took before Christmas was to make a firm decision to move to economic rates. However, Wyatt wanted some type of concession on top of economic rates. Both he and Jim were keen on the idea of matching the depreciation rates given in Australia – an approach whose logic mystified me. As for Bill, he was – as someone observed – 'a bricks and mortar man'. I tried every economic and political argument I could think of against a concessionary depreciation regime. I pointed out that, at a time of unprecedented unemployment, ministers were in essence proposing a cut in the company tax rate in a way that discriminated against job creation. It was to no avail. We announced a generous interim regime before Christmas. The work by officials to establish economic rates would be undertaken in 1992. There were strong hints that the final form of the depreciation regime, to be determined the following year, would involve matching international rates. One of the worst rows I had with Wyatt was over the exact wording of the press statement. Both of us knew it would be an important 'marker' for the battles on depreciation the following year.

A concessionary depreciation regime is expensive; just the interim 'loading' on depreciation rates was to cost roughly half of the money saved from our changes to national superannuation, which had been so damaging politically. To me it was the best possible example of how painfully acquired savings on the spending side of the ledger could be compromised by thoughtless action on the revenue side.

I would have no more luck the following year, when the final depreciation regime was determined. First Cabinet would agree on a highly concessionary regime. Then Wyatt would stir up the backbenchers, and caucus would settle on an even more concessionary regime.

Late in 1991 the Treasury produced a revised set of fiscal projections. Not surprisingly, they showed a considerably worse picture. The financial deficit for 1991-92 was now forecast to be $2.8 billion (compared with $1.7 billion in the budget), falling to just $2.3 billion in 1993-94 (compared with $0.5 billion in the budget). Government policy decisions since the budget had contributed to the deterioration, but the largest contribution had come from economic factors. Treasury had revised down its economic growth forecast for 1991-92 from 0.8 per cent to -1.3 per cent, in view of the latest information on the weakness in the economy over the first half of 1991. This had a significant flow-on effect on tax receipts.

Receiving the December projections was one of my more uncomfortable moments as Minister of Finance. In the budget I had spoken of how we were putting the fiscal problems of the past behind us. That phrase was now ringing somewhat hollow. The critics of the government's strategy could gather ammunition from the December projections, which could be taken as confirming that the government was chasing its own tail, that the expenditure-cutting programme was reducing growth, which was in turn widening the deficit. It had been a punishing year for domestic economic activity and for jobs. Though the economic news from the second half of the year seemed moderately encouraging, there was little talk of a general upturn. Now the government did not even appear to have solved the fiscal problem. We had, of course, still made huge progress compared with where we were 12 months before. I would continue to stress publicly that the government had strategies in place to control spending pressures. But I knew privately that there was little appetite in Cabinet for any major new assault on spending. I would have to hold the line as best I could and hope things came right.

A few days before the December projections came out, Jim held one of his last weekly press conferences for the year. By then he had been briefed on the fiscal situation. Jim's press conferences were often a liability. The press saw them as an exercise in taking potshots at the Prime Minister, and policy was sometimes made up at the podium. I was glad when in 1993 he cancelled his press conferences. On this occasion Jim told journalists that National might not be able to meet its first-term target of a balanced budget. He had given me absolutely no prior warning of this. It was, to say the least, unhelpful, and to my mind it sent quite the wrong signal. Naturally, I had doubts in my mind about whether we would reach budget balance in our first term, but it was too early to abandon the timeframe altogether. Only a few days previously I had given a speech of the 'no turning back' flavour, restating the commitment to budget balance in our first term.

Having made his surprise concession, Jim then referred further questions about the fiscal position to me! It was what they call in rugby a hospital pass. As chance would have it, end-of-year drinks for selected media and financial market analysts were starting in my office almost as soon as Jim had finished speaking, so the beginning of my function turned into an impromptu press conference. I had no option but to fall into line with Jim and make the best of it. I stressed that budget balance was still very much a goal of the government, despite the setbacks. I also stressed the government's continued commitment to controlling expenditure, and

I pointed to the still weak state of the world economy, which had adversely affected New Zealand's economic performance. This had added a large cyclical factor to the deterioration in the outlook.

As it turned out, having the analysts on the spot probably helped me. They were in a reasonably settled state regarding the government's fiscal policy. In the informal discussions that followed, they helped to calm down some of the wilder journalists. Seeing me handle a press conference also won me a sympathy vote from some of the analysts! Having never experienced one before, they were amazed at the aggressive and adversarial nature of some of the questioning; to me it had seemed par for the course. All things considered, the press conference did not go off too badly.

Jim was not finishing the year in the most settled frame of mind. Late in the year a group of senior ministers had a strategy session on Sunday night at Premier House, and Jim was at the lowest ebb I had seen him. All year I had regarded him as a man who had taken many courageous decisions against his own instincts. I had admired him for that. But on this occasion Jim was extremely negative about the strategy. He even suggested we change the Reserve Bank Act and loosen monetary policy, prefacing his remarks with 'I know you are going to hate this, Ruth, but …'. Ruth did hate it. To the credit of my colleagues, Jim received no support at all. Bill Birch was sensible on the subject, as was Philip Burdon, who was reporting a positive picture from the export sector. The idea was stillborn.

The minister who advocated by far the most substantial change of economic direction was Wyatt. Over the Christmas holidays my Associate Finance Minister prepared a long paper entitled 'A New Programme for New Zealand'. It was extremely gloomy about the political prospects for the government under existing policies and it was heavily critical of the economic strategy:

> The heavy emphasis on theoretical correctness in economic policy of recent years with the associated belief that the rigid application of a set of principles will solve all our problems conflicts with the electorates [sic] general commonsense results oriented pragmatic understanding of political activity.

In 36 pages of this prose, Wyatt argued that the fiscal strategy was flawed:

> Despite the frequently pronounced intent of the current economic strategy to achieve a growth in economic activity, no growth has emerged. On the contrary, the economy has diminished in size over the last year.

> During 1991 the main focus of much of the government's economic policy action was the attack, carried out with considerable vigour, on New Zealand's fiscal position. Efforts to control government expenditure have succeeded in reducing the gross outlay on particular votes compared to the 1991 departmental bids, but the accumulated consequential economic effects of the expenditure reductions have been to generally aggravate the depression of the internal economy to such an extent that the reduced revenue flows into the government's coffers have left a continuing fiscal problem in spite of the original expenditure reductions (for example, witness the results of the benefit cuts) ... More consideration of the downstream effects of expenditure cuts and allaying them should have been considered at the time cuts were introduced.
>
> Although Treasury advice remains wedded to the notion that growth is about to take off, it is doubtful it will come quick enough or be substantial enough to stop unemployment rising significantly. Certainly there is little sign of such an event occurring at the moment. It could easily be wishful thinking. Treasury's track-record is one of consistently producing over optimistic predictions of economic performance.

Without irony, Wyatt went on to call the government's expenditure control programme 'blunt and unintelligent'. His solution was to push for what he what he termed 'investment-led growth'. He wanted the budget-balance target abandoned, as well as the targets to reduce government spending and taxation as a percentage of GDP. He proposed a programme of infrastructure spending, paid for partly by selling state assets. He also proposed tax incentives for savings and investment. He wanted new venture capital to be encouraged by 'the government guaranteeing a part of the loan to small new businesses of a person who has little capital resources and no track record in business but who has a good idea'.

Wyatt did not want a significant general tax increase. However, he said that he supported 'a rate change for higher-income earners as a fairness measure'. On monetary policy, Wyatt thought Jim and Don Brash could come to a sensible understanding:

> Now that the current target has been met, the Prime Minister should approach the Governor of the Reserve Bank and discuss the appropriate line to take from here. Rather than select what would be an arbitrarily selected number, for the purposes of this paper the target should be to achieve an inflation rate that is less than the trade-weighted average of New Zealand's major trading partners and competitors.

It looked like being quite a discussion, because Jim and Don would also discuss 'what a competitive real interest rate might be as New Zealand prepares for an economic expansion'. The exchange rate would also be 'part of the proposed discussion with the Reserve Bank'.

Wyatt also proposed splitting the Treasury into two new departments, and transferring tax policy advice to Inland Revenue.

I shall resist the temptation to explore Wyatt's paper any further. Suffice to say that we were back in very much the same landscape as that inhabited by the 15 Auckland academics: the tendency to believe that you can buy prosperity with inflation, that you can reduce your debt by spending more, that you can live within your means by having one last binge.

Wyatt's timing was bad. Had he presented his paper before Christmas it is still unlikely he would have got anywhere, but he would have had a much greater chance than early in the new year. During the summer break something happened that many people did not expect. The economy began to look, at long last, as if it might be recovering.

13

A RECOVERING ECONOMY

The early part of the summer was filled with good economic news – on business confidence, on exports, on consumer spending, on gross domestic product. A short period of favourable statistics can be misleading, but by early February I was also receiving extremely positive feedback from my visits to businesses. At meeting after meeting I was told the conditions for business success were now in place. Exporters talked glowingly about price stability, about low interest rates and the competitive exchange rate. The Employment Contracts Act was praised to the skies. This confidence was all the more encouraging for being grounded in the fundamentals of our economic strategy. The positive feedback was not just coming from our export sector. Many domestic industries were reporting a strengthening of demand. And in the region previously most depressed, Auckland, the mood was almost buoyant.

Even on my visit to the Manufacturers' Federation I was not greeted with the heady blast of gloom that I normally collected from that forum. I had never considered the Manufacturers' Federation to be remotely my constituency. As protected manufacturers, they had long been vocal opponents of the economic reforms and issuers of dire warnings on the future of manufacturing. Yet on this occasion, fully half of the people sitting around the table were optimistic – a previously unheard of percentage. Some even praised aspects of the government's strategy. I considered it a most encouraging sign.

By early February I was all but certain the economic upturn had begun. The strong export performance we had seen in 1991 was enduring, and was supporting the upturn in domestic demand. Previously I had avoided public talk of recovery; I had wanted my language to be realistic. I had talked about the need for New Zealanders to adjust, and about our progress in laying the groundwork for sustainable economic growth. Any strongly optimistic rhetoric had been confined to the long term. But now my language made a sharp change. As far as I was concerned the economic upturn was under way and it was my business to 'talk up' that recovery. While acknowledging that not all businesses – and still less all individuals – were feeling the upturn, it was the language of recovery that now filled my speeches.

The strategy I had set for myself within Cabinet changed too. The last few months of 1991 had been dedicated to holding the line, in difficult political and economic circumstances. Now the task was not just to hold the line; it was to maintain the momentum of economic recovery.

All in all, I was starting 1992 in much better heart than I had ended the previous year. Over the Christmas break I had gone with my family to the Chatham Islands. There, the private-enterprise culture was a refreshing antidote to the negative attitudes so prevalent in the rest of New Zealand. If I started 1992 in much better heart, so did Jim. He had been receiving similar feedback to me; he was buoyed by his Christmas break and by all the good news. I immediately sensed Jim was closer to me than he had been at the end of the previous year, and more responsive to my suggestions. Nor was he in a mood to pay much attention to Wyatt's gloom-laden paper. I am not sure how many other ministers saw the paper, but Jim prevented Wyatt from placing it on the Cabinet agenda.

The new feeling of optimism was also evident at National's three-day caucus meeting. The mood in the past in caucus towards the government's economic strategy had often been distinctly mixed. Two National MPs had already left to set up their own party, while many others had bucked the party line or been critical of the economic direction. The critical elements had certainly not disappeared completely. In politics, however, nothing sways the middle ground like success. There was a new realism in caucus: an acknowledgment that we were on the right track and that we should not throw away the gains. This was firmly brought home to the two loudest mavericks – Winston Peters and Michael Laws. Both were given a very solid warning that if they continued with their public criticism of the government, they could face expulsion from caucus. That warning came not from Cabinet ministers but from ordinary backbenchers. Laws took the warning to heart and became noticeably quieter. Peters ignored it and was duly expelled from caucus later that year.

In March I took off for a two-week trip to Asia, accompanied by 15 top New Zealand businessmen. It was the first time I had travelled with a business retinue. It was exhausting, but a very valuable time was had by all. On many occasions the party undertook joint presentations: I would lead off, and sectoral presentations would follow from some of the businessmen.

This trip seemed particularly rich in bizarre incidents. When we arrived at Seoul, the greeting party mistook Anna, my press secretary, for the minister. Anna is blonde, very attractive and a good deal younger than me. Even the local film crew was trailing for a while the glamorous young 'Minister of Finance' from New Zealand.

In the historic Japanese city of Kyoto, Andrew and I went for an early-morning run that took us past an ancient temple surrounded by a dry moat. Succumbing to the temptation to take a closer look at the splendid temple wall, I climbed over the moat. Unfortunately, this set off the burglar alarm. Who or what came running I shall never know, and was not keen to find out. 'Richardson arrested in Japan' was not a headline I wanted my Cabinet colleagues to read. Highly abashed, Andrew and I fled the scene of the crime!

The same trip saw the loss of a different kind of innocence after I committed a major cultural blunder. Nomura Securities had invited our party to a meal in a very traditional Japanese garden restaurant. I had not been forewarned – or had perhaps forgotten – that such an occasion was strictly for social bonding between Nomura and the New Zealanders; any business talk was strictly prohibited. Unfortunately, I began by launching into a heavy disquisition on New Zealand's macroeconomic policy in a social faux pas akin to telling raunchy stories to the Queen Mother. I was soon on the receiving end of a kick under the table from Pat Duignan and a muttered aside that there should be no serious conversation.

Naturally, I was keen to retrieve the situation. I noted that Nomura had arranged for the New Zealander to be served Japanese beer. Hitherto the only alcohol I had drunk was wine; indeed, I had been brought up a teetotaller and had not tasted alcohol at all until I was 24. If I were to become 'one of the boys', I decided, the time had come for my first glass of beer. My announcement to this effect made me a considerable hit with my Japanese hosts. From that point on the evening went swimmingly, and increasingly swimmingly as the meal proceeded.

By the time of the trip I was already well into the cycle of work leading up to the 1992 budget. On the expenditure side, planning had started just before Christmas. Though the mood in Cabinet had been against significant new expenditure savings, I did obtain agreement to aim for an average 2 per cent reduction in departmental expenditure. In January, Cabinet held a strategic session in which we settled on our new expenditure priorities for the budget. Ministers decided that skills, employment and enterprise would be the key areas for new spending.

Early in the year, assisted by my associates, I held a series of bilateral meetings with all the other ministers and their chief executives. These went extremely smoothly. The only person who played up was not a minister but the chief executive of the Ministry of External Relations and Trade, who was as obstructive as he was impertinent. Apart from him, all departments made at least a reasonable effort to co-operate with the budget process. Nor could I complain about the general attitude from my ministerial colleagues.

Following the bilaterals, ministers produced their draft departmental budgets. New policy bids were held over to a late stage of the budget process. By then we had Treasury's new three-year projections, incorporating the new departmental baselines. The new spending in the budget was relatively minor, most of it taken up in expanding various job schemes. The new spending roughly matched the departmental savings. All in all, expenditure control produced few problems in the lead-up to the budget.

There were big problems on the revenue side, however. From early in the year I began receiving increasingly serious reports on further weakness in tax revenue. This weakness was of greatest concern when it related to income tax on individuals and companies. By the time it came for the Treasury to produce the April revised fiscal outlook for 1991-92, the projected financial deficit had again been revised upwards. It now stood at $3.4 billion, compared with $2.8 billion in December and $1.7 billion in the budget. The bulk of this deterioration was on the tax side.

A great deal of formal analysis and emotional angst was expended by the Treasury in an attempt to make sense of the tax shortfall. Some of it was due to the faster than expected reduction in interest rates and was an inevitable byproduct of the government's success in bringing interest rates down. But most of the shortfall was in business tax receipts.

A number of influences appeared to be at work, though it was not easy to sort out the most dominant. One factor was probably a previous underestimation of the tax shortfall due to the recession. In addition, avoidance activity using the schemes countered in the 1991 budget appeared to be greater than previously believed. A third factor was the large quantity of tax losses that had built up in corporate New Zealand in the wake of the sharemarket crash. Many companies were still in the process of using up these losses to offset taxable income. The speed with which these losses would eventually be worked off was a matter of considerable uncertainty.

From early in 1992 it seemed clear to me that in the coming budget I would be bringing down a fiscal outlook no better than, and probably worse than, the outlook in the December projections. The economy had begun tangibly to recover. But a moderate economic recovery had already been built into the December projections of tax revenue and benefit numbers. I would not be getting a large fiscal dividend from that source. The case some of my colleagues would make for tax increases was stronger than it had been 12 months ago.

I had now made my assault on spending, and another could not take place for another two years, if at all. Meanwhile, the deficits still had to be funded. In the long run, if deficits cannot be eliminated by reducing spending, the logic of tax increases is inescapable. But the long run was still some way off. Running with large deficits in 1992 would be a calculated risk, but to me it seemed a risk worth taking.

It was clear from my discussions with the Treasury that there was considerable uncertainty about the strength and timing of a rebound in tax revenue. The Treasury's tax forecasts were likely to be slightly on the conservative side, though none the worse for that. The economic recovery was only just getting under way. It seemed to me too precipitate to raise taxes when the need to do so was not yet firmly established; it risked compromising the recovery and it was a major negative signal to send to the business community. It would also punish New Zealand's wealth creators – the very people I had wanted this government to help. I wanted to give the economic recovery the benefit of the doubt.

I may have been certain in my own mind that tax increases should not be contemplated, but I needed to convince my doubting Cabinet colleagues.

I also needed to fashion a credible story for the financial markets in the 1992 budget. In both of these tasks the development of the tax-base maintenance strategy was to play an important role.

Tax-base maintenance was not, of course, new to the government. The measures to combat corporate tax avoidance in the 1991 budget had been substantial base-maintenance initiatives. In the past, however, we had tended to take one step back for every step forward. I was now trying to elevate base maintenance to become the guiding principle in our revenue policy. This would put me sharply at odds with Wyatt. In general I favoured as low a rate of tax as possible, applied over as broad a base as feasible. Wyatt had no such philosophical commitment.

I invested a considerable amount of time talking to Jim about the principle of base maintenance. Jim was not one for philosophical purity. To the economist, the basic appeal of a broad tax base is that it helps resources to flow into activities that have the highest rate of return for society as a whole. I did not bother with that argument with Jim. I wanted Jim to see base maintenance in two important ways: as an integral part of our fiscal strategy, and as a 'fairness' measure. The previous year I had had the Treasury think up the interim targeting regime in order to counteract pressure for higher taxes. This time around my weapon was base maintenance. Jim, like me, was worried about the fiscal deficit. He was also worried about fairness.

Gradually the momentum of the idea built up. As early as January, in our fiscal strategy meeting, I obtained Cabinet's agreement for Wyatt and me to report back on policies to 'maintain and where necessary enhance' the tax base. Wyatt and I had some meetings, making our usual slow progress. The emerging information on the weakness in business tax revenue added considerably to my case within Cabinet. Showing all the loyalty and courtesy that Wyatt had shown me, I put up a tax strategy paper to Cabinet while Wyatt was overseas. On more than one occasion the previous year I had tried to reach agreement with Wyatt over a tax strategy paper, but had never been able to do so. This time I was striking while the iron was hot. It was the only time I ever 'ambushed' another minister but, given Wyatt's own record, I had no qualms about doing it.

Wyatt got back into the country fizzing. He produced his inevitable alternative paper. He also told Jim, not for the first time, that he wanted sole control of tax policy. But the contest was largely won by me. Cabinet bought the idea of an active base-maintenance strategy: base maintenance would be one of the themes of the budget.

Like the interim targeting regime, the base-maintenance strategy was to prove more attractive to Jim in the abstract than in practice. Like the interim targeting regime, some of our base-maintenance initiatives would end up riddled with anomalies. Like the interim targeting regime, post-budget changes to measures in the base-maintenance strategy would leave it raising scarcely any revenue, but it neutralised any calls from within Cabinet for tax increases.

Another significant move prior to the budget was the establishment of a proper process for developing tax policy. Previously, tax policy had been an informal tug-of-war between Wyatt and me. Wyatt tried to do as much as he could get away with on his own, while I tried to intervene as often as possible and ensure that differences were taken to Cabinet to sort out. Jim, Wyatt and I all knew that there was both a process and a personality problem with tax policy. Jim's solution, which I both encouraged and applauded, was to form a specialist Officials Tax Committee (OTC), chaired by the Prime Minister's Department and comprising representatives from both Inland Revenue and the Treasury. OTC reported to the Cabinet Strategy Committee.

From my point of view OTC was a very useful vehicle. It made sure the officials' advice was on the table and out from under their respective ministers. It quickly became apparent that Inland Revenue and the Treasury had little substantive disagreement on most issues and could usually sign up to common positions. Likewise, I generally took a similar stance to the two tax policy departments. The odd one out was Wyatt.

It was through OTC that the base-broadening initiatives announced in the budget were developed. Some initiatives did not make it through to the budget. For the second year running Cabinet turned down the proposal – which I supported – for a contractor's withholding tax, designed to counter widespread tax evasion in the provision of services to households by tradespeople. Also considered but rejected was a proposal to bring employee tax-free allowances under the tax net. Three principal base-maintenance measures made it through to the 1992 budget. The least controversial was the extension of two-way interest back to the first provisional payment date for large provisional taxpayers. This was to counter the practice among some taxpayers of deferring payment of most of their tax liability until the third and last provisional payment.

The measure that would turn out to be the most controversial was the extension of fringe benefit tax to cover business entertainment. Business entertainment had not previously come under the tax net, despite the clear private benefits associated with it. The move to tax entertainment was fully consistent with the introduction of fringe benefit tax by the previous government. Some countries tax 100 per cent of business entertainment; we decided to tax 50 per cent, but with few allowable exemptions. This was fair, while keeping compliance costs to a minimum.

The third base-broadening initiative in the budget was the move to tighten up on the taxation of the foreign income of New Zealand residents. This was a highly complex area of policy. Though the budget contained a large number of announcements, the thrust of the decisions was to move New Zealand's regime closer to the ideal regime where one layer of taxation was imposed on the foreign income of New Zealand residents.

This was my ideal of New Zealand's international tax regime – not Wyatt's. I believed the rationale for taxing New Zealand residents once on their worldwide income was simple, strong and well-nigh irrefutable. It went as follows. My object as Minister of Finance was to maximise the total welfare of New Zealanders. Just as welfare is maximised when the tax system does not favour one type of domestic investment over another, so it is also maximised when the tax system does not favour investing domestically compared to investing abroad, or vice versa. We want a New Zealand company to invest abroad if, and only if, the return to New Zealand is greater from that investment than the return the company could get if it invested in New Zealand. To ensure this, we have to impose a layer of New Zealand tax on foreign-source income, even if the foreign country imposes tax on the investment.

Remember that what we are interested in is the return to New Zealand of each investment. There is a major difference between investment at home and investment abroad. For a domestic investment, the whole of the return from the investment constitutes a return to New Zealand. The taxed portion of the return goes to the government; the after-tax return to the private sector. This is not the case for an investment abroad: it is only the after-tax return that constitutes a return to New Zealand. The rest goes to a foreign Treasury. But from the point of view of New Zealand, taxes paid to a foreign government are no different from any other cost of doing business that comes off the bottom line.

The New Zealand company, however, sees it differently. To the company, tax is tax – something to be avoided whether it is paid here or overseas. It is always the after-tax rate of return that matters to the New Zealand company. If this rate is higher for an investment abroad than for an investment in New Zealand, the company will invest abroad. If it is lower, the company will invest at home.

It follows, then, that to maximise overall returns to New Zealand we must impose a layer of tax on New Zealanders' foreign investment income.

If we did not, some investments would take place abroad that yielded a lower rate of return to New Zealand as a whole than potential investments at home. These 'inferior' foreign investments are those whose after-tax return is higher than the post-tax return from domestic investments, but which is lower than the pre-tax return from domestic investments (the one that matters for New Zealand's welfare). The company invests abroad because it is guided by post-tax returns, but the domestic investment would have been better for New Zealand's welfare because of its higher pre-tax return.

In other words, in the absence of a layer of New Zealand tax imposed on the worldwide income of residents, there would be excessive investment abroad by New Zealand companies. The only way to ensure that there is the right amount of investment abroad is to impose a layer of New Zealand tax, regardless of whether tax has already been paid to foreign governments.

The logic of this rather abstract argument, once grasped, is irresistible.

The 1992 budget came together. It contained comparatively little in the way of new announcements and, compared to the mother of all budgets, was the height of blandness. That did not greatly concern me. Economic recovery had begun; the task of this budget was to keep a steady course – to maintain the momentum of recovery. My biggest problem was the fiscal deficits I would be presenting. As expected, the picture had deteriorated since the December projections. We were now forecasting a deficit of $3.3 billion in 1992-93, falling to $2.3 billion in 1994-95.

It was at such moments that I was grateful for the personal credibility built up, over a period of years, with the financial markets. But I was well aware that credibility can be lost in an uncomfortably short time. I needed to persuade the markets that the government still had a strategy capable of dealing with our fiscal pressures. I wanted the markets to give that strategy the benefit of the doubt. In truth, I had little new to say on controlling expenditure. Tax-base maintenance would be elevated to stand beside expenditure control as a key element in the strategy.

I also obtained Cabinet's agreement that any fiscal saving resulting from 'stronger-than-forecast economic, revenue or employment growth' would be 'applied to deficit reduction'. Though sounding somewhat like a new year's resolution, and never in the end fully carried out, this statement was useful in signalling where we saw our priority – making continued progress on the deficit.

Whenever market expectations of the fiscal position were out of line with numbers that I would shortly be releasing, it was my practice to push market expectations in the desired direction in advance of the announcement. There were various ways I could do this. I could write some appropriate lines into a speech, or, if I wanted my message to go solely to the financial markets, I could invite the Reuters and Telerate journalists to my office for an interview and give them an appropriate line. I wanted no negative surprises when it came to any announcement; I certainly did not want a major event dominated by media reports of interest rates going up. The 1992 budget was no exception: I was careful to telegraph broadly the deficit track in advance.

This was to be the first of my budgets delivered to the backdrop of an economic upturn. We knew that gross domestic product had increased in the last two quarters of 1991, and that the indicators for the early part of 1992 had been positive. Unemployment, however, was only just peaking – at best. The tone of my speech was one of guarded optimism – I was confident but realistic:

> The positive signs are here; they are unmistakable; and they are all around us. Slowly and surely, the economic recovery we New Zealanders have looked for is emerging.
>
> Many problems still remain to be solved; many obstacles still need to be surmounted. There can be no room for false optimism – for illusions about where we are and what we have to do.
>
> But there is no denying the new mood of confidence. It is there in the community, it is gaining strength, and it is spreading.

The words 'confident' and 'confidence' occurred many times in the speech, providing one of its main subliminal messages. When evaluating the fiscal outlook, I wanted to make a virtue out of frankness. I made no pretence of any complacency over the forecast deficits:

> The government's record on expenditure control, when combined with favourable recent trends in our current account, means the fiscal position is less damaging than when we took office 20 months ago. Nonetheless, the fiscal position remains far from comfortable. It represents the main domestic risk to the economic recovery now in progress.
>
> Tonight's forecast financial deficits are too high and need to be reduced. They leave New Zealanders too exposed to adverse events, either at home or abroad, that could further erode the fiscal position and further increase our debt.

I then outlined the government's fiscal strategy: expenditure control, tax-base maintenance, and any dividend from a stronger economy to be dedicated to improving the fiscal position. I dismissed any suggestion that tax increases had a place in our strategy:

> At present the government is faced with a shortfall of revenue and an erosion of the revenue base, particularly on business incomes.
>
> Some argue for an increase in general taxation to meet this shortfall. This would not be fair as it would penalise the thousands of ordinary wage and salary earners and smaller businesses who already pay their fair share of tax.
>
> Higher tax rates would encourage people and resources to move into activities where tax can most easily be avoided. This would increase the gulf between those who pay their taxes and those who know the loopholes. It would divert New Zealanders away from the true business of creating wealth. And it would threaten the economic recovery now emerging, for which all of us have waited so long.
>
> For these reasons the government will not be increasing tax rates.

The budget went down as well as could be expected. The financial markets remained impressed by the government's record on expenditure control, and by the strong downward trend in spending as a percentage of GDP. The markets were prepared, in the main, to give the government the benefit of the doubt over the deficit track. At my meeting with market economists the day after the budget, I received considerable favourable comment about the open way in which the government had gone about acknowledging the risks.

The steady-as-she-goes budget also went down well with the public. By now the media were talking the language of economic recovery, and some New Zealanders – though far from all – were beginning to feel the recovery in their own lives. This was a good period for the government. In the first Heylen poll taken after the budget we drew level with Labour; we had been behind in the polls for over a year. Now, after taking some very tough social policy decisions, the government was back level by the middle of its three-year term. Ahead of us lay 18 months of economic recovery. It was an auspicious position to be in.

I had other reasons to be pleased in the middle of 1992. The government's privatisation programme, which had started slowly, was now much more firmly under way. By now we had sold New Zealand Timberlands, the Crown's interests in on-shore Taranaki petroleum mining licences, and the Government Supply Brokerage Corporation. I had been keen from the beginning to develop a privatisation programme that added impetus to our growth strategy. Despite the gains from turning state trading activities into state-owned enterprises (SOEs), I was well aware that the proper place for most – if not all – of these businesses was eventually the private sector. It was not, however, until Maurice McTigue became Minister of SOEs that we began to make genuine progress. Shortly before the 1992 budget Maurice announced that studies would be undertaken to assess the suitability for sale of Works Corporation, Landcorp, New Zealand Rail and the computing company GCS Limited. The latter two were eventually sold.

In our privatisation programme we kept to some important principles that had not always been followed by our Labour predecessors. We did not fall into the trap of tying privatisation to a fiscal timetable. The previous government had run its asset sales programme with half an eye on the domestic borrowing requirement. Estimates of asset sales receipts had gone into their projected Table 2 deficit, which made for rushed sales and compromises on price. At one point Labour had even indulged in the scandalous practice of using the proceeds from asset sales for new social spending. We, by contrast, were interested in obtaining the best possible price for the Crown – not in massaging any particular year's fiscal numbers. Soon after I became Minister of Finance I announced that all proceeds from privatisation would be used to retire foreign debt. No forecast sales receipts were ever included in the National government's projected Table 2 deficits. This unhooked the privatisation programme from any direct connection with the government's domestic borrowing programme.

We also believed that, in assessing the privatisation programme, the best candidates for immediate sale were those in industries that did not involve difficult regulatory issues. The best sequence was first to work through the regulatory issues concerning an asset, and then to privatise only after the regulatory issues had been resolved. This would give maximum certainty to all the players in the industry.

Once a decision had been taken to sell, we ran a clear and structured sale process, so that bidding could take place in an atmosphere of certainty. We made sure that it was ministers who oversaw any sale process, not the board of the company, as sometimes happened overseas. In that way we avoided any potential conflict of interest on the part of the board. It was ministers, after all, who represented the shareholders, and who were in the best position to observe the shareholders' interests.

While ministers made the key decisions in the course of the sale, all sales were conducted on a highly commercial basis. The sale process was generally as open as possible. We placed very few restrictions on who could enter the bidding, and no restriction whatever on the extent of overseas ownership. It was important to provide as much information as possible on the asset. In settling on the final details of any deal, we saw our role as minimising overall fiscal risk to the Crown, not just gaining the highest price. This meant keeping to a minimum the number of warranties or indemnities provided to the purchaser, or at least structuring them in a way that gave the purchaser the incentive to manage the risks down.

Just before the budget, we announced the sale of a large portion of the Housing Corporation's prime-rate mortgages. Though Housing Minister John Luxton was the lead minister for the sale, I was also closely involved. The sale proved controversial two years down the track when Mortgage Corporation, one of the purchasers of the mortgages, became a market leader in setting interest charges, as well as enforcing the repayment penalty that had not been enforced by the Housing Corporation. By then out of Parliament, I was amused at the attempts by new Housing Minister Murray McCully to distance himself from the sale. At the time of the sale Murray was the minister leading the government's communications strategy and was kept well informed throughout the sale process.

By far the most satisfying privatisation, from my point of view, was the sale of the Bank of New Zealand. I had been convinced that the long-term performance of the bank and its contribution to the New Zealand economy would be best secured by its transfer to private ownership. The BNZ had proved a tar baby for the previous government, and could do so again. The political and financial downside of owning the bank exceeded any possible advantages.

As minister in charge of the BNZ, I was the lead minister for the sale. Following the rescue package in late 1990, the bank had rapidly returned to profitability. In 1991, after initially striking some resistance, I obtained Cabinet's agreement for the Treasury to begin exploring interest from potential buyers of the bank. Most privatisations involved a public announcement that the asset was for sale, and that the government was inviting bids. That was not the case with the BNZ. We judged that an open process was too risky in terms of confidence in the bank. We also believed it might weaken our bargaining power with any potential buyer. There was only a very limited number of institutions likely to be interested in the bank, which made a non-sale quite a strong possibility. If we had publicly announced the BNZ was for sale, a would-be purchaser might then have believed we would be reluctant to emerge from the process without making a sale. We did not want a potential purchaser to have that belief.

Instead, the Treasury sounded out a number of potential buyers for the BNZ. The number of foreign institutions even moderately interested in buying the bank was small; of these, National Australia Bank always looked the most likely aspirant. And so it proved. After a long period of negotiation we had an offer on the table from NAB to purchase all the shares in the BNZ at 80 cents. It was a fair offer: the government would receive $840 million for its shares. I took a paper to a ministerial subcommittee comprising Jim, Bill, Philip Burdon and myself at Premier House one Sunday afternoon. It was a long meeting. Jim was at first wholly against going through with the sale. 'Why are we selling?' he asked rhetorically. Bill and Philip, however, were both in favour. One by one, we talked Jim through the issues and by the end of the meeting he had been won over. The next day Cabinet ticked through the sale.

There were still hurdles to be negotiated. NAB undertook the 'due diligence' procedure on the BNZ, going through the bank's books in some detail, and pronounced themselves satisfied. Some 90 per cent of the bank's shareholders needed to agree to sell their shares if the deal were to go through. The government and Fay Richwhite, which had also announced it was selling, together made up about 85 per cent, which meant around one-third of the small shareholders needed to take the decision to sell. It looked probable, but not certain. Many had bought into the bank at 1.75 cents back in 1987 and would be getting out with a big loss. Many were understandably aggrieved, some loudly so. They were encouraged by Winston Peters, who had found a cause ideally suited to his populist rhetoric.

By now Peters' anti-BNZ campaign was in full swing. None of his numerous accusations, made under the cover of parliamentary privilege, gained any support from independent authorities. I had always disliked Peters, thinking him from my first acquaintance to be a person almost wholly interested in self-promotion. This dislike had now deepened into a total contempt for the man and his operating methods. Most of Peters' questions in the House on the BNZ were directed at me, as the minister responsible for the bank. Often these questions were on matters quite outside the purview of the government as shareholder in the bank. There were plenty of fiery exchanges. Though I generally reined in my natural pugilism, on occasion I let fly.

Peters' campaign – like the great majority of his campaigns – failed. In the end reality intruded. The government did not hold a 'full public inquiry' into the BNZ, and enough of the small shareholders decided that 80 cents was a reasonable price. The sale went through.

Where Peters did succeed was in seriously demoralising his own party. He had long been a negative influence, whose own popularity was bought

at a high price to team cohesion. From the time Peters began his BNZ campaign to the time his nomination for Tauranga was vetoed by head office, a period of nine months, his presence in our ranks was hugely destabilising. During these months Peters constituted one of the biggest political problems faced by the government. Not only did he substantially affect National's popularity, but caucus cohesion and morale was weakened almost to breaking point. Jim did not help himself by being too reactive and defensive in his dealings with Peters, but with the most assertive leadership in the world Peters would still have proven a handful. Only after he had been effectively ejected from the party would the government's political prospects improve.

In September I undertook a trip to the United States and Europe. The highlight was the Commonwealth Finance Ministers' meeting in New York, which I had been invited to chair. The high esteem in which the New Zealand reforms were held was undoubtedly one of the factors behind this invitation. The conference proved to be a fascinating occasion. It was a measure of the intellectual progress of market liberalism worldwide that the participants, almost to a man (and they were all men apart from me), took it for granted that a progressive agenda involved liberalising their economy. Many of those present had not made much progress down that road, but almost all saw it as the desired direction. Much of our discussion was political: how Finance Ministers could make progress in the face of the vested interests massed against them.

I had been keen from the outset to institute a new format for the conference. Instead of the usual, boring reading out of set speeches, I wanted much more cut and thrust, with genuine debate among the participants. Everyone liked this idea except the very junior British Treasury Minister, who insisted on being obstructive, and I had to deal with him firmly. It did not turn out to be a good week for the British. In the middle of the conference, despite reportedly spending one-third of Britain's foreign exchange reserves attempting to defend their currency, they failed to prevent the pound from hurtling out of the European Exchange Rate Mechanism. The news came through when the British minister was in full flight, extolling the virtues of Britain's economic policy. Reserve Bank Governor Don Brash, sitting with the New Zealand delegation, passed a note up to me in the chair. I watched the junior minister turn a whiter shade of pale as he was handed a similar note. Myth has it that he disappeared to the gents, not to be seen at the conference again.

The New Zealand dollar was unaffected by the turmoil on foreign exchange markets. Since New Zealand was seen as a haven where level heads were increasingly to be found, our own currency even strengthened. Not a single New Zealand dollar was spent by our authorities in defence of our currency (nor has it since the dollar was floated). That evening I digested a good deal of quiet satisfaction over our respective performances.

On exchange rate policy, I had always held to three principles that stood me in good stead.

- A country cannot get rich by getting poorer – that is what a depreciating currency really means.
- It is economic deeds that markets judge, not political words. You cannot talk your currency up.
- Policymakers end up with the currencies they deserve. If your policies are at odds with your ambitions for the currency then no amount of intervention will deflect the markets from their adverse verdict.

The events at the Commonwealth Finance Ministers' meeting further reinforced those principles for me.

14

LIFE ON THE POLITICAL HIGH-WIRE

So far I have described 1992 mainly in terms of budget issues and privatisation. But a great deal else was going on. Describing the events afterwards, one tries to group events together by topic, but that can give a misleading impression of what it feels like to be a minister. In reality, all sorts of different things are going on at the same time. The average politician's day is extremely messy and scrambled. There are always many different problems on the go – some large, some small, some soluble, some intractable, some growing, some receding, and some coming over the horizon. You are constantly having to fight short-term tactical battles while trying your best not to lose sight of your long-term strategic goals. And you are fighting on many fronts.

During 1992, one of the battle-fronts for me was the longer-term social policy reforms. The broad design of these reforms had been carried out in the lead-up to the 1991 budget. After the budget the government had moved into its 'implementation' phase. Health continued to be the most technically complex and politically difficult area, with the greatest potential for backsliding. Some slippage occurred early in 1992, when we took decisions on the form of Crown health enterprises (CHEs). In order to maximise the efficiency gains, I had wanted CHEs to be set up to resemble as closely as possible ordinary SOEs. I believed the government would be able to meet all its social objectives through the contracts entered into between the regional health authorities (RHAs) and the CHEs. CHEs themselves should concentrate solely on being efficient businesses. This model, however, was only partly achieved. While it was agreed CHEs would be taxed on their earnings and pay dividends to the government, their statutory objectives involved a weaker profit focus than the SOEs'. It was also decided that CHEs – unlike SOEs – could never be allowed to go bankrupt. A major incentive for CHEs to run profitably was thus removed.

Paul East had been appointed Minister for Crown Health Enterprises in Jim's October 1991 reshuffle. Under the new legislation the Minister of Finance was the second shareholding minister for all the CHEs. In the case of SOEs I had delegated the role of second shareholding minister to an associate. With CHEs I assumed the role myself, taking an active interest in the provider side of the health reforms.

Selecting the personnel for the new boards was one of the most important and difficult tasks. There were also tricky issues surrounding the treatment of existing area health board debt. We decided not to carry forward debt from area health boards to their successor CHEs as this would unfairly disadvantage the most indebted of the CHEs. The past was strictly history; we wanted all CHEs standing on a competitively neutral footing.

The further we went into the health reforms, the more horror stories we uncovered about the existing system. Setting up each CHE with its own balance sheet brought home the costs that had previously been hidden from the public. In 1993 we would be forced to make a substantial capital injection to boost CHEs' balance sheets.

Treaty of Waitangi issues came increasingly into prominence in 1992. One reason for needing to wrestle with Treaty issues was the transfer of Crown assets to new Crown-owned bodies in the course of a number of the government's reforms – the creation of CHEs in the health reforms, the creation of the rental SOE in the housing reforms, and the establishment of nine new Crown research institutes to replace the previous structures for public-sector science. There was considerable debate over the extent to which we should write Treaty provisions into the legislation governing these new structures – as had been the case with SOEs. In some of these instances I was influential in toning down Treaty references.

The wider debate among ministers on Treaty settlements hotted up considerably in 1992. One morning in Cabinet Doug Graham, the minister in charge of Treaty negotiations, brought up an oral item without having distributed any kind of paper whatsoever. It concerned a major Maori tribe. 'I propose we spend $1 billion in settling,' said Doug. 'Spread it out over 10 years so it is presented as $100 million per year. That'll sound fairly reasonable to the man in the pub.' I was not so sure that it would sound reasonable to the man in the pub. More to the point, I was far from impressed at the way Doug was operating in a vacuum, without any reference to a wider strategy. I made vigorous objection, both to the amount Doug was suggesting, and to the lack of any coherent process for settling Treaty claims. What were the principles we would use to settle claims? How could we proceed in a way that would satisfy both our Maori and European constituencies? How much could we afford in terms of our fiscal strategy? Those were the questions I was asking. Doug did not get his $1 billion; he was sent away to do more work.

Following this incident Doug returned to Cabinet with a proposal to establish a trust fund into which the government would pay a fixed amount of money to be used for settling Treaty claims. This was the origin of the fiscal envelope, which was the form taken by Doug's idea when it eventually saw the light of day. It was not true that I originated the idea of a fiscal envelope as some claimed in the wake of the fiasco on Waitangi Day 1995. However, it is true that the envelope proposal came about as a result of pressure on Doug to put forward a process that would limit fiscal risk to the Crown. The main person applying this pressure was myself, although I was not alone. When Doug proposed the concept of a fixed-quantum trust fund, I certainly supported it.

Doug's idea was refined by an officials' group chaired by the Prime Minister's Department, which helped prepare a strategy paper on the principles and procedures for determining Treaty settlements. Jim was closely involved in all deliberations. Ministers settled on some key principles for determining the amount of the fund:

- Affordability: The amount needed to be fiscally affordable.
- Acceptability: The amount needed to be acceptable to the wider community.
- Durability: The amount had to be sufficiently large to achieve full and final settlement of claims. An important quid pro quo for full and final settlement would be the eventual winding back of all special legal and institutional apparatus relating to the Treaty.
- Viability: The amount needed to be sufficiently realistic for claimants to think it worthwhile coming to the negotiating table.

A range of numbers was discussed for the size of the trust fund. Not surprisingly, I advocated a figure near the bottom of the range; Doug Graham a figure near the top. Eventually Cabinet settled on $1 billion. The idea of a stand-alone fund was dropped in favour of a simple 'fiscal envelope'. It was also decided that the whole subject was too sensitive for any announcement in election year.

As 1992 drew to a close, new problems confronted me. One of the most serious was the five-yearly redrawing of electoral boundaries by the Representation Commission. When the provisional boundaries came out, they contained a nasty surprise: my Selwyn electorate had become highly marginal. I had long decided that I was not interested in seeking another seat outside Selwyn. Andrew and I had made the electorate our home; our children were settled at the local school. If I lost Selwyn, that would be the end of my political career.

Submissions could be lodged to the commission before the boundaries were finalised. Andrew and I put a lot of work into a submission proposing alternative boundaries, but we reckoned without Jim Gerard, the National MP for neighbouring Rangiora. There had been bad blood between Jim Gerard and myself over boundaries ever since the last redrawing of the electoral map. On this occasion he lodged a counter-objection to my proposal. His move was completely unexpected. Under my proposal his own seat remained entirely safe – albeit with a reduced majority – and I had fully consulted him in advance. At a meeting where I presented my proposal to Jim, his electorate chairman and the divisional chairman, all in the room had appeared to give their assent. Jim's counter-objection floored me.

I was concerned enough to talk to Jim Bolger about it. Big Jim was outwardly sympathetic. He said he would ask Jim Gerard to withdraw his counter-objection. But Big Jim did not do so and the counter-objection remained.

Various reasons could be suggested for the Prime Minister's reaction, but it was a very disturbing signal for me to be receiving. In the end, the issue did not prove fatal for me. When the final boundaries came out, the redrawn Selwyn electorate was somewhere in between the provisional boundaries and the boundaries in my own submission. It was a marginal seat but it seemed probable I would hold it. What had not gone away, out of the whole boundaries affair, was the signal I had received from the Prime Minister.

Another source of tension was international tax. It turned out that Jim, along with many other ministers, had never understood the basic reasoning behind the international tax moves in the budget. He had never got his mind around why it made sense to impose a layer of tax on the international income of New Zealand residents when they had already paid foreign tax. In retrospect, the Cabinet Strategy Committee should probably have spent more time on all the tax moves in the budget, especially international tax. By not being careful enough to take my senior colleagues with me, I left myself exposed when the reaction to some of the budget measures came through.

I had certainly warned Jim that there would be major reaction to our international tax moves from business. And so it proved. Large corporates were not slow to protest, and were particularly vocal after the draft legislation had been published. They claimed double taxation was unfair. Wyatt had never supported the budget approach in the first place. Now Jim became gradually convinced that our international tax proposals were unfair and needed to be changed.

Jim invested a huge amount of his time delving into this extremely complex area. He called endless meetings at extremely short notice, which drove me to distraction. A prominent tax accountant was flown to Wellington to advise the Cabinet Strategy Committee on a subject he had done little thinking about. Some of the proceedings bordered on farce. To me it seemed a classic example of misapplied effort on the part of a Prime Minister. The government's general public positioning was now going badly, largely as a result of Peters' campaigns. Jim needed to be sitting back and doing some clear strategic thinking; instead he was micro-managing international tax. There was little politics in it. We still had the solid support of the business community, and as a public issue international tax was hardly ever further forward than the business pages.

Jim's solution to the double-tax 'problem' was to move to a regime that provided an underlying tax credit. He successfully sold that idea to Cabinet and late in the year he announced the U-turn himself in a speech in Christchurch.

There would be many more battles on international tax the following year as the details of the system were strapped down. In the end, our new international tax regime was probably no worse than the regimes of most other countries. But it failed to give the best signal to corporates about the choice between investing abroad and investing at home. It encouraged New Zealanders to over-invest abroad. And it raised less revenue than would have been raised by the proposals in the 1992 budget.

The final months of 1992 saw the government again significantly trailing Labour in popularity. Peters' campaigns on corruption in government, and on the BNZ, had proved hugely damaging to public perceptions. The health reforms were entering a delicate stage. There were some own goals scored by ministers. As usual, when Jim was unsettled about the state of his government, I felt him noticeably drifting away from me. Worries over international tax compounded his unease. I learned that there was a paper prepared in Jim's office on splitting the Treasury into two and I knew what that meant: two Ministers of Finance. I had more than once seen off attempts by various people to bring about that outcome when we were back in Opposition; it had been a standard tactic by those wanting to neutralise my influence. To this day I do not know how seriously Jim was taking the idea. Luckily, news of the paper found its way to the financial markets and then to the general media. Interest rates went up, various people became very alarmed, and Jim was soon forced to rule out splitting the Treasury.

For all the problems and tensions in the closing months of 1992, there was one policy initiative that gave me considerable satisfaction: the repeal of estate duties.

Deeply implanted in the New Zealand psyche is a strong notion of egalitarianism. Settlers throughout the ages brought a number of determinations to our shores. Maori matched a fiercely competitive tribalism with a caring communal spirit. European settlers sought to cast off the shackles of class and supplant it with a 'Jack's as good as his master' rubric. Whatever the individual motivation and drive, a strong ethic of equality came to characterise New Zealand's institutions and attitudes. What mattered most for some was equality of opportunity, while for others it was equality of outcome.

Unhappily, the latter often prevailed at the expense of the former. Our industrial relations regime, with its national awards killing both jobs and productivity, was typical of misapplied notions of equality. We levelled wages, but in the process smashed individual incentives. This was the suffocating side of equality. Within months of taking office we had taken steps to rid ourselves of this jobs and productivity handicap with the introduction of the Employment Contracts Bill. But there were other economic levellers still to be dealt with – especially our estate duty and land aggregation laws. These two pieces of economic envy owed their existence to the misguided notion that people should not be permitted to accumulate too much wealth. In practice, well-organised people could arrange their affairs to avoid the impact of both sets of legislation. The law is an ass if it can be so easily avoided.

Naturally, debate raged over the merits or otherwise of these regimes. The earlier debates generated more heat than light and little progress was made.

My father had made a name for himself at successive National Party conferences during the Muldoon era, advancing passionate and persistent arguments against estate duties. In essence he charged that estate duties were both unfair and unmanageable unless family members died in the 'right' order. A tragedy that had occurred on land he farmed on the Waitotara coast served to highlight the injustice of the regime. A neighbouring farmer and daredevil pilot always helped with the annual stock muster down at the beach. Stock roamed over both properties and mustering was a combined effort. On this fateful day John Hawken, then in his late thirties, buzzed a clump of lupin bushes at too low an altitude and lost his life as the plane spun out of control. John left a wife and four young children, all of whom attended the local Waitotara Primary School at the same time as my brothers and I. In truth that family paid twice for the tragedy – the emotional shock of John's death and the financial shock of a 40 per cent tax on John's estate. He was too young to have thought about arrangements to escape estate duties. With the injustice visited upon that and many other families uppermost in my father's mind, he concluded his conference speech in favour of a remit to repeal estate duties by turning to Muldoon and saying, 'If I live to 65 you won't get a penny out of me.' The conference was easily persuaded, but not so the politicians. Muldoon, ever a socialist, refused to budge.

I encountered no such resistance during my time with Federated Farmers to the idea that estate duties should go. But it was a different story when it came to the repeal of the land aggregation laws. For every Federated Farmers conference delegate who was prepared to make a case against the control of land aggregation there was one who would stand up and deliver a vehement counter-argument. I knew no government would dare move to repeal land aggregation laws if there was such division in the ranks of Federated Farmers itself.

Consequently, both issues were consigned to the political 'too hard' basket.

I was determined to use my political influence to repeal both regimes. The growth and development of New Zealand, by my reasoning, depended upon both the accumulation of capital and the most inspired investment of that wealth. Estate duties and land aggregation controls, besides being a barrier to wealth accumulation, created substantial investment distortions as people arranged their affairs to avoid the impact of the respective regimes. I believed that New Zealand suffered from a shortage of capital, that we could ill-afford second-best investments, and that our reliance on foreigners' savings to fund our growth and development was all the heavier for the fact that domestic policies penalised domestic savings.

The fate of death duties was squarely within my finance portfolio, whereas land aggregation responsibilities lay in the hands of others.

Round one of my repeal campaign had involved getting the caucus and the party to sign up to a manifesto commitment to repeal, among other things, estate duties. While privately very pleased to have secured a formal manifesto commitment, I deliberately never made much of it publicly. I was only too aware of egalitarian sensitivities.

In office, making good the promise was essentially a matter of timing.

Implementation in the first year, dominated by the need to make major fiscal savings, was clearly out. Action in the third year would, in my judgment, have unnecessarily inflamed election tempers, so I set my sights on the second year.

The obvious vehicle for the announcement of the repeal of estate duties was the budget. That did not, however, square with my sotto voce strategy. Just before Christmas 1992 proved to be the ideal time. With little fanfare and little comprehension from the talkback hosts and chattering classes, the repeal was announced, to the huge approval of those who have the capacity to move capital and generate growth in the economy.

Rescue on the land aggregation front came from a different and unexpected quarter in 1995 – a private member's bill promoted by David Caygill. Sensibly, Caygill appreciates that the only interests advanced by the existence of land aggregation laws are those of the lawyers who charge plenty to arrange the tortuous legal escape route from the legislation. If Caygill's bill goes through, it will be quite an irony that a law owing so much to socialist cant should be overturned by a parliamentarian ostensibly hailing from the centre-left.

As 1992 ended, I could be forgiven for having intimations of political mortality. I had long known that Jim would not keep me on as Minister of Finance out of sentiment. Jim is nothing if not a political survivor: he would retain me after the 1993 election only if he judged it to be in his interests. I knew that I had no guarantee of that. His inaction over my electorate boundaries had been particularly discouraging. I also knew that our second term, if we got one, would probably take place under the shadow of a change in the electoral system. The mixed-member proportional (MMP) system was favoured to win over the existing first-past-the-post system in the referendum at the 1993 election. The subsequent election would then be held under MMP. In an MMP environment it would be extremely hard to articulate successfully and drive through an agenda for reform. To me, MMP was a system of lowest-common-denominator politics – a recipe for political paralysis, totally at odds with how I saw myself operating. The lead-up to MMP would be fraught with political nervousness. I had no confidence that in my second term as minister, if I had one, I would be able to push economic reform into new areas. And even at the best of times, I had always seen myself as getting out of politics after serving five terms. That would mean just one more term as minister.

In politics, people come and go; institutions and legacies remain. I certainly did not regard my political mortality as inevitable – far from it.

Reports of my death had been exaggerated many times in the past. But by late 1992 I was increasingly thinking long term. I had always thought of my political career in terms of how many runs I scored, not in terms of how long I occupied the crease. I wanted to cement in the huge gains that had been made in economic policy. In my last year as minister, securing that legacy was to dominate much of my thinking, and become my most important concern.

15

LOCKING IN THE GAINS

My first task was to do all I could to cement monetary policy in place. Donald Brash's five-year term as Reserve Bank Governor was due to end in the second half of 1993. Don was highly respected abroad and already had a record most other central bankers could only envy. His name was virtually synonymous with the Reserve Bank Act. He had even been touted in the British press as a future Governor of the Bank of England. That the British would seriously discuss taking someone from their furthest colony to head the Old Lady of Threadneedle Street would have been quite inconceivable just 10 years earlier. Don had expressed to me his willingness to be reappointed Reserve Bank Governor and it was unthinkable that he not be. Don's reappointment would also be an appropriate time to negotiate a new policy targets agreement (PTA) between the government and the Reserve Bank.

I did not want either the reappointment or the renegotiation to take place in the run-up to the election. There was always the risk that political nerves could interfere with the smooth process of reappointment. This might happen if the timing was unlucky – if, for instance the Reserve Bank were forced to tighten monetary policy just prior to the renegotiation. I was also aware – as was Don – that there would be increasing market speculation about his reappointment as 1993 wore on. To give the best possible signal to the financial markets about the government's commitment to low inflation, I wanted both the reappointment and the PTA renegotiation to take place before Christmas 1992.

Technically, the Minister of Finance appoints the Governor on the recommendation of the board of the Reserve Bank. This recommendation was given unanimously. The renegotiation of the PTA was also a relatively straightforward matter. I started with a strong presumption in favour of the status quo. The government had built up considerable credibility with the existing PTA. The markets would scrutinise the new PTA for any signs the government was weakening in its anti-inflation commitment. In the event, both sides were happy to keep substantive changes to a minimum. The previous PTA had committed the bank to 'achieve and maintain' 0-2 per cent. Since by now we had achieved 0-2 per cent inflation, the new wording committed the bank simply to 'maintain' inflation in that range.

The existing approach to the treatment of 'shocks' that pushed inflation outside the target range was largely maintained: the Reserve Bank would publicly estimate the impact of a shock on the CPI and account for the way it would bring inflation back within the 0-2 per cent range.

In writing the PTA, there is a trade-off between designing a rule for the Reserve Bank that allows it to react sensibly to short-term shocks, and designing a rule that most strongly signals the government's commitment to price stability. So far New Zealand governments have opted for a simple, strong rule that minimises the Reserve Bank's discretion to go soft on inflation. Yet it would be wrong to assume that the current rule is perfect. One can construct scenarios in which such a rule is potentially unhelpful.

It might, for instance, be known that the real (i.e. inflation-adjusted) exchange rate is overvalued, and should depreciate. A depreciation in the real exchange rate could take place by New Zealand running a slower rate of inflation than its trading partners. This process, however, might prove too slow. In that case, to effect a sufficiently fast depreciation in the real exchange rate the nominal exchange rate would have to depreciate. However, the nominal exchange rate has a large impact on the rate of inflation, and in the short term has far more impact than interest rates. The Reserve Bank, following its existing 0-2 per cent rule, would most likely move to slow any market-led downward movement in the exchange rate. There are a large number of 'ifs' to this scenario – including the assumption that we can know when the real exchange rate is overvalued. But the bank's mandate could conflict with the desired adjustment of the exchange rate.

In the overall scheme of things, it does not greatly matter if the Reserve Bank fails to hit its target in any one year. What matters is the Reserve Bank's record over a long period. It could be argued, then, that a less rigid rule would enable the bank to treat short-term pressures in a more flexible manner. However, a less rigid rule runs into the danger of weakening the accountability of the Reserve Bank; with weakened accountability would go weakened credibility.

Between my first PTA and my second, the Treasury expended a good deal of effort in trying to formulate a rule that was less rigid, yet retained sufficient accountability and credibility. In the end they were not confident they had come up with anything better than the existing model. With the turbulence of the transition to MMP on the horizon, I was in no mood to experiment. I placed strong emphasis on having the Reserve Bank regarded as a sound, predictable, reliable institution in the years ahead, and that meant strong emphasis on credibility. The Reserve Bank itself was of a similar mind.

When I took the Governor's reappointment and the new PTA to Cabinet, I struck little serious opposition. The news was announced just before Christmas.

The next year, 1993, started very auspiciously for the economy. Just as in the previous summer break, there was a rash of good economic news. The recovery was now around 18 months old and was looking increasingly buoyant. Even unemployment appeared to have peaked and to be gradually moving down. But the government's fortunes were not matching the fortunes of the economy. Jim was going through one of his bad patches in which he made a number of maladroit moves and comments. The long-running conflict between Peters and the party continued to dominate the headlines. And the health debate was going badly for the government. National fell back further in the polls, a position that looked ominous for our re-election chances. For the first time during the Bolger government, there were growing rumblings in the National caucus about the leadership. They were not terribly serious, but caucus was definitely in unsettled mood. At one point Jim asked Cabinet whether they thought he should go on his next planned overseas trip.

With rattled ministers and a nervous caucus, the early months of the year were notable for the low quality of the government's decision-making. For much of this period we were acting as if we did not deserve to be re-elected. I still, however, had the occasional victory. I managed to block Philip Burdon's idea to 'harmonise' the New Zealand and Australian car industries. Philip's proposal had been floating around for some time. It involved the banning of used-car imports into New Zealand, along with measures to allow the car industries of the two countries to compete on a more equal footing. The proposal was strongly protectionist and bad news for New Zealand consumers. Fortunately, with Jenny Shipley and John Falloon lending me very strong support, I had the numbers to defeat it.

It was in the context of a fractious and unsettled caucus that the entertainment tax debacle took place. This initiative had not initially looked under threat. Murray McCully had reportedly vowed to have the tax scrapped. That, however, was not unexpected: Murray had consistently taken a soft line on tax avoidance. There had been little adverse public comment in the wake of the budget, and after that the legislation was put together. At this point the range of the proposed tax was significantly increased. In extending fringe benefit tax (FBT) to cover business entertainment, a number of boundary issues had arisen concerning the existing FBT regime. We decided to extend FBT to eliminate a number of anomalies, such as the exemption from FBT of in-house dining and recreational facilities. We also decided to alter the existing de minimus exemption from FBT from a per employee basis to a per employer basis. This move was designed to raise substantially more revenue while better addressing the compliance-cost concerns of small business.

Officials had suggested that they consult the private sector prior to the introduction of the legislation. However, at a meeting of the Cabinet Strategy Committee, Jim said, 'Don't consult. Just do it.' I had a similar view to Jim regarding consultation, and I do not recall Wyatt making any objection either. Jim was fully behind the entertainment tax at all stages, seeing it as a fairness measure more than anything else. The legislation was duly introduced into the House before Christmas.

In the new year, with the legislation before FEC, business was protesting noisily. This did not greatly surprise me: by now we were planning to take $95 million from the business sector by means of the initiative. Such an event can hardly expect to happen without protest. I was confident the objections would die down once the measure was through, just as they had died down once we had stood firm on the abolition of inter-corporate dividend exemption. Wyatt, who had initially supported the entertainment tax, had now turned on the issue. Past history suggested this was not surprising, either. More disappointing was that government members of FEC wanted a whole raft of amendments to the legislation. The quid pro quo for having only a 50 per cent tax rate on entertainment had been a broad tax base. FEC 'banked' the low rate, then immediately started working to chip away at the base. Yet even this was not especially surprising. Despite my attempts to bind government members of FEC into the fiscal strategy, their track record was one of caving in to pressure from special interests.

Two extra factors I had not bargained on probably served to push entertainment tax over the edge. One was the new mood in caucus, which was looking to punish the perceived sins of the executive. The other was Jim's departure overseas just when the issue was coming to a head. Jim had left deputy Don McKinnon with strict instructions to give as few concessions as possible on entertainment tax. Don, for all his charm and many virtues, is not a man for holding the line under pressure. He caved in on virtually every demand made by FEC members, short of scrapping the tax altogether. Designed as a broad-based, low-compliance-cost measure, the tax ended up riddled with anomalies, saddled with much higher compliance costs, failing to raise significant revenue, and lacking any raison d'être. My only victory – and an important one at the time – was that the government still had an entertainment tax.

It would have been a close contest to pick the most absurd of the amendments to the legislation. Perhaps the prize should go to the decision to exempt conferences held offshore. The rationale of the entertainment tax had, of course, been to bring into the revenue net non-taxed remuneration of New Zealanders; it did not matter where that remuneration was earned. I pointed out that the effect of the exemption would be to encourage conferences to be held offshore. And so it proved: no sooner was the ink dry on the final changes to the bill than the domestic conference industry was complaining – legitimately enough – that it had been unfairly discriminated against.

The best epitaph on the entertainment tax came later from someone who should probably remain nameless. I was discussing my second-term agenda when one person wondered aloud whether the entertainment tax might be better off abolished, given the state to which it had now been reduced. 'No,' said this gentleman firmly, 'it should stand as a monument to what happens when a select committee designs a tax.'

All in all, the fate of the entertainment tax was not one of my more memorable moments. My firm public defence of the tax had made me the minister by far most greatly hurt by the debacle. I had chosen to advocate strongly in public the agreed Cabinet position with the intention of holding the line, rather than covering my back by preparing to compromise (as Wyatt had done). I was aware of the risk I was running; it is an occupational hazard of any politician who is interested in setting a direction rather than just swimming with the tide. Not that the entertainment tax was unpopular with the wider public; almost uniquely among the government's reforms it was supported by a majority of New Zealanders. One of the ironies of the whole episode was that a *National Business Review* poll showing greater than 50 per cent support was not published until after the tax had already been reduced to a Swiss cheese. It may have given some of my more poll-driven colleagues pause for thought.

Perhaps I misassessed the forces ranged against me, but personally I think bad luck played a large part. Our biggest mistake was allowing the initiative to be called an entertainment tax. The name made business think we were attempting to play politics. They saw it as a populist smash-and-grab raid for revenue on the part of the government. If the measures had simply been called an extension of FBT – which they were – we might have received an easier ride. Despite the Prime Minister's equal enthusiasm for the initiative, I would have been naive in the extreme to imagine Jim would be rushing to share the odium. Quite the contrary: he had plenty of problems of his own.

NEALE McMILLAN

Obligatory pose as the 1991 budget rolls off the printing press.

My ministerial office 'family': Joyce Sapsford, Anna Symmans with son Harry, David Hunt, Katy Greco, Martin Hames and Pat Humphries (front).

DOMINION

ABOVE: Delivering the 'mother of all budgets'

OPPOSITE: The wags' verdict on my dumping from finance. (For those who haven't met me, I am surprisingly short!)

No. 432-98 July 14th, 1994

JOB VACANCY

Applications are invited for the position of New Zealand's fiscal guardian, due to an unexpected departure.

The job entails never-ending vigilance against politicians and interest groups who wish to spend money they don't have and incur further debt.

Applicants should be prepared to take abuse from almost anybody for their part in saving New Zealand's economy, and when successful, gracefully take being sacked from the job.

This is an equal opportunity position with no discrimination on grounds of gender, age, ethnic origin, sexual orientation and height.

Please forward all applications to:

The Prime Minister
Parliament Buildings

Previous applicants need not apply again.

THE NELSON MAIL

Running with 'the boys'. Caucus retreat at Nelson post-dumping.

DOMINION

Elect this woman! Campaigning in the Wellington Central by-election.

By now the grumbles about the leadership had reached their height. There was even an open discussion in caucus, though not a terribly fraught one. Jim came back into the country on Sunday, tired out, and made the mistake of calling a press conference. He looked terrible. He said that some ministers needed to improve their act. That got the press excited. It also got Jim's ministers excited and they rounded on him at Cabinet the next day. 'Which of us has to improve our act?' asked Jenny. Jim backed away very quickly. At the subsequent press conference he avoided criticising his ministers, which in turn made him look weak.

But a Cabinet reshuffle was coming up later that week. There was the usual speculation in the press. One story had me losing my responsibility for tax policy as a result of the entertainment tax debacle. The story might have been planted by Jim's staff; it might equally have been an educated guess by journalists. The action was to take place on the day Labour released its economic policy. The evening before, Jim called me up to see him. Bill was sitting in on the interview. I was well aware of their rattled state of mind. Jim told me he was putting Wyatt in charge of revenue policy. I told Jim that he had not thought the matter through. As budget minister, I needed to have responsibility for both sides of the fiscal ledger. I told him I could not be an effective Finance Minister for the government and for the country on that basis. 'Don't ask me to fly on one wing,' I said. 'If you are determined to proceed, then you can have my warrant.'

It was the first time I had played the resignation card with Jim, and it was no bluff. It was already difficult enough having to share the revenue responsibility with Wyatt; I was not prepared to be Minister of Finance and lose all control of revenue. The interview ended inconclusively. As was so often the case, I was unsure what Jim was now thinking, though I left him in no doubt as to what I was thinking.

I then had to go out to Avalon to do a live television interview with Labour's finance spokesman, Michael Cullen, on Labour's economic policy. After the interview Cullen, pleased with his day, poured me a glass of champagne. He little knew how uncertain I was of my own future beyond that very evening. Back in my office, very late, I had a visit from Simon Upton, who told me that Jim had decided not to give Wyatt sole control of revenue.

Simon's own shift out of the health portfolio ended up being Jim's biggest change. It was a change Simon had requested. Bill took on health and Simon became an Associate Minister of Finance. Maurice McTigue lost both his SOEs portfolio and associate finance. Maurice was unlucky: he had fallen out of favour with Jim, and his extreme loyalty to me had probably been to his detriment. The SOEs portfolio went to Wyatt – something he was far from keen to receive.

Jim must already have told Wyatt he would receive sole control of tax policy before his interview with me that night because Wyatt had arranged drinks in his room the next day with the government members of FEC. The drinks were cancelled.

Soon after this incident I left for what would turn out to be my final overseas trip as minister. The atmosphere within caucus was still highly unsettled. A challenge to Jim's leadership could not be ruled out. I was taking a risk in leaving the country. Some of my staff had understandably urged that I stay at home, or at least scale my trip down, but I hated the idea of walking away from the trip. In the event, little was to happen while I was away.

In planning the trip I had struck a hitch that illustrated Jim's state of insecurity. I had put in a standard request to Jim for permission to travel. I had received a reply through his office approving in principle all of the travel except the visit to Tokyo, probably my most important destination. Jim had declined permission for Tokyo on the grounds that my visit was taking place not long before a trip he himself was planning to Japan, and that he would 'focus strongly on the economic achievements of the government' and 'target the same audiences' as me.

It was a most odd missive. It was years since I had been seriously spoken of as one who might knock Jim off his perch. My period as Minister of Finance had seen to that. Even if our audiences were the same, I did not see why Jim should be the only show in town and our audiences were not, in fact, the same. Mine was largely foreign investors. When I wrote back to Jim, outlining the nature of the investor presentations I would be giving, I eventually received permission. But my office was told I was to give no speeches! Fortunately, none was planned for Tokyo.

In the early months of the year there was little sign of the improvement in the fiscal position that one might expect from a strongly recovering economy. By May, however, the news was far more positive. The Treasury had revised its forecast deficit for 1992-93 to $2.6 billion, compared with $3.3 billion on budget night. This was $2 billion lower than the post-election (PEB) projection for 1992-93 of $4.5 billion. Expenditure was down by almost $1 billion compared with budget night. Tight expenditure control meant there had been no need to use the provision for supplementary estimates in the budget. Spending on welfare benefits was down, owing to lower than expected benefit numbers. And debt servicing was well down on forecast. Contributing factors included lower interest rates, a stronger exchange rate, successful privatisations, and the lower expenditure in 1992-93.

For years the economy had been struggling to emerge from its vicious cycle of increasing dependency leading to higher spending, higher debt, higher interest rates, low growth and further dependency. Now, at last, there seemed to be tangible signs the fiscal tide was turning. Many of the key influences on government spending were working positively to reinforce one another.

It had been another smooth expenditure round in the lead-up to the 1993 budget. There was some new spending planned, but not so much as to make the government appear to be trying to buy its way back into office. For an election-year budget it was extremely restrained. There were a few titbits for industry, a moderate amount of new money for training programmes, and extra family support for teenagers. There was additional funding for community initiatives aimed at combating some of New Zealand's social problems. In a political sense, the new initiatives were fairly well judged. They were intended by Cabinet to project the image of a government that was compassionate but still fiscally responsible. In the lead-up to the budget I talked of its being a document that included New Zealanders in the recovery, and that looked after some of the casualties of the economic reforms.

The fiscal outlook to be published in the budget was growing brighter. The forecast deficit for 1993-94 was $2.3 billion – still high, but a great deal lower than the $5.4 billion forecast in the PEB for 1993-94. The deficit was now forecast to fall to $1.1 billion in 1995-96. In that same year, net public debt as a percentage of GDP was forecast to begin falling.

The Treasury had also produced for my information longer-term fiscal projections out to the year 2000. These projections were not forecasts as such; they were scenarios, based on a variety of growth assumptions. They assumed the government would continue to control government spending and maintain the tax base. The scenarios were extremely instructive. They suggested that, under plausible assumptions about growth and government spending, budget surpluses were not too far away. They also suggested we could begin making major inroads into government debt before long. Renamed 'progress outlooks', these scenarios were to become a feature of my third budget.

As the budget neared I was hard at work on my most important task of the year: my attempt to entrench over time the improving fiscal outcomes. Before Christmas I had done all I could to put monetary policy beyond reach of an unfavourable shift in the political winds. Now I was engaged in my second and much more difficult task: putting institutional constraints on the conduct of fiscal policy. I wanted to cement in the positive trends in government spending achieved under National. And I wanted to help ensure governments continued to place major priority on lowering the deficit and reducing debt. As far as possible, I wanted to do for fiscal policy what the Reserve Bank Act had done for monetary policy.

There was ample reason to believe that fiscal policy, both here and abroad, often suffered from political and institutional environments inimical to good outcomes. Future generations are not represented in the political system, or at best are represented only weakly. This leads to an inbuilt bias towards government deficits being financed by issuing debt. The benefits of government spending tend to be heavily concentrated among easily identified and easily mobilisable groups, while the costs of any given expenditure – higher taxation or higher interest rates – are spread widely but very thinly. This asymmetry gives the recipients of government expenditures a major inbuilt advantage in the political lobbying process over taxpayers, leading to excessive government spending. Often voters are ill-informed about the economic consequences of government action. As with monetary policy, the nature of the election cycle creates a bias in favour of short-term spending, with the full costs becoming apparent after the election is safely past.

All of these weaknesses – and many others – had been well in evidence in New Zealand in recent years. We had a history of entrenched and endemic deficits. We had seen a huge build-up in debt. We had seen excessive government spending, as interest groups increasingly captured the political process. And we had seen flagrant election bribes. In 1975 I had been so dismayed at Muldoon's national superannuation policy that I refrained from voting National for the only time in my life. Muldoon subsequently governed in a way that suggested he was only too aware of the strength of his aphorism that the average New Zealand voter would not know a deficit if they fell over one. In 1990 fiscal irresponsibility hit a new low, all the more dismaying for being perpetrated by a government once noted for its ability to take hard decisions. Labour in 1990 spent as if there were no tomorrow, failed to be honest with the public over the deterioration in the fiscal position, failed even to keep a running tally of new spending commitments, and even risked starting a run on the BNZ in its determination to hide from the voters the need for a rescue package.

While we had made major progress in fiscal policy since 1990, I had no guarantee a future government would not revert to the spending habits of the past. I was only too conscious of the fact that fiscal responsibility is hard won but easily lost. With MMP coming up, I had every reason to fear that the siren calls of fiscal irresponsibility would grow stronger. But in searching for an institutional framework to cement in responsible fiscal behaviour, my task was a hard one. Fiscal policy is a far more diffuse and intractable beast than monetary policy. Unlike monetary policy, fiscal policy has a multitude of legitimate objectives. It involves some very technical measurement problems. Taxation, spending and the fiscal balance also vary considerably during the course of the business cycle. For all of these reasons we cannot specify a single objective and then monitor a chosen statistic that tells us unambiguously whether we are succeeding or failing in meeting that objective.

Still less can we make one measure the basis for a hard and fast rule. The most widely advocated fiscal rule is probably the proposal for a mandatory balanced budget. Yet such a rule is as problematical in theory as it has proved infeasible in practice. First, we know that the budget will vary naturally over the course of the business cycle: it can be in deficit when the economy is in recession, and should be in surplus when the economy is growing strongly. Attempting to run a strictly balanced budget during recession can be counterproductive. If we are trying to balance anything, it is the 'cyclically adjusted' deficit; yet defining and measuring a cyclically-adjusted deficit is a complex and far from clear process. Another technical difficulty is that when budgets are brought down they are forecasts of the fiscal position, but it is the actual out-turn that ultimately interests us.

A strict budget-balance rule is also an open invitation for politicians to find ways around the rule. They can shift expenditure off-budget or devolve the responsibility for these expenditures to a lower tier of government. They can try to substitute regulation for government spending, often in a way that leads to less efficient overall outcomes. They can also write rosy growth scenarios and over-optimistic expenditure numbers into their fiscal forecasts. All of these dodges, and others, were employed by the United States Congress in the 1980s to make nonsense of the Gramm-Rudman targets, which had been intended to bring the US budget into balance. The experience of Gramm-Rudman suggests that, without the political will, a seemingly strict budget-balance target is no match for politicians determined to evade it.

New Zealand has one advantage over the US when it comes to fiscal accountability. There, power is widely dispersed among different branches of government, whereas here it resides clearly in the government formed from the House of Representatives. When fiscal policy goes wrong, the governing party cannot shift the blame to some other body. We also have a high quality of fiscal reporting in this country. And if fixed rules do not seem feasible, there are other ways of improving accountability. One of these is openness.

In a report published in 1991, the Ombudsman had traversed a number of the issues surrounding the Labour government's failure to disclose information before the 1990 election. One of the Ombudsman's suggestions was that an economic update be published just prior to each general election. At first I was sceptical about the proposal, thinking it might politicise the Treasury to an untenable extent. But as time went on, and as I continued to turn the idea over in my mind, it seemed to me that a pre-election update could be genuinely feasible. If it were feasible, it could become a powerful weapon against election-year fiscal extravagance.

A pre-election update would ensure all political parties had the latest economic and fiscal information, and they would need to justify their manifesto commitments in the light of that information. Not only would there be less incentive for a government to embark on a spending spree in election year, there would be less incentive for Opposition parties to make extravagant promises. No longer would there be an 'opening the books' after the election, where a victorious Opposition expressed shock and horror and then ditched the election promises that had proved vote-winners on the campaign trail. The books would already have been opened.

At the beginning of 1993 I had several sessions with the Treasury in which I set out my objective for entrenching good fiscal behaviour through a stronger fiscal constitution. I put to them the idea of a pre-election economic and fiscal update. Most of the Treasury people were less than enthusiastic, for the same reason I originally had been: they saw it putting them in the political firing line. But they undertook to consider the issue further.

We also discussed the more general question of fiscal reporting. Already major advances had been made since I had entered Parliament. As a result of the Public Finance Act the Treasury had produced, for the 1991-92 fiscal year, the first operating accounts for the government on an accrual basis. They had also produced the first estimate of the Crown's overall balance sheet, as at 30 June 1992. These had so far been backward-looking exercises, produced after the event. Labour's David Caygill had begun the practice of publishing three-year forward projections with the budget, rather than just the single year previously available. I had carried on this practice, and initiated the publication each December of similar three-year projections as a regular update to those in the budget. I had also introduced a further update of the expected fiscal position for the current fiscal year, released in the April-June period. These were important developments in fiscal openness. All forward projections were still, of course, undertaken on the old cash accounting basis.

No other country in the world provided such comprehensive and high-quality fiscal information as New Zealand. However, there was no legislative requirement for the government to bring down any of the forward projections. Nor was there a requirement for the government to be transparent about its fiscal strategy and intentions in the budget documentation. That was something I had followed because I believe in fiscal openness. A future minister could undo it, without the embarrassment of amending an Act of Parliament. There seemed a good case for entrenching in legislation the good reporting practices that had been built up. It was also timely to assess what new practices could be initiated.

These were the themes I developed with the Treasury at the beginning of the year. They undertook to do the work and come back to me. By budget time our thinking was significantly advanced. The Treasury were warming to the idea of a pre-election update, which is just as well since I was determined to press ahead with it. I also wanted to entrench in legislation all the good reporting practices, including the publication of progress outlooks. From 1994 the Treasury would be in a position to bring down forward projections on an accrual basis. All budget financial reporting would be meeting generally accepted accounting practice. I believed the government should also be required to be as transparent as possible in its intentions for fiscal policy: at budget time it should be required to state its longer-term fiscal objectives and report on its progress – or lack of progress – in achieving those objectives. I believed all of these requirements should be entrenched in legislation.

Shortly before the budget I took a paper to Cabinet seeking agreement for legislation to be drafted incorporating these initiatives. I was not expecting much resistance to most of my proposals but I did expect considerable discussion over the pre-election update. After all, we did not know in advance whether the pre-election update would be good or bad for the government's fortunes at the 1993 election. The fiscal numbers could move in either direction between the budget and the update. Jim normally dislikes binding himself in advance if he can avoid it; that was one reason he had opposed the Reserve Bank Act. But on this occasion my paper went through with little objection, from Jim or anyone else. Presumably Jim thought it was good politics. I was delighted at the success of my proposals and made the fiscal innovations a feature of my budget-night speech.

The budget had a strong fiscal flavour. The progress outlooks were especially instructive:

> The progress outlooks show that current fiscal policy settings are sustainable. They show very clearly that within three years we can start to reduce our net debt, and that by the end of our second term we can move into budget surplus without sharp cuts in expenditure or increases in tax rates. In short, they show that the government's fiscal policy is succeeding.
>
> The government has firmly ruled out increases in tax rates as a means of balancing the budget.

In the election campaign, the government would strongly attack Labour as the party that would put up taxes. This passage positioned the government on the high ground in that debate: tax increases were not necessary and would compromise the recovery.

When I came to announce the pre-election update, my speech bordered on the party political. But if ever a politician could be excused a degree of righteous indignation, this was such an occasion:

> I am also announcing a major new initiative for honest and open government. This initiative will ensure that no government can fool the people of New Zealand as to the true state of the nation's accounts the way the last government did.
>
> It is of crucial importance that the public is well informed about the economic outlook of the country and the financial position of the government during the lead-up to a general election.
>
> In 1991 the Chief Ombudsman expressed strong concerns that the previous government withheld information prior to the 1990 election. The Chief Ombudsman suggested that Parliament consider a means by which a survey of the state of the economy could be published for all to see and understand before a general election.
>
> The government believes the case made by the Ombudsman is sound. The government has therefore decided that prior to each general election there will be a public release of an economic and fiscal outlook. The first of these releases will take place prior to the general election this year.
>
> The requirement to continue this practice in the future will also be built into legislation. This initiative will enable this year's election to be conducted with all the relevant information available for public scrutiny. It reflects our continued commitment to openness in government.
>
> This government is not afraid to be judged on the true facts of its economic stewardship.

After the budget, drafting got under way on the bill to entrench fiscal responsibility. The bill codified the practice of laying before Parliament three-year economic and fiscal updates, one at budget time and one in December. The bill specified the information to be forecast in these updates. The pre-election update would contain the same material as an economic and fiscal update. It would be presented four to six weeks before election day or, in the case of a snap election, within 14 days of the dissolution of Parliament. For a normal general election held towards the end of the year, the pre-election update would essentially constitute the bringing forward of the December update for that year.

In a clause that would be considerably strengthened the following year, the bill also required the government to specify its long-term fiscal objectives clearly. At budget time the government was required to report on its objectives for expenses, revenue, the gap between expenses and revenue, and debt; on how it intended to achieve those objectives; and on its progress so far. Progress outlooks giving forward projections for the next 10 years would need to be included in this report.

Requiring the government to specify its objectives had many advantages. It would encourage governments to think long term. It would give the financial markets, media, parliamentary Opposition and the wider public a benchmark by which to assess the consistency of the government's actions. And it heightened the likelihood that irresponsible or inconsistent fiscal policy would be detected and punished.

Some of the most difficult issues to think through concerned the exact nature of the fiscal disclosures in the economic and fiscal updates. My guiding principle was one of fullest possible disclosure. All policy decisions and other material factors that could be reasonably quantified would need to be disclosed. A government could no longer bring down a budget, as Labour had done in 1990, where some initiatives were simply not in the fiscal numbers. But the level of disclosure in the bill went further than this. Each update would include a statement of fiscal risks, whether or not those risks could be quantified. Those risks that were quantifiable were to have a number or range beside them. Unquantifiable risks were to be simply listed. Risks had never been dealt with in such a systematic manner in the past.

There were safeguards. Information could be withheld if disclosure would prejudice New Zealand's substantial economic interests, security or international relations, or compromise the Crown in its commercial activity, or in negotiation or litigation, or if disclosure would result in material loss of value to the Crown. For instance, a risk might be left unquantified if to do so would compromise the Crown's negotiating position with a foreign country. However, simply triggering one of these conditions would not be enough to allow a government to temporarily sweep under the carpet a politically inconvenient fact. A further test needed to be passed. The government could withhold the information only if it could not 'reasonably or prudently' make a decision prior to the update that would mitigate the loss or prejudice that might occur.

The BNZ is the example nearest to my heart. Had the fiscal responsibility legislation applied in 1990, and had Labour had enough time to come up with a rescue package before the pre-election update, Labour could not have avoided disclosing the BNZ's plight. If the Ombudsman's report on the affair is accurate, Labour did have enough time. Under the bill, they could not have hidden the matter from the voters.

Considerable time was spent on the clause of the bill dealing with the statement of responsibility each update would carry. This was not a clause that attracted much attention. However, for me the statement of responsibility was an important advance in accountability and transparency in the public sector. The statement would be signed by both the minister and the Secretary to the Treasury. The Secretary testified that the Treasury had used its best professional judgment in producing the update, on the basis of the information supplied to it. In this way, the Treasury took responsibility for the technical judgments in the forecasts. Previously it had been constitutionally unclear as to precisely whose forecasts they were.

I had never myself as minister attempted to substitute my technical judgment for the Treasury's, even when sceptical about an aspect of their forecasts. However, I cannot speak for my predecessors. In future there could be no question of the minister 'leaning' on the Treasury to produce politically useful numbers. The right and responsibility for the judgments underlying the forecasts were squarely vested in the Treasury.

The bill required the minister to testify in the statement of responsibility that she has supplied the Secretary of the Treasury with all fiscal decisions, and with all fiscal risks known to her. The minister was also responsible for the overall integrity of the disclosures, and with the consistency of the update with the Act. The clarification of the respective roles of the minister and the Secretary was particularly important in view of the political sensitivity of the pre-election update.

In September I took the draft bill to the Cabinet Legislation Committee. I had decided to call it the Fiscal Responsibility Bill. No significant changes were made to the bill by Cabinet, and soon after I was introducing it to the House:

> This legislation will enforce on New Zealand governments an unprecedented level of openness and honesty about public finances.
>
> In the past governments have often kept hidden from the electorate the full fiscal consequences of their decisions. Responsible fiscal policy has often fallen victim to short-term considerations of political expediency. In the process the country has built up a crippling burden of public debt, amounting to over $11,000 for every man, woman and child.
>
> We are now paying the price for the bad management of the past. That is why the legislation I am introducing today is so important. It will prevent the abuse of the electorate's trust that we have seen in past years. It will bring about more open and responsible fiscal policy far into the future.

The bill was referred to the Finance and Expenditure Select Committee. I was disappointed in the reaction to the bill. The media all but ignored it. Many in the business community and financial markets seemed slow to appreciate that here was a bill of major importance. But perhaps I should not have been surprised. In my experience, institutional measures whose focus is long term often meet initially with a muted response. Only later does their full significance become apparent to many people. That has certainly been the case with the Fiscal Responsibility Act.

National's opinion poll ranking had started to pick up before the budget and recovered further after the budget. Soon National was leading Labour by a large amount. There were a number of factors working in National's favour: the economy was continuing to improve, Jim had abolished his Monday press conference in a long-overdue move, the negative spirit of Peters had been finally exorcised from the party, and the budget had been well received. Confidence within the government's ranks was expanding rapidly.

This was a good period for me. I had been working on a proposal to liberalise non-resident withholding tax on dividends for foreign indirect investment. Portfolio investment was more mobile than direct investment, and was thus more sensitive at the margin to a change in its rate of return. Like the earlier substantial liberalisation of NRWT on interest, removing the double tax on portfolio investment was aimed at sparking the maximum inflow of new capital for the smallest possible loss from the tax base. As before, Wyatt opposed the move. Jim, however, was always more amenable to tax changes that involved reducing the tax base rather than extending it. He backed me, as did a sufficient number of others in Cabinet. The announcement immediately had a positive effect on the sharemarket.

The new mood in Cabinet was an important factor in the sale of New Zealand Rail to a consortium lead by the American company Wisconsin Central Railroad. I was especially pleased to bring off this sale, as it was secured in the teeth of dogged opposition from Wyatt, who by now was Minister of SOEs. Politics aside, the commercial aspects of the sale went extremely smoothly. We ran an excellent process and received a very good round of bids. The most attractive bid was from a party with strong credentials in the rail industry and a commitment to adding value.

As the process came closer to resolution, Wyatt came up with ever more inventive arguments in an attempt to head off the sale. One issue he raised was the fate of branch lines; Wairarapa just happened to be his example. Perhaps surprisingly, given how close we now were to the election, Cabinet decided to sell. It was unlikely I would have secured that result earlier in the year, when political nerves were much weaker.

Naturally, I was greatly enjoying my successes during this phase of the government. But they did not extend to heading off the concessions given by the government in the multi-party accord on superannuation.

There had been a long lead-up to the superannuation accord. In 1991 the government had set up the Todd Committee to look into the options for private provision for retirement. If truth be told, the Todd Committee was partly a means of extricating ourselves from our election commitment to introduce a tax incentive for private retirement savings. By then I had come to the view that designing a tax incentive would create more problems than it would solve. Jim himself was uncertain whether to proceed with a tax incentive. A number of others in Cabinet were keen on compulsory savings for retirement.

The Todd Committee duly looked at the three broad choices: voluntary provision, compulsory savings and a tax incentive. It consulted widely. The Treasury played a valuable role in assisting the committee, which in the end recommended voluntary provision. It also came up with a raft of other recommendations, some of which I was less than enthusiastic about. On the strength of the Todd Committee report, the government chose voluntary provision. Jim's next move was to make another attempt to reach a multi-party accord on the long-term shape of superannuation, using the Todd Committee report as a starting point. He wanted to neutralise the political advantage Labour had gained on superannuation as a result of our own political contortions.

I, naturally enough, sensed fiscal concessions in the air, and was suspicious throughout the process. Jim appointed Wyatt to front the negotiations for the government, and the accord was wrapped up soon after the budget. We did make concessions. Indeed, our intelligence from the Labour Party was that they were surprised at how many we had made. One of the casualties of the accord was the pure linkage of superannuation to the CPI, which Simon and I had worked so hard to have adopted as National policy when in Opposition. A band of 65-72 per cent of the average net wage for couples was established. A temporary transitional benefit was also agreed for those New Zealanders over 60 who had been affected by the accelerated shift to 65.

It was here that Labour outfoxed us with their policy of a '60-plus allowance' – effectively a proposal to make the transitional benefit permanent for those between 60 and 65. Labour kept the 60-plus allowance separate from their negotiations on the accord. They signed the accord, then came out with their extra policy on the side. It was our fault: we knew the 60-plus allowance was being mooted by Labour and did not insist on its being put on the table and dealt with. Mike Moore was able to look statesmanlike, while simultaneously outbidding National in the electoral auction.

Jim was to become highly defensive about the 60-plus allowance. Shortly afterwards, when I showed him the press release I had prepared on the cost of Labour's election commitments, Jim asked for that particular policy to be taken out of the list of costed promises: he did not want me drawing attention to it! Since the 60-plus allowance was projected to cost around $100 million by the year 2000, it was not an inconsiderable omission from our armoury.

The superannuation accord seemed a backward step to me at the time. In hindsight, it was probably a fortuitous move. In August 1993 no-one realised how rapidly the fiscal outlook would improve the following year. In the absence of the accord, 1994 may well have seen the start of another bidding war between the parties on superannuation. At the time of writing that has not so far happened.

One of the final policy issues to be played out before drawing up stumps for the election campaign was Doug Graham's proposed takeovers legislation, drawn up by his takeovers panel. I believed that the takeover – or the threat of a takeover – was an important market discipline. Takeovers kept management honest and in general led to a better use of resources in the corporate sector. I favoured a liberal takeovers regime. At first I took my eye off the ball on this issue. When Doug's restrictive code was being considered by the Strategy Committee, I was in the House speaking to the

Electoral Law Reform Bill, giving one of my anti-MMP blasts. After that, however, I focused more successfully. At Cabinet, two of us made so much noise – myself near the front and Maurice Williamson near the back – that Jim kicked the issue back down for further consideration.

Thereafter we fought to a temporary draw. There was heavy business lobbying against the code, which undoubtedly made a difference. In the end we reached an interim, compromise solution: Doug's code was dropped, but we legislated for another code to be drawn up the following year.

I never had confidence in the people advising Doug on commercial law, but they seemed to have captured the policy process exceedingly effectively. Despite my attempts, the Companies Bill had passed into law without the Treasury or the Commerce Department having any serious input. Amazingly, the bill did not even come back to a Cabinet committee after all the work that had been done on it by the Justice Department. I was also told that Labour's Geoffrey Palmer, when introducing the bill, had not taken it to a Cabinet committee either. If true, that means the Companies Act was never once considered by any Cabinet, despite straddling two governments.

The good news was that in 1995 the commercial law policy function of the Justice Department was transferred to the Commerce Department – a far better home for this important area of policy advice. It was a move I had wanted to facilitate while Minister of Finance, but had not managed to bring about. It should certainly improve the quality of our future commercial law.

By now the election was fast approaching. The economic picture we were taking to the voters was extremely good. The recovery showed no sign of slowing or hitting capacity constraints. Job growth was accelerating – we were increasingly seeing a job-rich recovery. We appeared to have achieved all but two of the first-term targets we had set for ourselves in the Vision document back in Opposition (it now seemed a lifetime ago). We had achieved 0-2 per cent inflation, single-digit business and mortgage interest rates, 3 per cent growth and a substantial reduction in government spending and taxation as percentages of GDP. We did not appear to have balanced the budget, though we had made very substantial progress. And we had not come near to halving unemployment, though the trend in unemployment was at last turning around.

Unbeknown to us, we had in fact balanced the budget for 1993-94, but this would not become apparent until the fiscal revisions during the following year. We received the first instalment of these positive revisions in the pre-election update. In the update, the forecast 1993-94 deficit had fallen to $1.4 billion from $2.3 billion in the budget. For 1995-96 the Treasury was projecting virtual budget balance. By now the Treasury had also produced the actual out-turn for 1992-93: at $1.8 billion, it was well down even on the May update. The improved outlook in the pre-election update reflected three main factors: stronger than expected tax flows, lower than expected benefit numbers, and lower than expected interest rates.

From the government's point of view, the update could scarcely have been better. The improvement in the fiscal position was welcome in itself: it reinforced the perception of National as the party of responsible fiscal management. And if the improvement had been much greater it would have begun to undercut one of National's principal campaign themes – that Labour's spending promises meant they would be forced to put up taxes.

When the update came out the tax campaign was already well under way. The Treasury, in conjunction with other departments, had undertaken at my request costings of all of Labour's final election policies. These costings were to prove highly controversial. The problem started because Labour's policies were not always 100 per cent clear. In six of the costings Treasury made assumptions as to the most likely interpretation of Labour's policy. These assumptions were in every case the most plausible in the circumstances. However, making assumptions at all, without reference to the minister concerned, was contrary to standard protocols on departmental costings of election promises, as the post-election State Services Commission review, requested by Michael Cullen, would point out. The review would not say that the costings in those six cases were wrong, or the assumptions unrealistic – only that assumptions had been made when they should not have been made. The review cleared the Treasury from Cullen's charge of political bias. Had the Treasury not made those assumptions in the six cases, I as minister would have asked them to recost the promises making precisely the same assumptions.

The Treasury costings of Labour's policy amounted to a very expensive set of policies – quite expensive enough for the government to claim quite plausible that Labour would put up taxes. Jim and I launched our tax attack at a press conference, when I released all the Treasury reports backing the costings.

A day or two later in Parliament Cullen made a savage attack on the Treasury costings and the integrity of some of the Treasury officers who had performed them. I can understand Cullen's disappointment at the way the costings had come out. But this attack under privilege, on officials who were in no position to answer back, was contemptible. The tax saga would rumble on for much of the campaign. Labour released an Infometrics report they had commissioned, which stated that Labour's policies cost less than the government claimed. I accused Cullen of giving Infometrics a specially tailored version of Labour's policies. Lange made a speech which – wittingly or unwittingly – was grist to our mill. Cullen was refusing to rule out tax increases, a point I was naturally enough capitalising on in our media debates. I signed a statement in front of the media saying National would not put up taxes, although Jim refused to sign a similar statement. Labour leader Mike Moore succumbed to the pressure and unilaterally ruled out a tax increase, and Cullen's staff worked through the night to produce numbers backing Moore's new position.

If Labour were often at sixes and sevens, things were not entirely smooth in the government camp either. At one point Jim, feeling under pressure on the jobs issue, hinted that National would be spending more on employment schemes the following year. It looked like a promise on the hoof. The media naturally asked me if this was a new spending commitment by National. I was forced to stress that any new money in this area would be treated as a new policy bid in the coming budget round. The media ran the story 'Richardson overrules Bolger'. But, whatever the hiccups along the way, the campaign appeared to be going well enough for National. We had started with a lead in the polls, and we were ending with a lead in the polls. I also looked to be comfortably in front in my own electorate of Selwyn.

16

SCAPEGOAT

By election night I was in a confident mood. But the first results in Selwyn looked far from clear-cut. Nationwide, there was a big swing against the government, but I was not following events outside Selwyn in much detail. I was still at my desk, fielding calls from my party scrutineers. Selwyn continued to hang in the balance. It was going to be a very long night. The press were growing increasingly insistent, but I was not going to comment until I was certain of the result. By the time it was clear I had held Selwyn, we looked to be headed for a hung Parliament. In addition, MMP had narrowly defeated first past the post in the referendum on the electoral system. It was not the result I had wanted, and it was almost the worst possible result for the financial markets. I spoke briefly by phone to the Reserve Bank Governor and the Treasury Secretary. Only then did I make it out to my party workers, who had waited so patiently in the marquee. I did my best to give a victory speech, but the celebration was more than a little muted.

What had gone wrong? It certainly cannot have been the economic strategy. On the strength of the government's economic record, the election could not have been lost. Yet now we had a hung Parliament. Three main factors appeared to have led to our downfall. Our broken promises on superannuation were still a vivid memory with voters. The health reforms had been extremely unpopular: we improved the health system but we lost the public relations battle. And we did not have a political strategy of the same quality as our economic strategy. Political strategy is driven very much from the top, and our leader had largely failed to explain our policies or gain the confidence of the public. Roger Douglas had had a David Lange to charm New Zealanders. I had not.

The next day I was back in Wellington. If the election-night result held, National would probably be a minority government. The budget process would need to be radically rethought. I had a strategy session with my officials. Whatever happened on the special votes, there would no reforming second term for me as Finance Minister. But I was still interested in holding the line, in playing the role that would clearly be important – protecting the legacy of 10 years of economic reform. Would Jim reappoint me? The temptation for him to search for a scapegoat might be irresistible.

There had been speculation in the press that I might lose my job following the election. There was always such speculation; I had lived with it for five years. My closest advisers had warned me that once the economy was in good enough condition Jim might dump me – and I had not forgotten the signal Jim had given me over my electorate boundaries the previous year. Other rumours had drifted back to me – reports of Jim musing out loud to his drinking friends about my future and testing the water for reaction to the idea of my removal.

For my part, I suspended judgment. I had always tended to put such thoughts out of mind. The job had been too important to be distracted by constantly looking over my shoulder for advancing knives. But now, in the days following the election, I developed with Andrew and my advisers litmus tests that would guide my future actions. Would the reform momentum live or die? If it died, I died with it. Would Jim opt for power or the programme? I could not operate in an environment where maintenance of office was more important than the pursuit of policy. Finally, and this was the clincher – would the leadership continue to win my respect?

At first the immediate post-election atmosphere looked bad for me. Jim had set the tone in his election-night speech. That tone was 'consensus'. As the peppery little conviction politician , there was a good chance I would be seen by Jim as not in tune with the new political mood. Jim Anderton inadvertently helped my cause by appearing to say that he expected me to lose finance. The PM now risked looking as though he was simply doing Anderton's bidding if he sacked me.

At last the result of the special vote count in the cliffhanger Waitaki electorate came through. We were confirmed in government with a bare one-seat majority. Jim could now sit back and concentrate wholly on sorting out his new Cabinet. But he seemed to take forever to do so; it was several days before he called me up to see him.

Jim started off by saying, 'I'm asking all my ministers this question: what portfolio would you like if you didn't have your present one?'

'That's like me asking you what job you would want if you were not Prime Minister,' I replied.

'Touché,' said Jim. He then said he was uncertain whether to retain me in finance. He asked me to outline how I saw the finance job in National's second term. I said that in our first three years we had been forced to spend a lot of political energy getting New Zealand up off the back foot. It had been extremely hard, but a great deal of progress had been made. Our second term would be much more about New Zealanders capitalising on the opportunities opening up. It was a term that would see us much more on the front foot. I wanted Jim to see me as looking forward, not looking back.

On my suitability for the finance job, I did not put in any pleas. I just said, 'You've worked with me as minister for three years. You know what you're buying.' I reiterated that finance was the only portfolio I was interested in. However, I did not explicitly say that I would refuse any other. I did not want to hold a gun at Jim's head. I intended to stay on as his Finance Minister only if he genuinely wanted me to.

From the tone of the interview my chances did not look good. Still, there was a possibility Jim would shrink from the messy task of shifting me. There was nothing to do in Wellington until Jim made up his mind, which – judging by past history – could take quite some time. Rather than wait around, I went up the coast with Anna Symmans to stay at her bach.

Later I received a call from Don McKinnon. I was on very friendly terms with Don, and he had clearly been deputed for that reason. He wanted to know what I really wanted to do if I was not given finance. I firmly gave Don the same message I had given Jim.

At midday the next day – Friday – Jim himself rang. He offered me the portfolios of justice and transport. I told him I wished to be Minister of Finance; if that were not his intention, I would do the honourable thing and go to the back bench. Jim was surprised, rattled and angered by my response. He had never imagined I might do such a thing. He had worked closely with me for six years, yet how little he had known me! Jim was doubly rattled because he had been planning to announce his new Cabinet at 2pm that day. This would clearly have to be postponed as he reconfigured his line-up. Jim and I had a tense exchange. 'You always were too inflexible,' he said. 'This just shows why I was right to shift you from finance.' The conversation did not end happily.

In politics I had always been interested in policy, not in positions for their own sake. Once Jim had signalled that the fire was to go out of policy, the fire had gone out of my enthusiasm for office. To have stayed would have been a betrayal of what I had stood for and why I was in politics – a venal act.

Later, Don rang. Again, he was doing Jim's bidding. Could I be persuaded to change my mind? Don, ever the team man, was genuinely distraught. I felt sorry for him. But he would not be changing my mind.

Later still, I received a ring from Jenny – one of my closest friends and allies in Cabinet. She was the right person to choose for the task. Perhaps they were hoping, too, that one woman would persuade the other, but it was not to be. Jenny's attempt was the last.

When I got back to the Beehive, I went up to see Jim and Don for a final courtesy call. I told them that I left the Cabinet with my head held high. Then I flew down to Selwyn. I had, of course, kept Andrew abreast of developments. Now it was time to tell the children. I also phoned some of my other allies in Cabinet, who were aghast. One even talked of resigning himself. He did not, but it was sweet to have such a spur-of-the-moment reaction.

On Sunday I flew back up to Wellington for the announcement of the new Cabinet. After Jim's press conference the media filed into my office: the room was packed. It was the last time I would be addressing the Press Gallery as Minister of Finance. Whether they loved me or hated me, many were finding it an emotion-charged moment. Even the press are human. I would take no questions. I did not want to go out looking bitter, but I wanted to go out fighting. The media sat in complete silence. Only the repeated click of cameras could be heard as I read out a statement Andrew and I had prepared:

> I deeply regret that the Prime Minister has chosen to remove me from the finance portfolio.
>
> The Prime Minister's decision will not deflect me from the goals that I entered politics to pursue and the causes that mean so much to me. I have sought throughout my political career to champion the causes of

individual opportunity and responsibility, low inflation, fiscal responsibility, openness in domestic and international markets and competitiveness in the economy.

I am proud to be a member of a government that has taken the tough but necessary decisions that are now delivering very real economic results for New Zealanders. Last week it was revealed that 41,000 new jobs were created in the economy over the last year, and in the next few weeks we are likely to learn that growth over that same period will be nearer 4 per cent than 3 per cent.

These are the very dividends that the policies we have pursued have been designed to produce. I do not believe New Zealanders voted to put these gains at risk ...

I have decided to move to the back bench, where I can be best placed to ensure that the government remains committed to this programme of economic success. My decision to go to the back bench is motivated by my desire to remain true to the principles that have guided me throughout my political career.

As Minister of Finance I have always placed a high premium on New Zealand's economic and political stability. I have no desire to introduce any further element of instability into the political process. I intend to be an effective but responsible member of both the government back bench and the New Zealand National Party.

After the press had gone I signed away my warrant.

Only one man knows the exact reasons for my sacking. I was later to learn that Jim's close political advisers had pushed for it, arguing that it was his head or mine. Whether Jim felt that or not, he clearly believed he could not present a new image for his government with me as Finance Minister. And Jim had grown tired: tired of my reforming zeal, my constant sparring with Wyatt and – more significantly – tired of reforming the economy. He wanted to slow down, and enjoy his leadership. He also knew I would not be prepared, if reappointed Minister of Finance, to live with a diminution of the programme.

The next day there was a stream of messages and tokens. The floral bouquets poured in: my office was almost afloat. Being a female Minister of Finance had its advantages: I am sure Roger Douglas did not get half as many flowers when he resigned. Naturally, many of the messages came from the business community, but over the next few days I would receive a gratifyingly large amount of mail from ordinary people. Most of the letters were handwritten, almost all of them supportive. Many said Jim had made me his scapegoat for the election result. As a politician I had almost

always avoided any sort of populist pitch. I had never been the nation's pin-up, and still wasn't. But at the end, I discovered a large vein of people who thought I had been unlucky, or shabbily treated, or had just done a difficult job with integrity.

My hardest task by far was to go across to the Treasury and give my farewell address. The Treasury had its share of human frailty and fallibility. But they were a superb team – the best in the public sector. I owed them so much, and now could give them so little. I respected them hugely and they – I know – had come to respect me. It was more than that: everywhere I looked was the face of someone I now regarded as a friend. I had joked with them, debated with them, plotted strategy with them, poured them wine at midnight to celebrate our victories or to commiserate over our defeats. Now it was all ending. I can remember little of what I said, but the applause at the end almost brought out the woman in me. The longer it went on, the more I could only think: 'If I took another portfolio I would be losing all of these people.'

Back in the Beehive, in the elevator, I did something I was not accustomed to doing. I cried.

17

EXIT ON A HIGH NOTE

Encouragement is a rare but precious commodity in politics. Not the encouragement of those who tell you what you want to hear, nor the encouragement of fair-weather friends. The encouragement that counted was of the genuine and often unexpected kind. From Jim I neither expected, nor received, encouragement. Only once privately and once publicly did he single me out for praise. The private praise came in a letter (it may have been sent to all the other ministers for all I know) at the end of our first week post-election, which Jim aptly termed a 'baptism of fire'. It was a letter of appreciation, thanking me for 'your sound counsel and support over the past few days'.

The public praise, of a more ritualistic nature, was to come in the final months of my tenure as Minister of Finance. Along with the Minister of Finance from Malaysia, Anwar Ibrahim, I had been named runner-up Finance Minister of the year by the international magazine *Euromoney*. (Roger Douglas had achieved in his time the highest accolade.) I was very conscious that such recognition is of no great moment domestically. In a very public display, Jim made much of congratulating me in the House. Given that fresh rumours of my demise had resurfaced at that time, I took it all with a grain of salt. Deputy Don McKinnon, by contrast, was all encouragement and made genuine and frequent efforts to acknowledge that Jenny and I, in particular, were carrying heavy and often unpopular burdens for the government.

The encouragement of friends was always such a boost. At the outset there was Sue Wood, a substantial but spurned talent in the National Party. Sue celebrated her 40th birthday with me as the National Party's first female president. In turn I celebrated my 40th birthday with Sue as New Zealand's first female Finance Minister. Sue's encouragement came in the form of strong personal friendship and sound political advice. I remember well being bailed up by Sue and Dorothy McNab, a true matriarch of the National Party, at Federated Farmers' annual cocktail party in Wellington in 1980. Nominations had been called in the safe seats of Hauraki and Selwyn for the 1981 election. Sue and Dorothy, who had obviously got their heads together before the function, laid out before me a highly persuasive strategy for securing Selwyn. While I was not particularly in need of reassurance, looking back I see that that was the critical moment at which I committed myself to that course of action. Sue and Dorothy can take credit for my finally taking a successful step into the political arena.

Philosophical soul-mates tended to become friends as well. During the decade of economic reform the private-sector leaders typically saw economic liberalism as the hero of the story of New Zealand's transformation. This philosophy was consistently practised by governments of the left as well as the right and the private sector was quick to embrace and encourage those of us who lived by this philosophy. Their support was invaluable.

While I was extended numerous courtesies and kindnesses throughout my political career, encouragement from four quarters in particular meant a good deal to me personally. Sir Ronald Trotter, a towering figure in the private sector, was a highly persuasive ally in the quest for high-quality public policy. Douglas Myers, whose sense of civic duty saw him championing both political and sporting excellence, was generous in committing his time and energy to the advocacy of principled reform. Jenny and Alan Gibbs, she the soft heart and he the hard head in their respective public personae (but both all head and heart privately), were fearless and tireless in their support for market liberalisation. And Sir Peter Elworthy, a brave and caring farmer leader, ensured that the highest level of economic literacy came from those on the land. Peter and his wife Fiona gave me encouragement in good times, comfort in bad times, and wise counsel at all times. Public policy is the richer for the generosity of spirit displayed by souls such as these.

Friends continued to play a vital role throughout my political career. While a politician does not exactly leave the human race, the artificiality of the lifestyle, being constantly in the public eye, managing a commuter marriage and practising long-distance parenthood all add up to abnormal stresses and strains. Normality was so often restored by family and friends. But finally everything hung on the stability and support of my family. I could not have functioned without Andrew. I had made clear in my maiden speech that I would not sacrifice my family on the altar of politics. But while intentions are one thing, deeds are another. It was only Andrew who enabled me to make good that proposition.

Conscious of the corrosive impact of public on private life, Andrew and I deliberately structured family events to help create a number of politics-free zones. The children's birthdays were always big family affairs, with grandparents journeying from the North Island. Elaborate birthday cakes were baked (never by me, I'm afraid) and it was a great social occasion for Andrew and me to match the children's mood with a parents' party.

Easter brought with it the treat of a high-country excursion to great friends Mike and Karen Meares of Ryton Station at the head of Lake Coleridge. Mike, articulate, immensely practical and with a keen interest in my style of politics, was a great sounding-board, and Karen, the 'women can do anything' farmer extraordinaire, was great personal inspiration to me. While Andrew packed picnics, I packed Cabinet bags, and all three budgets were mulled over in their final stages on Mike and Karen's sunny deck looking over the shimmering lake and under the towering mountains. I could think of no better climate in which to advance the twin concepts of private enterprise and personal responsibility that my friends were putting into such obvious practice.

August often took us up to Lake Rotoiti, into the hospitable arms of Alison and Philip Graham at Rainbow Station. Philip's parents, Doug and Myra, had played a significant part in launching my political career but with their son and family it was purely personal enjoyment. Happy in the hills, we tramped, skied and got some colour in our cheeks, taking time out in glorious style. In later years Wanaka was to feature more heavily in our summer and winter plans. We were befriended by the Fogarty family as we shared the weekly rounds of cubs, cricket and hockey, and the skiing, fishing, canoeing and tramping from Sue Fogarty's family bach in Wanaka were a natural and highly enjoyable extension of our friendship. Bright and breezy Sue, sending risqué faxes from the highly respectable medical specialist practice in Christchurch where she worked as a nurse, was just the real-world tonic that we needed.

Guy Fawkes was another excuse for putting family and friends in the diary. I will never forget November 1990. Elected the previous Saturday and down a BNZ bunker ever since, I resurfaced seven days later to be with my family and friends to 'enjoy' our Guy Fawkes party. The strain of confidentiality was immediate and obvious and our close friends found my behaviour puzzling. I had been sworn in as Minister of Finance the day before and they were thrilled for me that I had achieved my political ambition.

Yet throughout the early evening and night, as splendid food (as always, supplied by friends) and supervised fireworks (supplied by us) were enjoyed by parents and children alike, I seemed curiously detached: BNZ issues weighed heavily with me. It was only on the following Monday, Guy Fawkes proper, that Jim and I were able to take to the Beehive stage to announce the scale of the BNZ's problems and the scale of taxpayer commitment necessary to fund the solution. Only then did my friends understand the personal toll of public policy pressures.

Time and again over the following three years I would return from Wellington at times frustrated, at times exhilarated, but always exhausted. The staff in my Beehive office, ever sensitive to the pressures on me, did all they could to create a home-away-from-home environment. Many had been with me from long before my Beehive days. The longest-serving was Pat Humphries – highly capable, fiercely loyal and possessing a wicked Irish wit. Private secretaries are both a shield and a sword for an MP and minister, and Pat excelled at both. We were a cosmopolitan lot in our office, with the copious filing cheerfully carried out by Katy Greco, of an Italian family in Island Bay, and the Treasury liaison undertaken by Joyce Sapsford, a stunning Samoan woman who was a wonderful influence on the whole office.

Their collective kindness made a huge difference; but home is where the heart is, and it was to Andrew, the children and my Selwyn network that I always turned to restore my equilibrium.

Equally long-serving staff ran a professional but very personable service for my Selwyn constituents. Hazel Bull fronted the constituency work while Aleida Dodd, who had turned my dreadful writing into typewritten copy from my earliest days as a candidate in Selwyn, was in charge of the office. These two became seasoned hands at caring for constituents, who soon found that, whether I was in the electorate or not, or in the country or not, there was virtually nothing Hazel and Aleida at the Selwyn end, and Pat at the Wellington end, could not fix.

Then there were the magnificent midwinter political parties at Sheffield, thrown by the Malvern Women's Group, who canvassed and baked their collective hearts out for my cause and that of the National Party. These well-organised women, typically much older than I, taught me a great deal about how families and communities function, and were incredibly kind at a personal level but incredibly exacting at a political level.

While it is invidious to single people out, there was a trio of women and a trio of men in Selwyn who were more inspirational and influential than most. Hazel Bull, my electorate agent, Frances Smith, my electorate secretary, and Margaret Baylis, my electorate publicity officer, guided me, baked for me, corrected and counselled me throughout my political career. They helped bring up our babies, they nursed my political hurts, and they pushed my political barrow. Of this I can be confident: no male MP could be the recipient of such kindness and care. Despite the higher hurdles that women face in politics, the compensations are enormous and unparalleled.

Likewise, three men stood out as beacons throughout my political career: Chris Charles, my electorate treasurer and consistently successful campaigner; Bill Taylor, campaign chairman and generous neighbour; and Bill Studholme, who held the key posts of campaign chairman in 1987 and electorate chairman thereafter. These three provided the crucial political drive and gave me the best political infrastructure any MP could have. Their formidable machine was not only successful time after time in the face of the worst that the Representation Commission could throw at us but, crucially, carried my successor, David Carter, to success in a tight by-election. Having not failed me once, and at a vital time of need not failing the party, these three political musketeers truly earned the honourable political discharge they would seek after the Selwyn by-election in mid-1994.

My political career did not end when I walked out of my Beehive office: I was to have a brief but productive political afterlife. There were two circumstances for which I was immediately thankful. First of all, Jim had named Bill Birch as my successor. Bill had wanted my job and lobbied Jim to sack me, just as he had played a major role in ending the careers of Derek Quigley and Jim McLay before me. There were several other ironies in Bill's appointment. The former Muldoonist was now the Treasury Minister, enjoying the benefits from the policies he had so long opposed. And Jim's explanation for shifting me from finance – that he wanted a more 'consensus' approach – sat oddly with Bill's history as the minister of Think Big and the National Development Act. Despite these circumstances, I was extremely grateful Bill had been given the job over Jim's other favourite, Wyatt.

The process may have been painfully slow, but Bill had come a long way since his Muldoonist days. Unlike Wyatt, he now supported the Reserve Bank Act. Unlike Wyatt, he supported the strategy of controlling expenditure. Bill was essentially a fiscal conservative. Unlike Wyatt, Bill did not have a hang-up about officials. The opposite was closer to the truth: Bill was easily captured by officials. Bill was a builder, not an architect. With a bad department drawing up the plans, Bill could be positively dangerous. But, as the Treasury Minister, he would have an excellent department to steer him. For all of these reasons, I was pleased that Bill had inherited the Treasury. There was another good aspect to Bill's appointment that I had not anticipated: Bill would approach the task of paying off government debt as almost a personal mission. The reason is not hard to see: Bill did more than anyone else alive to create the debt.

The minister with most reason to be grateful over my exit from Cabinet was Warren Cooper – though he may not have known it. 'Supercoop' had been marked down by Jim to lose both his defence portfolio and Cabinet rank, becoming a minister outside Cabinet. With my demise Warren earned a reprieve. Doug Graham, who had been intended for trade negotiations when I was offered justice, ended up keeping his justice portfolio.

My second piece of good fortune was Jim's agreement to making me chair of the Finance and Expenditure Select Committee – the committee to which the Fiscal Responsibility Bill had been sent. I was now in the best possible position to help the bill in its progress through the House – better even than if I had remained Minister of Finance. Already I had been thinking in terms of strengthening the bill. The advent of MMP and the closeness of the election result were good additional reasons to consider further fiscal safeguards. As the bill stood, open disclosure – along with open capital markets – was the principal mechanism for encouraging responsible fiscal behaviour. I was now interested in making the bill more prescriptive in its demands on government, without going all the way to mandatory targets.

Early in the new year I gave an interview to *Dominion* journalist Jane Clifton. I said I was considering strengthening the bill to give clearer legal status to factors such as budget balance and debt repayment. Bill's response was to say that no further strengthening of the bill was necessary. As for Jim, he said he did not know what I was getting at.

The select committee process, however, went well. At first there had not been a great deal of interest from the business sector, but in January I wrote to a wide range of people inviting submissions. I wanted high-quality scrutiny. I also saw the select committee process as important for creating the widest possible constituency for the principles in the bill. In the end we received some excellent submissions, particularly from the Business Roundtable, former Treasury Secretary Graham Scott and John Zohrab, also ex-Treasury. Some submissions proposed writing various fiscal objectives into the bill, either as mandatory targets or indicative guidelines. The government members of the committee, as well as the Treasury, believed mandatory targets were not feasible but that guidelines were.

We agreed to replace the clause requiring the government merely to state its fiscal objectives with a new and much more powerful clause. The new clause specified that the government 'shall pursue its policy objectives in accordance with the principles of responsible fiscal management'. Under the new clause, the government could depart temporarily from the principles of responsible fiscal management, but not permanently. Any temporary departure needed to be accompanied by a statement justifying the departure and outlining the approach the government intended to take to return to the principles.

The principles were:

- Reducing total Crown debt to prudent levels so as to provide a buffer against factors that may impact adversely on the level of total Crown debt in the future, by ensuring that, until such levels have been achieved, the total operating expenses of the Crown in each financial year are less than its total operating revenues in the same financial year; and
- Once prudent levels of total Crown debt have been achieved, maintaining these levels by ensuring that, on average, over a reasonable period of time, the total operating expenses of the Crown do not exceed its total operating revenues; and
- Achieving and maintaining levels of Crown net worth that provide a buffer against factors that may impact adversely on the Crown's net worth in the future; and
- Managing prudently the fiscal risks faced by the Crown; and
- Pursuing policies that are consistent with a reasonable degree of predictability about the level and stability of tax rates for future years.

These constitute demanding requirements. The first principle recognises that our debt is too high and needs to be reduced by running budget surpluses. By the time this principle was drawn up it was plain we would be achieving a budget surplus for the 1993-94 year. We had a window of opportunity over the next few years to reduce our debt. The first principle requires the government not to squander that opportunity.

The second principle requires the government, once prudent debt levels have been achieved, not in general to increase its debt. This will mean roughly balancing the budget over the course of the business cycle. However, it does not require the government to run a balanced budget literally every year, come what may.

The third principle recognises that what ultimately matters is the whole of the Crown's balance sheet. For instance, unfunded liabilities such as public-service pension liabilities are not 'debt', but certainly have implications for the financial position of the Crown. The reference in the third principle to 'factors that may impact adversely on the Crown's net worth' is intended to cover elements not captured in the balance sheet, such as the future demands of an ageing population. The fourth and fifth principles further reinforce the concepts of prudence, stability and certainty in fiscal management.

The five principles considerably strengthened the bill. They constitute an invaluable benchmark against which government policy is now being evaluated. They focus on the long term, while still allowing for short-term fluctuations. They are explicit about the direction and tenor of fiscal policy, without falling into the trap of imposing overly simplistic rules. They put the onus of proof on those who would seek to increase government spending. As with the Reserve Bank Act, short-term deviation by the government is allowed but it must be temporary, and it comes at a price: the government must account publicly for its fall from grace.

The second major improvement to the bill was more directly a reflection of the MMP environment we were moving into. In a world of coalition or minority governments, the Minister of Finance is likely in each budget round to be seeking an early sign-up from other parties on the broad principles of the budget. With this in mind, a new clause in the bill required the government to publish a budget policy statement no later than 31 March each year.

The statement would specify the government's long-term objectives for fiscal policy – including operating expenses, operating revenues, the balance between expenses and revenue, debt and net worth – and explain how these objectives accord with the principles of responsible fiscal management. The budget policy statement would also set out the government's broad strategic priorities for the 12 months covered by the coming budget, and indicate, by means of ranges, ratios or other means, the intended path of the key fiscal aggregates listed above. Any departure from the principles of responsible fiscal management, from the previous budget policy statement, or from the previous fiscal strategy report published with the budget, must be explained.

By providing such a full disclosure of the government's intentions, the budget policy statement should lead to wider ownership of the budget process. It should also separate out debate about the overall fiscal strategy from debate over the detail of individual departmental votes. In the past the two have tended to become mixed.

I was extremely pleased when Bill Birch agreed to the amendments proposed by the committee. Getting him up to speed on the fiscal responsibility legislation had been a crucial task for the Treasury. Before the election he had been scarcely aware of the bill at all, and his initial response to my proposal to strengthen it had not been encouraging. The Treasury, however, had invested a great deal of time in Bill. Luckily, he was keen to demonstrate to the financial markets that he was a fiscally responsible Finance Minister, and there could be no better way to do this than by

signing up to the Fiscal Responsibility Bill. After his initial learning period, Bill presented few problems.

Jim was different. With the election out of the way, he was no longer thinking of the bill in terms of its political usefulness in election year. He was sceptical about institutional rules that limited the freedom of movement of politicians. He was instinctively averse to any attempt to strengthen the legislation. Eventually Bill, not without difficulty, managed to persuade Jim of the merits of the proposed amendments. With Jim on side, carrying Cabinet presented no problems. I was less impressed when Bill gave a speech detailing the agreed changes while the bill was still in front of the select committee. He even issued a redrafted version of the bill. Not only was this a blatant attempt to hog the political limelight, it was contrary to the Standing Orders of the House.

That, however, was a minor irritant. I was so confident the changes to the bill would be acceptable to caucus that I had gone on holiday with my family at the time caucus considered the matter. I could scarcely have been more pleased at the way the bill had developed. It now ranked as one of the most important measures of the entire economic reform programme, now 10 years old. In one sense, the bill completed that programme. So long as the Act stays in place, it will make a permanent difference in the area of economic policy that had proved hardest, and most intractable. It has removed the last major policy risk.

When Bill brought down his first budget the fiscal outlook was extremely rosy. An operating surplus of $1.3 billion was forecast for 1994-95, rising to $5.0 billion for 1996-97. There was, admittedly, a considerable amount of new spending, but in view of the huge improvement in the fiscal position, the imminence of MMP and the government's one-seat majority in the House, the new spending might easily have been a great deal higher. This suggests the Fiscal Responsibility Act might already be having a valuable impact on government fiscal policy.

In the budget Bill hinted that there would be tax cuts in 1996-97 if two conditions were met: continued expenditure control and continued growth. Surprisingly, Bill had not taken this major positioning statement to Cabinet; the 'Bill and Jim' team had worked it out between them. Bill also hinted in the budget that tax cuts would not occur until net public debt was reduced to the sustainable range of 20 per cent to 30 per cent of GDP. A debate ensued within the government over whether New Zealanders should be awarding themselves tax cuts so soon, or whether we should be applying all surpluses to debt repayment. For as long as I was in caucus, I was firmly in the latter camp. By the time of the December update a subtle shift had taken place. If anything, the fiscal outlook was even more favourable. But, partly in response to pressure from backbenchers such as Max Bradford and John Robertson, Bill had imposed a new condition on any tax cuts: they would not happen until the government had repaid all of its foreign debt. Bill also stressed that, even with tax cuts, the government would still be planning to continue repaying debt by repaying surpluses.

In February 1995, in the first budget policy statement under the Fiscal Responsibility Act, Bill repeated his condition that net public debt would need to fall below 30 per cent of GDP before tax cuts occurred. On current projections that was achievable for 1996-97. Bill also stated that 'following any tax cuts, and if strong economic growth is maintained, the government would expect to run operating surpluses of at least 3 per cent of GDP. With this level of surplus committed to debt reduction, net public debt would fall below 20 per cent of GDP by the turn of the century.' Though the wording was not watertight, it did appear to be a signal that the government was continuing to place high priority on reducing debt – as it should under the new fiscal legislation.

The Fiscal Responsibility Bill went through its last stages in the House in June 1994. Seeing the bill successfully through to enactment brought me to a very natural point of repose in my parliamentary career. It would be

foolish to pretend that all possible reforms had been completed, or that all was perfect in government policy. This was manifestly not so. There were a number of areas that still awaited the energy and vision of those in politics who really wanted to make a difference. But I had been in Parliament, as an activist, for well over a decade. It had been a long haul. For the next few years there would be low returns for my style of activism. If I wanted to go on making a difference I would need to take my seat again for another long haul, just as I had waited out the long winter of Muldoonism. In the early months of the year I had spent a great deal more time in the company of my family and was finding it addictive. I had done my dash in politics, at least for the meantime. I was still young. A period in the private sector would be refreshing and invigorating. And in the very long term, who knows? The economy was buoyant. Unemployment was falling. We were headed for a budget surplus in 1993-94 – New Zealand's first for a generation. When Bill brought down his first budget, it showed a string of surpluses, as far as the eye could see. We were already repaying our debt. I could hardly leave politics on a higher note.

One night I rang Jim and told him I would be resigning my seat the next day. I had not trusted him with the information in advance; I had wanted to manage my own exit. The next day Andrew flew up for my press conference.

Asked by the media if I was bitter I replied: 'I do not have a bitter bone in my body.' And that is true. I had a huge amount to be thankful for. I had never entered politics expecting it to be 'fair'. Politics was not fair to Derek Quigley or Jim McLay. It was not fair to Roger Douglas, or to others in the Labour Party. They never lived long enough, politically, to be associated with the success of the policies they espoused. With me it was different. I was a privileged person: I was going out on a winning note.

NEW SUCCESSES
TO MATCH THE OLD

BLUEPRINT FOR THE FUTURE

It is tempting to believe that all the hard work for policymakers is over, that from now on governments can coast along on the strength of a rising wave of economic prosperity. A case can certainly be made for a 'rosy scenario'. Since the upturn began, in the third quarter of 1991, New Zealand has consistently grown faster than the OECD average. During that four-year period we have also grown by considerably more than in the nine long years of the Muldoon era. The 1994 growth rate of between 6 per cent and 7 per cent was not sustainable, but even with the monetary brakes having now been applied we look set to grow at a highly respectable rate in 1995 and again in 1996.

Even better, New Zealanders are now reaping a jobs harvest from the economic expansion. Since the Employment Contracts Act came into force, around 150,000 new jobs have been created. By New Zealand standards this is a hugely impressive rate of job growth. Unemployment has already fallen substantially, and is significantly below the OECD average. The jobs story is one that few had expected. Even most of the commentators sympathetic to the National government's strategy did not anticipate how rapidly labour market reform would combine with growth to produce a job-rich recovery. The Reserve Bank – hardly a hotbed of Keynesian economics – was at one stage predicting unemployment to top 13 per cent. It is now half that.

Our job-rich recovery is all the more impressive for showing every sign of being sustainable. We have swapped debt-ridden stagnation for a growth path in which we are now making substantial inroads into our debt burden. No real balance of payments pressures have yet emerged. We continue to see rapid expansion in sophisticated manufactured exports. The government's budget has moved into surplus. Less than four years after fighting off a double downgrade from Standard and Poors we were upgraded again. The other prominent international rating agency, Moody's, has also upgraded New Zealand recently. At the current rate of progress, further upgrades should not be far away. The Reserve Bank continues to implement its mandate for price stability.

Yes, it would be easy to become complacent, especially as New Zealand's reforms have caught the attention of the world. When ministers travel abroad they talk glowingly of the resurgence of our economy. But that resurgence did not happen by accident: it happened because successive governments had the courage and the wisdom to make far-reaching reforms. We did not content ourselves with matching the quality of policies elsewhere in the world. In many cases we led the world. That is what is bringing so many visitors to New Zealand, eager to learn about our policy environment. Yet it is precisely this attitude – a willingness to lead the world – that is now largely absent from the minds of today's policymakers.

This is worrying. Our economic position is not nearly as rosy as some would have us believe. Our progress has been impressive, but from a starting point no-one remotely in their right mind would have chosen. Eleven years ago we were the most severe basket-case in the OECD. We have changed that position, but we still have one of the lowest standards of living of any OECD country. Most New Zealanders are now better off than they were 10 years ago, but they are also working harder. Our real wages remain substantially below those of our nearest neighbour, Australia. As recently as 1983 we had a AAA credit rating. We are still an indebted country. Our growth rate may compare favourably with many other OECD economies, but a comparison with the Asian 'tigers' is not nearly so flattering.

Most important, there is a large group of New Zealanders still untouched by the recovery – our dependent underclass. Achieving an unemployment rate below the OECD average is a small boast in view of the chronic rigidities in most European labour markets. Unemployment today is not greatly lower than the level of unemployment National inherited when it took office – a level we had attacked in Opposition as scandalously high. And unemployment today is still much higher than the level the Lange-Douglas government inherited in 1984 – a level they had attacked in Opposition as scandalously high. Just as worrying, there is a huge disparity between the employment rates of Europeans and Maori, with the unemployment rate for Maori standing at around 20 per cent compared with 5 per cent for Europeans. Other dependency indicators are not even falling. The number on the domestic purposes benefit continues to climb. More children are being reared in poverty. We are increasingly becoming two societies: the mainstream of New Zealanders who are taking advantage of the new economic opportunities, and an underclass still trapped in a cycle of dependency.

If we are to continue to lift our economic performance, it will require more than self-congratulation over past initiatives and a complacency that we have at last located the 'up' escalator. It will require new thinking on strategies in areas so far little visited. We need to tackle vested interests that successive governments have shrunk from confronting. We have created, by and large, an enterprise culture in business. Now we need to create an enterprise culture where so far it has hardly reached – in education, in the delivery of social services, in our urban ghettos. We need to borrow some lessons from our near Asian neighbours. If we do that, we can continue to push out the boundaries of the reform programme and create new successes to match the old.

First, however, we need to complete the task of creating an enterprise culture in business. Two areas stand out as major anomalies in the economic reform programme. One is the producer boards. The other is the government's continued ownership of a large number of SOEs.

PRODUCER BOARDS

If our government set out today to design agricultural marketing arrangements from scratch, it is extremely unlikely it would come up with the current structures for producer boards. To enter the world of New Zealand's producer boards is to enter a world of distorting mirrors, where the normal market relationships between price and quantity, investment and return do not apply. It is a world where competition with outsiders is severely rationed, where it is allowed at all. Yet such is the tyranny of the status quo that any suggestion that agricultural marketing might benefit from substantially greater competition, or that farmers might prefer to receive proper market signals for their activities, is met with derision from the producer boards, and blank incomprehension and fierce resistance from many farmers.

The producer boards are strange beasts. First, they have a large degree of monopoly power. Some, such as the Dairy Board, are the sole agency empowered to purchase the farmer's product and sell it on world markets. Others do not have the sweeping powers of a 'single-desk seller', but do have the power to license exporters. Yet everything we know about the importance of competition suggests such arrangements are unlikely to produce the best outcomes. Competition breeds ideas, and in the battle of ideas, good ideas tend to win out over bad. All our experience of the reform programme suggests competition brings improved performance, from better air services to cheaper clothing.

Producer boards, naturally enough, claim no-one could do a better job than they are currently doing. So long as they face no competition they will not be contradicted. The same claim was made by many a government trading organisation, protected manufacturer or licensed operator in the old days. We discovered how hollow those claims were. If producer boards think they can beat all comers there is a simple test for that hypothesis: the market.

Not only are producer boards to a greater or lesser extent commercial monopolies, but many boards are themselves regulators of the industry they dominate. One of the themes of the New Zealand reform programme has been the separation of commercial from regulatory activities – and for good reason. The incentives faced by a regulator will be hugely affected if they have a commercial interest themselves in the regulations they are making. A regulator should consider the total public welfare, including all the second-round and flow-on effects of a regulation – not just the welfare of one interest group. If the regulator happens to be that interest group, one would need to be a Pollyanna of superhuman faith in human nature to imagine regulation would be undertaken even-handedly. Giving producer boards power to regulate is like asking the old, unreconstructed Manufacturers' Federation to set tariff policy.

The monopoly and regulatory powers of producer boards have seriously discouraged new ideas and new investment in agriculture. They have been particularly serious in discouraging foreign investment. The flow of foreign investment into manufacturing, retailing, tourism, forestry, transport and many other sectors has been an important element in New Zealand's economic transformation. It has not happened in agriculture and horticulture, and these sectors are undoubtedly the poorer.

The third and most bizarre feature of our producer boards is their unique organisational form. Typically, the farmer is both a supplier to the producer board and an implicit equity-holder in the board's wide range of commercial activities. Yet the dairy farmer, for instance, is paid purely through a single payout on the basis of milk supplied to the Dairy Board. The payout to the farmer is a 'bundled' average return from a wide range of activities: his or her on-farm investment and a variety of off-farm investments. This bundling of returns can, and almost certainly does, produce serious resource misallocation. Imagine if the equity-holders in Fletcher Challenge were the same people who supplied Fletcher Challenge with logs, and that both the return to equity and the return to the logs were paid in a single payment as a price per log. No-one would call that an efficient economic arrangement.

It is inefficient because such an arrangement will probably give quite misleading signals to suppliers. Producing milk and marketing milk and other products are quite different activities. A farmer's investment in the production of milk should be determined by the return on producing milk, not the return on other activities. Under current arrangements, if the Dairy Board has a good year in the wide range of other activities it is involved in, such as selling Belarus Russian tractors, dairy farmers will take this – other things being equal – as a signal to produce more milk. If the Dairy Board has a bad year in its other activities, dairy farmers will produce less milk. That is plainly nonsensical. At the same time, dairy farmers have little information by which to assess whether their investment in the board's processing and marketing activities is earning a decent return. If they decide it is not earning a return, there is no way in which they can transfer their equity holding to someone else – short of ceasing to be a milk supplier at all. Normal market disciplines simply do not apply.

Those advocating reform of producer boards are often told a single seller is necessary in order to maximise price. But that is to vastly overestimate the degree of market power possessed by our pastoral products. We are largely price-takers in almost all the markets we sell to. We face a high degree of competition, and it is unlikely competitive forces will lessen in the years ahead. In such circumstances, inhibiting competition among New Zealand sellers is both pointless and harmful. In the small number of cases – such as the British butter quota where there is a market rent for New Zealand as a whole to capture, alternative arrangements could capture the rent in a more efficient manner. The British butter quota, for instance, should be put up for tender.

The idea that New Zealand producers need to band together in order to be a 'strong seller' was a major concern back in the inter-war years when many of the producer boards were established, and remains a strong sentiment among farmers today. Yet it demonstrates a misunderstanding of the nature of market forces. To many farmers, unfettered competition will lead to their being repeatedly ripped off by processing and marketing industries further down the chain. It is a view of the market one expects to hear coming from the Council of Trade Unions or a left-wing academic, but not from New Zealand farmers. Ironically, farmers have been happy to urge unfettered market forces on other areas of the New Zealand economy, while considering themselves to be immune from the logic of such arguments.

Major reform is required if New Zealand is to capitalise best on its strong natural advantage in meat, dairy, wool and other land-based products. First, producer boards should be reorganised along more conventional corporate lines. In political terms this would be the easiest step to take. The equity in the boards would be given to farmers, thus separating out the return on a farmer's investment in downstream activities from the return from on-farm investment. Farmers would then face a more rational set of price signals. The equity in the new structures should be tradable between farmers; there is no reason at all why every farmer should necessarily wish to hold shares in a company undertaking downstream activities. The logic is also strong for allowing the purchase of shares by third parties. Listing on the sharemarket would provide a much improved set of disciplines on management and boards.

In tandem with restructuring the producer boards, all of the boards' activities should be fully opened up to competition. The regulatory functions of the boards should be abolished, and agriculture made subject to broadly the same regulatory disciplines as other industries. The Commerce Act should apply to the successor corporates of producer boards, and to new entrants into the market. Research and development of a 'public good' nature undertaken by producer boards could be maintained by producer board successors and their competitors bidding for funds from the contestable pool for public-sector science. As a second source of funding for research and development, the industry has the power to levy itself under the Commodities Levies Act. The farming industry would continue to be subject to standard regulations on hygiene. However, it would not be able to self-regulate for 'quality control'. There is no reason why all industry players should necessarily wish to meet the same quality standards. The question of which market niches to aim for is best left in the hands of individual producers and marketers.

These initiatives would hugely improve the environment for the processing and marketing of agricultural products. Currently the primary sector is flagging in its performance. If these trends continue, non-commodity manufactured exports will soon overtake the traditional trio of meat, wool and dairy exports. Psychologically, this could be an important moment. Despite having believed for generations that they are 'the backbone of the country', the news for New Zealand's farmers will be that – statistically speaking – the townies are out in front.

Producer board reform is so long overdue that one might well ask why it has not already happened. One reason is that producer boards are extremely effective lobbyists. When Australian economist Denis Hussey, in association with the New Zealand Business Roundtable, recently produced his lengthy and cogently argued study of the industry problems, the reaction from the boards was precisely what we have come to expect: rage, a great deal of declamation from high horses, protestations that Hussey did not know what he was talking about – everything except an attempt to meet Hussey's arguments in a rational fashion .

Another reason for the endurance of producer boards is that for generations they have been an article of faith for New Zealand farmers. Faith is the operative word, because logic has rarely entered into it. National, as the farmers' party, has reflected this deeply ingrained instinct. There is no doubt that producer board reform would face opposition from many farmers and near-hysterical opposition from the boards themselves. As Finance Minister I would have dearly loved to push reform into this area. Yet Jim, Bill, Agriculture Minister John Falloon and even his associate minister, Denis Marshall, were all solidly in favour of producer boards. I would have received some support from the lower ranks of Cabinet, but the key people were all against me.

Ironically, Bill, judging by his recent speeches, may now be waking up to the merits of reform. His conversion, however, came too late for the two of us to form a Cabinet coalition on the issue.

The best political chance for producer board reform probably came under Roger Douglas. Since farmers were not Labour's political constituency, there was perhaps a greater likelihood a reforming Labour government would grasp the nettle. Whatever the reason, Douglas – like me – could not muster the numbers around the Cabinet table. Yet I still live in hope that some government, before too long, will initiate producer board reform, even if it begins simply by corporatising the boards and making the shares tradable between farmers. Such a policy, scarcely objectionable in itself, might produce some very interesting political and economic dynamics, particularly if – as I suspect – farmers find that some of their investments in the new corporate structures are earning less than spectacular returns.

FURTHER PRIVATISATION

Producer boards remain the largest area of uncompleted business in microeconomic reform. But they are not the only area. In recent times the privatisation programme has become decidedly half-hearted and needs to be accelerated.

I have always regarded SOEs as constituting an intermediate phase in the reform programme. As an Opposition politician I sometimes referred to SOEs as 'corporate transvestites – all tarted up in private-sector clothes but with the same old state body underneath'. Though this line usually got a laugh, the initial gains to corporatisation were admittedly considerable. The next step for most remaining SOEs, however, must be their transfer to private-sector ownership. So long as businesses remain owned by the government, there will be a tension between the ambitions of management and the preferences of the Crown. Managers generally wish to undertake new investment, diversify their operations and pursue often aggressive business strategies. The Crown is reluctant to provide new capital, and naturally wishes to minimise business risk. Nor does Crown ownership and monitoring provide the same market discipline as shares freely tradable on the stock exchange.

There is an additional reason why we should press ahead with privatisation. The danger of SOE policy going backwards increases the longer SOEs remain in public ownership. There are all manner of political temptations for a government to fall into: political board appointments; overly aggressive or lax dividend policy; interference in pricing. We have already seen some slippage in board appointments and in pricing policy under the Bolger government. Jim has never become completely comfortable with the SOE model; part of him still hankers after a greater degree of ministerial control. Perhaps this unease is reflected in his having already gone through four SOE ministers. If even our 'conservative', supposedly pro-business government has an ambivalent attitude toward SOEs, the risks will be all the greater from political parties further to the left.

The government should press ahead to privatise New Zealand Post, Landcorp, Workscorp, Timberlands West Coast and the Forestry Corporation. The electricity generating industry should be privatised. The natural monopoly of Transpower should be separated into balanced club ownership where both producers and distributors are represented. Coalcorp should be privatised once its associated Treaty issues are resolved. There is no reason why Television New Zealand and Radio New Zealand should be left in state hands; in a free society the proper place for the media is the private sector. The Crown's interests in airports could also be sold. The regulatory regime governing ports should be addressed, so as to make it easier for regional authorities to divest themselves of their port company holdings.

There is also the large equity holding – some $2 billion – tied up in the rental housing SOE. Some voluntary sales of state houses to their tenants are already proceeding. However, with the government's social objectives continuing to be met through the accommodation supplement, there is no reason to prevent the sale of the whole of the Crown's rental housing stock. By placing the rental business in the private sector, where it belongs, we would also be making it much harder for a future government to reinstate the old, inequitable and inefficient system under which state house tenants in fact received a better deal than equally deserving people in the private sector.

REDESIGNING WELFARE

The government should by all means push on with microeconomic reforms to farming and industry. But for me the biggest agenda lies elsewhere: in social welfare, in education and training, and in completing the reforms to the labour market. It lies in rethinking what we really mean when we talk about income distribution. It requires asking some extremely basic questions that in the past have been too little asked by New Zealand policymakers. What constitutes well-being? What is a government really trying to achieve when it makes a social policy intervention? How do we measure whether a government is succeeding or failing in its objective?

In the past, too much of the debate on the welfare state has been couched simply in terms of its affordability. I would be the last to deny that affordability is an important consideration. We can never forget that it is wealth creation that enables social services to be funded. The requirement to support a welfare state dulls the incentives driving the creation of wealth. It results in reduced work effort from taxpayers, and from many of those in a position to capture the benefits of the welfare state. There is reduced private-sector investment. There is also an artificial reduction in household savings, further reducing capital formation and economic growth. The exact magnitude of these effects is highly uncertain. What is certain is that they exist, are substantial, and are ignored by policymakers at their peril.

But to argue merely over the affordability of the welfare state is to assume far too much. It assumes that the welfare state is a 'good thing', and that the only discussion we can have is over how much of a good thing we can afford. That begs a huge number of questions. Sadly, the public debate over the trimming of welfare in 1991 rarely got beyond the question of 'affordability'. At the time affordability was certainly a powerful argument running in favour of the government. It was this argument that persuaded many – perhaps even most New Zealanders – that the benefit cuts were justified. Yet the more acute commentators noticed something of a difference in rhetoric between Jenny and myself on the one hand, and most other ministers – including Jim – on the other. Jenny and I were more likely than Jim to talk about the benefit cuts in moralistic terms. We were certainly not oblivious to the question of affordability, but equally we saw the cuts as a statement about the types of lives people should be encouraged to lead, about the types of activities that should be more highly valued, about personal responsibility and integrity.

The welfare state has become so ingrained in the New Zealand psyche, and its benign effects so widely assumed, that it almost sounds 'extreme' to question the reality of those benign effects. Yet the essence of sound public policy is a preparedness to critically evaluate existing assumptions and existing institutions. And the most cursory examination of the welfare state would suggest that over the past generation it has gone badly wrong. It set out to reduce poverty and ended up increasing poverty. It set out to provide a safety net and ended up creating a dependent underclass. It set out to reduce income inequality and ended up increasing inequality. It set out to allow people to live in dignity, and ended up creating ghettos where lawlessness and hopelessness are rife. If that is success, its ways must be mysterious indeed.

Back in 1990 I repeatedly drew attention to the huge rise in dependency that had taken place since the early 1970s. Numbers on the unemployment benefit had risen enormously. Almost as spectacular had been the rise in domestic purposes benefits (DPB). Numbers on the DPB had more than quintupled since 1975, and by 1990 stood at around 90,000. Even numbers on the sickness benefit had more than doubled over the same 15-year period. It defied all common sense that New Zealanders had become more than twice as unhealthy over that time. Yet the welfare statistics would have had us believe so.

Now, five years later, the dependency problem appears as intractable as ever. The numbers on the unemployment benefit – though still very high – are at least heading down. But the numbers on the DPB, after an initial check following the benefit cuts, are on the rise again and have topped 100,000. New Zealanders still seem to be categorising themselves as sick or injured in escalating numbers. The rise in numbers on the sickness benefit shows no sign of abating, while accident compensation payouts set new records annually.

The superficial answer, often heard from critics of the government, is that the increase in dependency results from 'uncaring' government policy – and specifically the market reforms of the past decade. Yet there is very little evidence for this view. All the upward trends in numbers of social welfare beneficiaries were firmly established by 1984. In my maiden speech, back in 1981, I was already pointing to the rising cost of welfare. Long periods of economic recession have certainly played their part in adding to beneficiary numbers. But the state of the general economy cannot be the whole of the explanation. The rise in numbers on the DPB is remarkably unresponsive to the state of the business cycle. Today, four years into a strong economic expansion, DPB numbers show no sign of having peaked.

Our system of social welfare benefits is substantially a 'categorical' one. If you can persuade the bureaucrats that you fall into a certain category, you can receive a benefit indefinitely – so long as you remain in that category. There is little follow-up from Social Welfare. If you stay unemployed, you keep receiving the unemployment benefit. If you continue to be a non-working sole parent, you continue to receive the DPB. If you stay 'sick', you continue to receive the sickness benefit. What the designers of our social security system did not sufficiently appreciate were the strong incentives our categorical benefits would create for people to alter their circumstances, either to become eligible for a benefit or to remain eligible for a benefit.

It is in the case of the DPB that our categorical benefit system has had the most serious social consequences. The DPB was intended as a short-term benefit to assist a limited number of sole parents, who for one reason or another had been left without a partner. Yet its effect was almost the opposite. Instead of alleviating poverty, it created a new underclass of dependants – sole parents. Worse, it ended up increasing the number of children growing up poor and disadvantaged.

Like many social policies, the introduction of the DPB affected social behaviour in a way that was to have deep and undesirable consequences. It substantially altered the incentives and moral sanctions surrounding human relationships and child-rearing. For men, the DPB made it easier to be more casual about family ties. Suddenly, abandoning one's family became a far less costly exercise. The DPB reduced the expected financial cost; just as important, it reduced the cost of social disapproval. For women, the DPB also meant they had less at stake when investing in a relationship. For both men and women who were casual about relationships and careless about the consequences in the form of any child that might follow, personal irresponsibility was officially sanctioned.

Twenty years down the track we can see the consequences. By making it supposedly 'easier' for the parents, we have undoubtedly made it worse for the children. Far more children today are brought up in sole-parent households, and there are also far more children in families where there has never been a father. In a few short years we have created an underclass that shows every sign of being self-perpetuating. Children of sole parents disproportionately become sole parents themselves; we are already into our second generation of welfare dependency.

One of the huge disadvantages of our categorical benefit system is that it tempts people into making short-term choices that seem rational to them at the time, but that turn out to have serious long-term consequences. This is particularly so for the young, the unsophisticated and the low-skilled. The DPB for young unmarried mothers is an obvious case. So, too, is the unemployment benefit. This, like the DPB, can be paid indefinitely so long as the recipient continues to meet the eligibility criteria. Like the DPB, the unemployment benefit has major behavioural consequences. To a low-skilled, low-motivated individual, taking the unemployment benefit in preference to a low-paying, perhaps unpleasant job may seem rational at the time the choice is made, but it can trap them into a cycle of poverty, dependency and continued low motivation.

For most people on the unemployment benefit it is not true, in a strictly literal sense, that they cannot find a job. If their lives depended upon it, most unemployed people would find jobs in short order. In most cases, people remain unemployed because they are searching for a type of work, or for a level of remuneration, that they have not yet found. A person's job search often necessarily involves a downward adjustment of their expectations regarding the quality of job they can secure in the marketplace. This adjustment, if the gap in expectations is large, can be a difficult process.

Most people passing through the unemployment register do find the work they want, or manage to adjust their expectations satisfactorily, and move off the register in the course of a few months. Some, however, fail to make the mental adjustment into the world of work, and become long-term dependants. By so doing, they cut themselves off from their key route to advancement: a job in the marketplace. They deny themselves by far the most important type of training: on-the-job training. They deny themselves a record of work experience, and they lose motivation the longer they are unemployed. It might well be objected that this is their choice. That is undoubtedly true. But the question we need to be asking is: should the state be subsidising bad choices?

Having trapped people into dependency, our current policy regime further discourages workplace participation by imposing high effective marginal tax rates (EMTRs) on those seeking to shift off welfare. The shift is especially difficult for those wishing to move off the DPB. Not only do they generally face high EMTRs, those with young children have the added problem of the cost of childcare.

The situation in some of our urban ghettos today may seem desperate. But it would be quite wrong to take a fatalistic attitude to it. Many people once took a similarly fatalistic attitude to our long economic decline. Yet bad public policy had largely been responsible for that decline. As soon as enough people recognised what had gone wrong, we could go about designing better public policy, thinking issues through from first principles. The economic reforms made a huge difference, despite being roundly written off in many quarters as too radical. The same goes for the problem of our underclass. The first step is admit to ourselves that current policies are not working. There is then no reason why better-designed policies cannot make a difference. But to design better policies we need clear thinking and a minimum of preconceptions. We need to go back to first principles. We need to ask ourselves this question: what are really trying to achieve in social policy?

Every person will probably give a slightly different answer. I like to think of social policy in terms of 'personal well-being'. Obviously, material well-being is an important component of personal well-being. But it is far from being the only component, or even the most important. The satisfaction we derive from our work or other activities we engage in, the quality of our relationships with others, and the range of choices available to us are all key components of our well-being.

Well-being is an active concept – not a passive one. It will not do to think of human beings as essentially inert creatures, passively awaiting a range of socially engineered satisfactions. None of us, if we are honest, thinks of our own lives like that. And few of us, when we consider others, think that life in general is like that. Life is much richer, more complex, and more dynamic.

We know that all lives are lived actively, and that it is largely the process of living that imparts the satisfactions to be derived. A person's quality of life is far more a product of their self-esteem than it is of their bank balance, and self-esteem comes from realising one's capacities. It comes from earning a living, taking responsibility and meeting a challenge. It comes from successfully raising a family. It comes from standing on one's own feet while keeping one's integrity intact.

There are two concepts of key importance. One is control, the other is choice. Everything I have learned about human nature tells me that being in control of events is fundamental to well-being. Where people feel they have a high degree of personal control, there is a much higher chance that they will derive satisfaction from their lives. Control means 'ownership' in the widest sense of word. People in control feel they can influence the world around them and shape their destiny. For a person in control it is their job, their family, their friends, their lives.

Choice, too, is fundamental for well-being. All of us are different, with a huge variety of needs, capacities and preferences. Each of us knows more about our own circumstances than any other person does. The more choice we have, consistent with the rights of others, the more closely will we realise our well-being.

There is a poverty of debate in New Zealand today about the real goals of social policy. Too often it is implicitly assumed that the main object of social policy is to alter the pattern of incomes. Overwhelmingly, the social policy debate today is about whether current incomes are fair. Income adequacy is part of that debate, and a legitimate part. But most of the debate concerns the distribution of income. It is taken for granted that an object of government policy is to bring about a more 'equitable' distribution of income. Precisely why that should be such an important object is rarely explained. If statistics come out seeming to show that, in a static sense, income inequalities have widened, a predictable debate takes place. Commentators and the parliamentary Opposition use the information to condemn the government. The government, for its part, often plays down the accuracy of the statistics or claims government policy will address the problem. Both sides treat widening income disparities as a problem.

Yet to me this is one of the most arid debates we could have. The overall distribution of incomes, in a static sense, has very little relevance to issues of well-being and how a government might improve well-being. First, because it is not true to assume the rich are rich because the poor are poor. As we know, any attempt by a government to redistribute income away from the highest earners will lower the average income available to all. Second, a snapshot of income differentials at one point in time fails completely to capture the dynamics of changing incomes over time. These changes can be very considerable. Viewing income distribution in a life-cycle context can have radically different implications.

Even in the limited context of static income distribution, current social policy can be seen as failing. By locking people into dependency, it keeps them on low incomes. In the wider context of any meaningful definition of well-being, current social policy fails even more clearly. It erodes the degree of control people have over their own lives; it erodes self-esteem; it takes away choices.

We need to substitute a new approach to social policy. The theme of the new approach would be personal opportunity combined with personal responsibility. It would be based on empowering the individual yet holding that individual more responsible for their actions. It would be designed to encourage New Zealanders to take more control over their own lives, while better equipping them to that end. It would be concerned, not with the static distribution of income, but with the income mobility. That means changing the incentive structures facing individuals in a way that encourages mobility. It also means strongly encouraging the development of human capital.

Action is needed in two key areas: we need to redesign the welfare state, and we need to boost the quality of education and training available to New Zealanders, especially to the least advantaged. A third task also awaits us: we need to complete the liberalisation of the labour market that National largely accomplished but left unfinished. All of these initiatives would be aimed at equipping New Zealanders for workforce participation and ending the cycle of dependency.

The unemployment benefit should cease to be an open-ended payment. It has a legitimate role to play as support for those who are out of work temporarily. Its purpose is readying people for re-entry into the workforce. It has no role in supporting unemployment as a permanent lifestyle choice. Six months is the maximum length of time the state can reasonably be expected to pay unemployment benefit to any person. It gives ample time for unemployed people to assess options in the labour market and find a job that suits them. Beyond six months the only payment available should be an emergency benefit for those with children. The emergency benefit should be strictly work-tested. It should not be seen as merely an extension of unemployment benefit, and going onto the emergency benefit should not be seen as merely a cosmetic shift.

Imposing a time limit for unemployment benefit would not be without overseas precedent. Should such a limit be set, it is also possible a market would develop offering insurance for unemployment. We take out insurance for many contingencies that we do not expect to come about, but that nevertheless may occur. Unemployment is another such contingency. If there is a substantial demand for unemployment insurance, there is no reason why a market could not develop.

The DPB also needs to be rethought. There should be no automatic assumption that the DPB is a permanent benefit. We should also distinguish between a genuine family breakdown and the situation where there has never been an established partnership between the parents of the child. In the latter case, where the sole parent has had no relationship in the nature of a marriage with the father of the child, the benefit should not be available. We have been following the previous path for far too long, and its social consequences are all too evident. By paying the DPB in these circumstances, we have sent all the wrong signals about responsibility in personal relations. It has to stop. Thus a young, unmarried mother who had not been in an established partnership, under my proposal would be entitled only to the unemployment benefit, on exactly the same conditions as everyone else. In addition, a sole parent with children from an earlier marriage or de facto relationship, who had an additional child outside an established relationship, would not be eligible for extra monetary assistance for that child.

As early as the December Initiative in 1990, the National government declared an intention to work-test sole parents whose children were old enough for the parents to reasonably undertake at least part-time work. The government's proposal was to work-test those sole parents whose youngest child was seven or over. The sole parent would be required to be available for paid work of at least 20 hours per week, or to be undertaking some form of work-related training. Sole parents of older children would thus have been required either to be participating in the workforce or readying themselves for work. Despite further discussion of this idea in the 1991 budget, the government eventually backed off. When Jenny took her detailed proposals for benefit reform to Cabinet in 1992, she received a rebuff. Jim was among those least enthusiastic about work-testing sole parents. The high level of unemployment, which was then close to its peak, was an important factor with ministers. So was a feeling from Jim and others that the government had undertaken quite enough controversial social policy measures for its first term in office. The idea died and has not been resurrected.

I believed then, and believe now, that such a work test is long overdue. It is particularly appropriate now in view of the much stronger labour market conditions than existed during National's early period in office. Rather than imposing the work test when the youngest child is seven, I would bring it down to five – the age at which the child starts school. This is the point where the demands on the parent are reduced considerably and it is reasonable to require them to be available for work or training.

The government should continue to enforce a child-support payment from the non-custodial parent. The child-support regime embodies an extremely important principle – that a parent's obligations do not stop simply because he or she leaves the household.

In order to further encourage workforce participation, we need to substantially reduce, where possible, the high effective marginal tax rates faced by many beneficiaries. By far the best method of doing this is to cut marginal rates of income tax. Once government debt has been reduced to a responsible level, we should make it a priority to cut marginal rates. We should eventually aim to introduce a flat rate of income tax. A flat rate was a good idea in 1987, and it remains a good idea today.

There are other initiatives the government should undertake in the welfare area. One is to tighten up the eligibility for the sickness benefit. The huge and continuing rise in the number of sickness beneficiaries suggests something is badly wrong with its administration. It takes only one doctor to certify a person as eligible. Doctors do not bear the cost of their decisions; the taxpayer does. It would take only a small number of 'soft touch' doctors greatly to expand numbers on the benefit, which appears to be what has happened. The state is entitled to a second opinion.

Having muffed its opportunity properly to reform accident compensation in 1991, the government, if it wishes, can keep the costs of accident compensation within reasonable bounds. Like the sickness benefit, this is an area where the medical profession has been given far too free a rein, with little or no incentive to contain costs. We need to re-establish some rationality in the debate and rediscover a sense of proportion. The Accident Compensation Corporation processes well over a million claims annually. Around 80 per cent of these are for injuries requiring fewer than three medical treatments: these cost $1.1 billion out of the annual cost of the entire scheme of $1.7 billion. Yet there is a vast difference between a traumatic long-term injury and the very large number of short-term injuries, often sustained on the sports field, that are occasions for rich and poor alike to dip into the public purse. For short-term injuries there should be a much greater degree of self-insurance. There should also be much more equal treatment of sickness and injury. These were the themes National had developed prior to the 1990 election. We should revive them.

By far the largest item of government spending is our state pension scheme. Successive governments have taken important steps – at considerable political cost – to trim the worst excesses of national superannuation. Our scheme is no longer the extravagant model employed by Muldoon to woo the voters 20 years ago. We have bought ourselves a breathing space. But national superannuation as presently constituted still risks placing an unsustainable burden on the working population in the longer term. A graph published with the 1994 budget, showing the fiscal implications of New Zealand's ageing population, makes ominous reading. From early next century the costs will begin increasing, and are expected to rise steeply from around the year 2020. Currently the proportion of the population aged over 65 is less than 12 per cent. By the year 2031 that proportion is expected to be 19.5 per cent. Clearly, we have a limited period of time in which to fashion a superannuation scheme that will be viable for long into the next century.

Faced with looming demographic pressures, some advocate a scheme funded by compulsory savings. I believe this would be a mistake. Compulsory savings would be a tax by another name and would cut across one of our cardinal principles of economic management: maximum freedom of choice. A compulsory scheme would also have many practical drawbacks. It would require a large and expensive bureaucracy. It would also inevitably be too prescriptive of the form in which people prepare for their retirement. Many younger people prefer to save by initially paying off a mortgage. Others may regard the acquisition of human capital as a viable form of preparation for retirement, by increasing expected lifetime earnings. Compulsory superannuation schemes also raise issues of 'moral hazard'. Whether to place a government guarantee on retirement funds is a question with no wholly satisfactory answer. If the funds are guaranteed, the incentives facing the managers of those funds are severely weakened. If they are not guaranteed, a fund that strikes financial trouble poses a real dilemma for the government.

Over the next few years we should move instead to place the existing state superannuation scheme onto a more sustainable footing. We could go a long way towards that end by further raising, over a period of time, the age of entitlement to superannuation. With modern nutrition and medicine, the age at which the average New Zealander begins to feel that he or she is 'past' working continues to rise. If they have no specific physical ailment, most 65-year-olds still have the energy and the capacity to work. I believe it will soon be appropriate to raise the age of entitlement for superannuation to 70.

We should also move to improve the robustness of the targeting mechanism for national superannuation. At the moment there is widespread avoidance of the surcharge by wealthy individuals through the use of unit trusts and other mechanisms. This is perceived as unfair and leads to considerable revenue leakage. The government is well aware of the problem, but so far has shrunk from the political consequences of introducing anti-avoidance legislation. Avoidance activity can only increase as the population ages. National superannuation should be established as a social welfare benefit, targeted on family income, and the government should be aggressive in policing the new benefit. In many overseas jurisdictions there are asset tests for state pensions, or deemed income is applied. We should introduce provisions for deeming income in New Zealand, just as it is applied in Australia. We should also resume the indexation of national superannuation solely to the CPI.

Just as we should endeavour to put the gains in housing policy beyond reversal, so we should push on with our market reforms to the health system. Two developments are needed both to maximise the benefits from the reforms and to make it substantially more difficult for a future government to reimpose an inefficient, producer-driven system. First, we should privatise Crown health enterprises. There is no reason at all for CHEs to remain in the hands of the Crown. All the government's social objectives in health care can be met through the regional health authorities contracting with health providers – that is the role of the RHAs. Their task would not be compromised if most of the providers were in the private sector: some providers are already in the private sector.

Retaining CHEs in the public sector has two major disadvantages. First, with CHEs unable to become bankrupt, there is significantly reduced incentive to perform to maximum efficiency. Second, it increases the risk that bad commercial habits will be allowed – or encouraged – by politicians to creep back into the running of CHEs. The sale of CHEs would constitute National's most ambitious privatisation, and undoubtedly would be a complex undertaking. But the logic of the reforms leads us in that direction. Before sale, the CHEs should be set up as genuine SOEs. Once in the private sector there should be no presumption that a CHE cannot fall over, though a failing CHE would quite likely be quickly taken over or merged with another. It would be up to the RHA to ensure that, by their purchase contracts, health services continued to be supplied to the region affected.

Our second initiative for completing the health reforms should be to allow individuals and groups to opt out from under the umbrella of their RHA. We should revisit the 1991 budget proposal, dropped subsequently by the government, to allow New Zealanders to take their share of RHA funding and invest it in a health-care plan in the private sector. Those with higher health costs could be permitted to take with them a larger-than-average share of funding. Plans would provide a complete health service for their clients, and would be regulated by the government.

We already have an infant private-sector market in health care in New Zealand. I am confident it would expand considerably if we allowed genuine contestability. By allowing genuine choice and competition, we would be putting in place a dynamic that led over time to substantially improved health services.

EDUCATION: MAKING THE CONSUMER SOVEREIGN

Reform of the welfare state will place greater incentives on New Zealanders to move off welfare into work. However, in equipping New Zealanders to participate as productive members of the workforce, the quality of New Zealand's education system remains crucial. Just as we have successfully achieved excellence in economic policy, I believe we should aim to make our education sector the best in the western world.

Education is a notoriously difficult area in which to make progress on public policy. Like health, there has been a high degree of provider capture. The teacher unions are one of the most recalcitrant special-interest groups confronting the government. Any initiative involving greater accountability for teachers is greeted with extreme hostility bordering on obstruction. In this environment Lockwood Smith has made a good fist of a very hard portfolio. But despite his efforts, we have a great distance to travel if the education sector is to perform to its full potential.

For most of the postwar period in New Zealand there was low participation in both tertiary and higher secondary education, despite few barriers to access at either level. Low participation mainly reflected the type of economy New Zealand had become. The insulated nature of the economy and the bizarre logic of our industrial relations system meant skills were comparatively little rewarded in the marketplace. After 1984, however, the incentives facing young New Zealanders began to change rapidly. Not surprisingly, over the past decade there has been a strong increase in participation at higher education levels.

There has not, however, been a remotely commensurate increase in the quality of education produced by our schools and universities. Some advances have been made by the National government. The introduction of voluntary bulk-funding of schools, the design of a national curriculum and new assessment procedures, and the moves to better integrate school and training programmes have all been important initiatives. But their impact has been limited, given the institutional structures that operate in the education sector.

Education in New Zealand is largely a government monopoly. The percentage of children attending private schools is low by international standards, while the university sector is almost wholly government-run. At all levels the system is heavily centralised and unresponsive to consumer requirements. It is difficult to know just how effective our education system is, since educators are rarely in a hurry to see their performance evaluated. However, there is little drive for excellence in education, and every reason to believe we could considerably boost our performance. Since the 1960s, various briefly fashionable North American fads have swept our schools, usually with the same palpably deficient results they achieved in the United States. Excessive emphasis by educators on social engineering is as much a feature in New Zealand as in many countries elsewhere in the English-speaking world. The huge numbers of first-year university students requiring remedial English is a standing reproach to a school system that cannot, by the time they are 18, satisfactorily teach many of our brightest young people how to use our most basic cultural tool: the English language.

As in so many areas of social delivery, it is the upper-income groups who capture the greatest advantage from the state-run education system. While low-income areas receive a greater share of resources, the overall quality of schools remains much higher in high-income areas.

Educators are among the least accountable professions in New Zealand today. Pay and conditions remain centrally negotiated; there is no performance pay; a teacher can rise 10 steps on the pay scale simply by teaching for a sufficient number of years. A poor teacher has to be appallingly bad before he or she faces the sack. Our universities mirror the system of tenure found in most countries overseas. In short, industrial relations throughout the education sector remain stuck in a time-warp that looks increasingly at odds with the new labour market climate throughout the rest of the economy.

Recognising the highly centralised structures applying in education, the Lange Labour government introduced reforms to devolve power to local schools. Each school is now run by a board of trustees, most of whom are parents of children at the school. However well motivated, Labour's reforms took in practice precisely the wrong approach. There had been a widespread feeling that parents did not have enough control over their children's education. What parents really needed was greater control as consumers. Instead, Labour's reforms gave them greater control – at least in theory – as producers of education. There is a huge difference. As consumers, most parents can tell a good school from a bad school. It is not nearly so obvious that parents have a comparative advantage in producing education. In fact, there is every reason to believe parents have no such advantage. They are not education professionals – indeed, many parents run the risk of becoming captives of the teaching staff of their school. What parents would like is to be able to exercise choice over which professionals they entrust their children to.

I have taken a close interest in education policy ever since I was given the job of education spokeswoman during National's first term in Opposition. Labour's Education Minister was then Russell Marshall, who epitomised many of the woollier trends in educational thinking. My own philosophy was in considerable contrast to Marshall's. National's education policy stressed the teaching of core skills, the importance of regular and objective assessment methods, and more accountability from teachers. The theme of our policy was excellence in education. There was a clear brand difference between the two sides: surveys taken at the time showed education as one of the few areas where National was besting the government in the eyes of the public. My philosophical allies in the Labour Party confessed in private to me that they would have dearly liked a similar hard-headedness in the government's own education policy.

There was one idea, however, that I could not persuade my caucus colleagues to adopt. That policy was education vouchers – the proposal to turn education into a consumers' market by giving to parents a voucher that could be spent on any educational institution of their choice.

In my advocacy of vouchers I met from colleagues the familiar failure of political nerve that has so far defeated almost all efforts by market liberals around the world to introduce vouchers on a wide scale. The palpitations are understandable enough. Voucher proposals are anathema to the teacher unions, who vigorously oppose any attempt to have vouchers tested or introduced. There would also be major transitional issues to think through. Despite that, I remain convinced that we are unlikely to see significant progress in education in New Zealand until we give purchasing power directly to parents. All other change is a distant second-best: it has to be imposed from the top down, meeting with all sorts of obstruction.

The idea of giving purchasing power directly to parents, rather than investing in a monolithic state education system, is not new. John Stuart Mill, who saw a universal state-imposed education as social engineering, was making this point as long ago as 1859:

> Were the duty of enforcing universal education once admitted there would be an end to the difficulties about what the state should teach, and how it should teach, which now convert the subject into a mere battleground for sects and parties, causing the time and labour which should have been

> spent in educating to be wasted in quarrelling about education. If the government would make up its mind to require for every child a good education, it might save itself the trouble of providing one. It might leave to parents to obtain the education where and how they pleased, and content itself with helping to pay the school fees of the poorer classes of children, and defraying the entire school expenses of those who have no-one else to pay for them.
>
> The objections which are urged with reason against state education do not apply to the enforcement of education by the state, but to the state's taking upon itself to direct that education; which is a totally different thing. That the whole or any large part of the education of the people be in state hands, I go as far as anyone in deprecating. All that has been said about the importance of individuality of character, and diversity in opinions and modes of conduct, involves, as of the same unspeakable importance, diversity of education. A general state education is a mere contrivance for moulding people for being exactly like one another.

To Mill, the freedom of the individual was paramount. He naturally favoured a system that involved choice. And choice is one of the huge advantages of any scheme to give spending power to parents. All children are different. They have a wide range of backgrounds, aptitudes and inclinations. The more choice we give parents, the greater the chance a child will go to a school that meets his or her needs.

A voucher scheme would transform the New Zealand education system into a competitive market. In many other areas of the economy the injection of competition has markedly improved services – despite protestations that the service prior to competition was already efficient. There is little reason to believe education would be different. As in all competitive systems, diversity would allow stronger ideas to prevail over weaker. Many issues in education are a fierce battleground, from the correct method of teaching reading to the optimal size of classes. These are the inputs into the education process. The government need have no concern about prescribing for inputs. From the parents' point of view it is outputs that matter: how much their child is learning, how much their child is gaining in confidence and social development. Parents can observe most of those outputs directly, which is why they can choose a school for their child. It is only outputs that need concern the government.

The introduction of education vouchers would improve the quality of education throughout the state school system. But the biggest quality improvement would be seen in the education available to economically disadvantaged families whose parents take an interest in their children's education. At the moment this group is generally condemned to live in areas where property prices are lowest and the quality of state schools is at its worst. Despite the assurances of those defending the status quo, it is sheer cant to pretend these families are currently placed by the state in an equal situation to families in affluent neighbourhoods. Often the neighbourhood of a poor family is also becoming increasingly lawless. The ability of these families to use a voucher could radically transform the educational performance of their children. Yet currently they are completely denied that opportunity.

Various objections are made by the teaching profession whenever a voucher system is proposed. One objection is that parents are not sophisticated enough to choose their schools wisely. Such an attitude is hugely patronising. Its obnoxious élitism should be repugnant to anyone who believes that, in the main, people are entitled to make their own choices in life. A variant of this argument admits that better-off parents might be able to choose schools, but claims that the less sophisticated parents, i.e. those from the lower-income groups, are not capable. In this argument the paternalism is directed purely at the working class. The argument remains, of course, nonsense. It is undoubtedly true that some parents would not be very good at choosing schools, just as they are not good at bringing up their children in many other ways. But to pretend that most low-income parents are not capable of choosing schools is simply not credible.

The 'parents cannot be trusted' argument also betrays a fundamental misconception about the nature of competitive markets. For a competitive market to be of benefit to all – or nearly all – consumers, it is not necessary that all consumers be sophisticated: it is only necessary for enough consumers to be sophisticated. By shifting from product to product on the basis of price and quality, the sophisticated consumers keep all producers more honest. Thus, it is not necessary for a failing company to lose all its customers for it to receive a strong market signal that it needs to improve its performance; the company only needs to begin losing customers at the margin. It would be no different with education: vouchers would most likely improve the quality of education available to even the great majority of unsophisticated consumers.

Another argument against vouchers is that, because of the distances between schools, most children have little choice but to attend one school. If true, this argument would make education effectively a natural monopoly. However, with modern transport and an urban-based society, this argument certainly does not apply to the great majority of schools. There may be a few rural schools that are effectively natural monopolies. That does not constitute an argument against vouchers; it merely suggests that the organisational form of these schools should reflect their monopoly status. Clearly a profit-maximising company would not be an appropriate model in these instances. However, there are other options. The government could continue to run such schools directly, or communities could take their schools over and run them as non-profit trusts – probably the preferred option.

A third argument used by opponents of the voucher is that it would lead to a stratification of schools by socioeconomic group, race and other supposedly undesirable characteristics. This argument is particularly rich in view of the high degree of stratification built into our current system. At the bottom are the state schools for the urban ghettos; at the top are the small number of private schools for the genuinely wealthy. Almost certainly, vouchers would lead to much greater mixing of children from different backgrounds. The less well-off would be able to purchase private education, or an education in a different neighbourhood. Nor is it true that most New Zealanders want to separate themselves into ethnic and socio-economic enclaves. Some may, and they are entitled to, so long as they stay within the law on human rights. But the majority of New Zealanders are not instinctive segregationists. Most of us, given a choice, would want our children to attend schools that reflect, within reason, the main currents in New Zealand society.

A final argument advanced against vouchers is that the system would not cater for the most disadvantaged children – those with special problems and learning difficulties. Again, the opposite is probably closer to the truth. The parents of these children would now have purchasing power, and the market abhors a vacuum. For these children the government could add to the value of the voucher, or make some other appropriate arrangement.

In introducing a voucher system for New Zealand schools, it would be important to move on both sides of the ledger – funding and provision. At the moment funding and provision are merged; under a voucher system they would be separated. On the funding side all children would be provided with a voucher, which could be spent on purchasing education at any state or private school. Parents could, of course, supplement the voucher out of their own resources, where fees exceeded the value of the voucher. However, the voucher would be pitched at a level that would pay the fees for an average school. Simply by offering a voucher, we would expect to see almost immediately a big expansion in private education. Besides funding, the government would also be involved in setting standards in primary and secondary education. A core curriculum and nationwide examinations would be retained.

On the provider side we would be aiming to bring about a major cultural change. Schools that are largely producer-driven, with little customer focus, would need to become much more businesslike. However, since we do not as yet have a free market in education to observe in practice, we have little idea what the characteristics of a competitive market would be. Would there be large conglomerates or myriad single school enterprises? How much vertical or horizontal integration would there be? We can make only educated guesses a priori on such questions.

I suggest that those state schools not destined to become community trusts should be placed into a large SOE, or perhaps several regional SOEs. Just as most doctors are not business managers, so most teachers are not equipped to manage resources in an entrepreneurial fashion. The SOEs should be looking to inject private-sector entrepreneurship into those schools that are performing badly. Education entrepreneurs could be expected to purchase state-sector assets, or bid for franchises to run schools using state assets. The SOEs would have a strong incentive to match the quality of education provided in the private sector. They would have complete control in all dealings with their most important resource – teachers. If they chose, they could make staffing decisions, and conduct negotiations on salaries and conditions, at the level of the individual schools.

Once the system is in operation, with a mixture of state and private schools funded through the voucher, the next step would be for the government to gradually divest itself of all schools it owned. In conducting such a programme, the government could learn a great from observing developments in the private sector. The government would continue to play a crucial role as funder of education and as setter of standards.

At the tertiary level the argument for vouchers is just as strong as at the primary and secondary level. Tertiary institutions, like schools, have little incentive to be responsive to consumer needs. And because of the way fees are structured, students have equally little incentive to take into account costs when choosing courses. At the moment, students taking low-cost courses such as commerce and arts degrees receive a much smaller real level of subsidy than students taking high-cost courses such as medicine. Funding should instead go directly to the student, and the universities should be restructured along corporate lines. Tenure should be abolished. Universities would then charge fees that better reflected their real resource costs. This could also open the way for new private universities to compete with government institutions on a fair basis.

DOMINION

DOMINION

Resignation day, 14 July 1994. Andrew and I enjoying our new politics-free zone.

Selwyn stalwarts: (above, l-r) Lois Mulholland, Malvern Women's Group, Frances Smith, electorate secretary, Myra Graham, campaigner, Margaret Baylis, publicity officer; (below, l-r) Chris Charles, electorate treasurer, Bill Studholme, electorate chairman, Bill Taylor, campaign chairman.

Hazel Bull, my Selwyn electorate agent 1981-94.

Hamming it up with comedian Mark Wright at Aoraki's 'Champagne on the Lawn' immediately post-dumping.

JOHN McCOMBE

Rejoining the human race: a week after my resignation, with Andrew and our tame deer, who both approve.

EVENING POST

Home on the Range, late 1994. Preparing a computer-driven presentation on public-sector reform for Malaysia with a little help from our pet magpie.

THE ROAD TO FULL EMPLOYMENT

We have seen the huge gains, both in productivity growth and job creation, brought about by the Employment Contracts Act. The progress has been so encouraging it is tempting to become complacent about the structure of our new labour market. But in reality we have no grounds for complacency. Unemployment is still high in historical terms. The government can do more to bring about a labour market in which all New Zealanders have a chance to participate. It can remove the last major impediments to job creation. Doing so would be an important quid pro quo for tightening benefit eligibility. We cannot make increased demands on beneficiaries to move off dependency if there are regulations still in place preventing them from competing fairly in the labour market.

The most serious of these regulations is undoubtedly the minimum wage. It is an elementary economic law that a minimum wage, provided it is struck at a level that raises any wages, will have the byproduct of costing jobs. This follows from the laws of supply and demand. The jobs lost are those that are only profitable for the employer at a wage rate below the legal minimum. No employer will pay someone the minimum rate if their productivity does not justify that wage. The minimum wage thus raises the returns for some while freezing others out of the labour market altogether.

The victims of a minimum wage are inevitably those whose productivity is lowest: the young and the unskilled. These are the very people politicians profess to be most concerned about, yet a minimum wage is the worst policy if we are genuinely concerned about the welfare of this group, rather than simply being concerned to appear concerned. A minimum wage is also a particularly good example of a misconceived policy based on a view of the distribution of income in a static sense, rather than a dynamic sense. For the young unskilled person, there is no choice between high pay and low pay. The key choice is between obtaining their first job and failing to do so. Viewed in the context of the life-cycle, there is a huge difference between a young person getting their foot on the first rung of the employment ladder and failing to get a foothold. The first job is easily the most crucial, leading to on-the-job training and a valuable work record. Not allowing people that first chance is criminal.

Given their relative position in New Zealand society, Maori are especially disadvantaged by minimum-wage laws. Milton Friedman has repeatedly pointed out that the most anti-black law in the US is the minimum-wage law. A parallel statement can be made here: our most anti-Maori law is our minimum wage.

Far from abolishing the minimum wage, the government recently extended its scope. Until 1994, the minimum wage applied only to those aged 20 and over. Soon after the 1993 election, however, there was pressure from within caucus to extend it to those under 20 and Cabinet cravenly buckled under this pressure. It was a decision to which I made vigorous public objection.

As well as abolishing the minimum wage, we should take steps to combat the disturbingly high degree of judicial activism found in our courts on industrial relations issues. The Employment Court (formerly the Labour Court) has a long history of disregarding fundamental principles of contract law in its eagerness to introduce a variety of concepts of fairness. Like much judicial activism, the approach of the Employment Court comes with a downstream and largely hidden cost: the integrity of market processes. The uncertainty generated by the court in the minds of employers has undoubtedly flowed back to workers in the form of lower wages and fewer jobs. If truth be told, there is no need for a separate Employment Court at all. A separate jurisdiction only encourages judges to see labour market contracts as in some way different from other types of contract. The courts should be viewing labour contracts as essentially the same as normal contracts. That process is not helped by having an Employment Court.

It is not, however, simply a matter of abolishing the Employment Court. A remarkable split judgment of the Court of Appeal last year, in a case involving Brighouse Ltd, showed that even our Court of Appeal was prepared to disregard in cavalier fashion the spirit of the Employment Contracts Act. In the Brighouse case the Appeal Court upheld a judgment of the Employment Court that had read redundancy terms into an employment contract containing no mention whatsoever of redundancy. It is unlikely this judgment will be the last controversial decision from our courts; they will most likely continue to chip away at the principles in the Employment Contracts Act. We need to amend the Employment Contracts Act so that it more unambiguously stresses the paramountcy of freedom to contract in labour relations. Better still, we should replace the Employment Contracts Act with legislation similar to the statute I placed on the Cabinet table back in 1990.

SECURITY FOR ALL CITIZENS

There is one final area of public policy in which we still face major challenges: personal security. Like most western countries, New Zealand has experienced a substantial rise in crime over the last generation. Violent crime is now an especially pressing problem. Those who commit violence to themselves are increasingly looking to commit violence to others. Those who abuse themselves with drink and drugs are increasingly liable to abuse others. Crime hurts the well-off, but it hurts the poor far more. In some neighbourhoods, increasing contempt for the law is a major factor detracting from personal well-being. It creates fear and suspicion, inhibits social interaction and weakens a sense of community. Crime has a multitude of causes, but its effects are clear enough.

New Zealand has one of the highest imprisonment rates in the world. We spend very large resources combating crime. Yet there is little sign the government's existing strategy is working, or even that it has a strategy at all. Crime is not one of those problems that will simply go away. If our policymakers fail to tackle the problem, our crime levels will remain a serious reproach to our society.

Many of the policies recommended in this book should assist in lowering crime. The initiatives to discourage welfare dependency and eliminate barriers to job creation would undoubtedly help. So should the policy to boost the quality of our education system by introducing vouchers. But we would be naive to imagine measures such as these would alone be sufficient. Too many people today simply do not respect the law, from the repeatedly delinquent teenager to the white-collar fraudster. That lack of respect is further reinforced by what the offenders think is a high probability of escaping detection and a low risk of being asked to pay any sort of price for the crime.

Technology can help. The deadly accuracy of DNA testing and matching improves immeasurably the prospect of violent crime being met with punishment. The incentives on criminals must change radically as the scientific certainty of being caught and successfully prosecuted is perfected. And then we need to ensure that punishment really does fit the crime.

Sadly, we need to stiffen sanctions at all levels of the penal system. It is time we paid more attention to the needs of the law-abiding majority, and less attention to the needs of those who break the social contract by infringing the law.

We need to make much more imaginative use of sanctions. Prisons as presently constituted are successful only in taking people out of the community for the period they are serving a sentence, during which time the criminal is allowed to congregate freely with other criminals. The record of prisons on the habilitation of prisoners is very poor, and so is their record of deterrence. We should not be afraid to use community-based sentences for minor or first-time offences, in order to keep people out of prison. But where committal to prison is appropriate, the prison environment should be substantially altered in a way that reinforces deterrence and encourages habilitation. The current penal philosophy is that a person's punishment consists merely of their being deprived of their freedom. That needs to change so that it is the way in which the sentence is served that is regarded as the punishment. An austerity programme should be devised so that a prison sentence means something rather more than an enforced spell of idleness in insalubrious company. Under austerity, a prison sentence would mean real deprivation. At the same time, we should be putting much more effort into devising programmes to reorient prisoners and ready them for their eventual return to society.

To combat crime we need to become smarter across a wide range of public policies. One area with substantial room for improvement is policing. In the past, police effectiveness has suffered from a poor ability to focus on the outputs produced by the policing system. When Minister of Finance, I found discussion of the police vote still substantially conducted in terms of inputs. For instance, National implemented a policy of increasing police numbers by 900. I never felt confident that ministers were in a position to evaluate the outputs produced by the police or make decisions about their relative priority. The police were in no hurry to help ministers take an output approach, while we as ministers failed to call them fully to account. That needs to change.

CONCLUSION: REFOCUSING GOVERNMENT

The New Zealand reform programme has seen big changes to the manner in which the government conducts economic and social policy. Not only have the rules governing private-sector behaviour changed fundamentally, but the government itself has moved away from directly providing many goods and services. Yet these changes are far from complete: in some areas of social policy they have scarcely begun.

We need to continue the process of refocusing government. There are few, if any, areas where the state should be a provider of goods and services. For this reason, we need to complete the privatisation of SOEs. We should also transfer to the private sector the government's current provider functions in social services. The government does not need to own services in order to ensure their consumption. In housing, health and education the government holds major assets that could be better managed in the private sector.

Under my proposals the government would retain a crucial role as funder of social services and setter of standards – as payer of the accommodation supplement or education voucher, as purchaser of health services for those remaining under the RHA umbrella, as regulator of the health system and as the setter of standards in education. These are fundamental roles of a government. By taking provision out of the hands of government, we would enable it to concentrate – indeed would force government to concentrate – on the really crucial questions of social delivery. What outcomes in schools should we regard as basic and universally enforceable? What is a fair allocation of education funding between children of widely different socioeconomic status? How should health-care plans be regulated? What should be the rules for determining how much of their share of RHA funding a person wishing to 'opt out' can take with them? We will find a number of these questions difficult – even novel. But that just shows we have not been asking the right questions in the past.

Almost everything I am recommending involves greater choice for individuals, or a greater reliance on individual initiative. I make no apology for that. The individual has for too long taken second place to a misconceived collectivism. Collectivism has been one of the most melancholy themes of our century. In New Zealand we escaped – though we lost lives fighting – the horrific versions of collectivism that arose in Europe in the early decades of the century. We did not escape a kinder, gentler collectivism that took opportunities and responsibilities that should have been ours as individuals, and vested them in government. We did not escape the paternalism that assumed the government knew more than ordinary individuals, and could do things better. New Zealanders suffered inferior economic performance, reduced vitality, a sapping of the spirit. Our new economic renaissance is based on the initiative and enterprise of the individual. So can be our social renaissance. That is our challenge for the 21st century.

APPENDIX

New Zealand now probably boasts the best framework for monetary and fiscal policies of anywhere in the world.

The Economist, 1 April 1995

RESERVE BANK OF NEW ZEALAND POLICY TARGETS AGREEMENT

This agreement replaces that signed under section 9(2) of the Reserve Bank of New Zealand Act 1989 (the Act) on 2 March 1990.

In terms of section 9(4) of the Act, the Minister of Finance (the Minister) and the Governor of the Reserve Bank of New Zealand (the Governor) agree as follows:

1 Price Stability Target

Consistent with section 8 of the Act and with the provisions of this agreement, the Reserve Bank shall formulate and implement monetary policy with the intention of achieving a stable general level of prices by the year ending December 1993 and maintaining price stability beyond that date.

2 Measurement of Price Stability

(a) In pursuing the objective of a stable general level of prices, the Bank will monitor prices as measured by a range of price indices. The formal price stability target will be defined in terms of the All Groups Consumers Price Index (CPI), being the measure that is monitored most closely by the public.

(b) For the purposes of this agreement, annual rises in the CPI of between 0 and 2 per cent will be considered consistent with price stability.

(c) The CPI is unusual amongst OECD consumer price indices in its treatment of housing costs. The Bank is to continue to publish quarterly its housing-adjusted (consumer) price index (HAPI), which incorporates a different approach to the measurement of housing costs compared with the CPI.

3 Deviations from the Targets

(a) There is a range of possible price shocks arising from external sources, certain government policy changes, or a natural crisis which are quite outside the direct influence of monetary policy. The Bank shall generally react to such shifts in relative prices in a manner which prevents general inflationary pressures emerging.

(b) This approach means that the CPI inflation rate can be expected to move outside the 0-2 per cent range in response to particular shocks. The principal shocks are considered to be:

- significant changes in the terms of trade arising from an increase or decrease in either import or export prices;

- an increase or decrease in the rate of GST, or a significant change in other indirect tax rates;

- a crisis such as a natural disaster or a major disease-induced fall in livestock numbers which is expected to have a significant impact on the price level;

- a significant price level impact arising from changes to government or local authority levies; and

- a significant divergence between the CPI and HAPI inflation rates.

(c) In the event of such shocks, the Reserve Bank shall be fully accountable for its handling of the price effects, and, in particular, for any movements outside the 0-2 per cent band. In each Policy Statement made under section 15 of the Act, the Bank shall detail fully its estimate of the direct price impact of any such shock and the impact on the Bank's achievement of the price stability target. The Bank shall also detail what measures it has taken, or proposes to take, to ensure that the effects of such shocks on the inflation rate are transitory.

4 Renegotiation of the Targets

The policy targets are established on the understanding that the monetary policy instruments available to the Bank are adequate to achieve the objective. The Governor shall inform the Minister if he considers that any changes in these policy instruments impair the effective conduct of monetary policy. The Minister and the Governor may then set new policy targets.

5 Implementation

(a) The Bank shall implement monetary policy in a sustainable, consistent and transparent manner.

(b) Each Policy Statement released by the Bank under section 15 of the Act shall contain a statement of how the Bank proposes to formulate and implement monetary policy to ensure that the price stability is achieved and maintained over the succeeding five years. The Policy Statement should also contain a projected path for inflation for each of the years until the price stability target is achieved.

Ruth Richardson
Minister of Finance

Donald T. Brash
Governor
Reserve Bank of New Zealand

19 December 1990

ANALYSIS

1994, No. 17

An Act to improve the conduct of fiscal policy by specifying principles of responsible fiscal management and by strengthening the reporting requirements of the Crown and, in particular,—

(a) By requiring the Minister of Finance to report regularly to the House of Representatives on the extent to which the Government's fiscal policy is consistent with the specified principles of responsible fiscal management and to justify in his or her report any departures made by the Government from those principles; and

(b) By requiring all the Crown's financial reporting to be in accordance with generally accepted accounting practice; and

(c) By requiring the Minister of Finance—

(i) To publish, at least 3 months before the start of each financial year, a budget policy statement containing the Government's long-term objectives for fiscal policy, its broad strategic priorities for the Budget for that financial year, and its fiscal intentions for that and the next 2 financial years; and

(ii) To lay before the House of Representatives, on the day on which the first Appropriation Bill relating to a financial year is introduced, a fiscal strategy report assessing the consistency of the Budget with the budget policy statement and providing progress outlooks for the next 10 years, and an economic and fiscal update prepared by the Treasury for the next 3 years; and

(iii) To publish, in December of each financial year, an economic and fiscal update prepared by the Treasury for the next 3 years; and

(iv) To publish, before each general election, an economic and fiscal update prepared by the Treasury for the next 3 years; and

(v) To lay before the House of Representatives, towards the end of each financial year, a fiscal update prepared by the Treasury for that year, including forecast estimated actual financial statements for the Crown

[27 June 1994

BE IT ENACTED by the Parliament of New Zealand as follows:

1. Short Title and commencement—(1) This Act may be cited as the Fiscal Responsibility Act 1994.

(2) This Act shall come into force on the 1st day of July 1994.

2. Interpretation—(1) In this Act, unless the context otherwise requires, "Budget", in relation to a financial year, includes—

(a) The statement delivered by the Minister when moving the second reading of the first Appropriation Bill relating to that financial year; and

(b) The fiscal strategy report laid before the House of Representatives under section 7 (1) of this Act for that financial year; and

(c) The report containing an economic and fiscal update laid before the House of Representatives under section 8 (1) of this Act for that financial year; and

(d) The Estimates laid before the House of Representatives under section 9 (1) of the Public Finance Act 1989 for that financial year.

(2) In this Act, unless the context otherwise requires, the terms "commitment", "contingent liability", "Crown", "department", "expenses", "financial year", "generally accepted accounting practice", "Government", "Minister", "Secretary", and "Treasury" have the meanings given to them by section 2 (1) of the Public Finance Act 1989.

3. Act to bind the Crown—This Act shall bind the Crown.

4. Principles of responsible fiscal management— (1) Subject to subsection (3) of this section, the Government shall pursue its policy objectives in accordance with the principles of responsible fiscal management specified in subsection (2) of this section.

(2) The principles of responsible fiscal management are—

(a) Reducing total Crown debt to prudent levels so as to provide a buffer against factors that may impact adversely on the level of total Crown debt in the future, by ensuring that, until such levels have been achieved, the total operating expenses of the Crown in each financial year are less than its total operating revenues in the same financial year; and

(b) Once prudent levels of total Crown debt have been achieved, maintaining these levels by ensuring that, on average, over a reasonable period of time, the total operating expenses of the Crown do not exceed its total operating revenues; and

(c) Achieving and maintaining levels of Crown net worth that provide a buffer against factors that may impact adversely on the Crown's net worth in the future; and

(d) Managing prudently the fiscal risks facing the Crown; and

(e) Pursuing policies that are consistent with a reasonable degree of predictability about the level and stability of tax rates for future years.

(3) The Government may depart from the principles of responsible fiscal management specified in subsection (2) of this section, but when the Government does so—

(a) Any such departure shall be temporary; and

(b) The Minister of Finance shall, in accordance with this Act, specify—

(i) The reasons for the Government's departure from those principles; and

(ii) The approach the Government intends to take to return to those principles; and

(iii) The period of time that the Government expects to take to return to those principles.

5. Generally accepted accounting practice—All financial statements included in reports required under this Act shall be prepared in accordance with generally accepted accounting practice.

6. Budget policy statement—(1) The Minister shall, not later than the 31st day of March in each year, cause to be published a budget policy statement.

(2) The budget policy statement shall specify the Government's long-term objectives for fiscal policy and, in particular, for the following variables:

(a) The Crown's total operating expenses; and

(b) The Crown's total operating revenues; and

(c) The balance between the Crown's total operating expenses and the Crown's total operating revenues; and

(d) The level of the Crown's total debt; and

(e) The level of the Crown's net worth,—

and shall explain how these long-term objectives accord with the principles of responsible fiscal management specified in section 4 (2) of this Act.

(3) The budget policy statement shall, for the financial year commencing on the 1st day of July after it is published and the 2 financial years following that financial year,—

(a) Specify the broad strategic priorities by which the Government will be guided in preparing the budget for that financial year; and

(b) Indicate explicitly, by the use of ranges, ratios, or other means, the Government's intentions regarding each of the variables specified in subsection (2) of this section.

(4) The budget policy statement shall—

(a) Assess the extent to which the intentions indicated under subsection (3) (b) of this section are consistent with the principles of responsible fiscal management specified in section 4 (2) of this Act and with the objectives specified under subsection (2) of this section; and

(b) Where the intentions indicated under subsection (3) (b) of this section are not consistent with the principles of responsible fiscal management specified in section 4 (2) of this Act or with the objectives specified under subsection (2) of this section or with both, specify—

(i) The reasons for the departure of those intentions from those principles or from those objectives or from both; and

(ii) The approach the Government intends to take to ensure that its intentions regarding each of the variables specified in subsection (2) of this section become consistent with those principles and those objectives; and

(iii) The period of time that is expected to elapse before the Government's intentions regarding each of the variables specified in subsection (2) of this section become consistent with those principles and those objectives.

(5) The budget policy statement shall—

(a) Assess the consistency of the objectives specified under subsection (2) of this section with the objectives specified in—

(i) The immediately preceding budget policy statement; or

(ii) Where the objectives specified in the immediately preceding budget policy statement were amended in the report most recently prepared under section 7 of this Act, the objectives specified in that report; and

(b) Where the objectives specified under subsection (2) of this section are not consistent with those in the immediately preceding budget policy statement or in the report most recently prepared under section 7 of this Act, justify the departure of the objectives specified under subsection (2) of this section from those in that immediately preceding budget policy statement or in that report.

(6) The budget policy statement shall—

(a) Assess the consistency of the intentions indicated under subsection (3) (b) of this section with the intentions indicated in—

(i) The immediately preceding budget policy statement; or

(ii) Where the intentions indicated in the immediately preceding budget policy statement were amended in the report most recently prepared under section 7 of this Act, the intentions indicated in that report; and

(b) Where the intentions indicated under subsection (3) (b) of this section are not consistent with those in the immediately preceding budget policy statement or in the report most recently prepared under section 7 of this Act, justify the departure of the intentions indicated under subsection (3) (b) of this section from those in that immediately preceding budget policy statement or in that report.

(7) The Minister shall not later than 3 sitting days after the date of the publication of a budget policy statement under subsection (1) of this section, lay a copy of the statement before the House of Representatives.

7. **Fiscal strategy report**—(1) The Minister shall, for each financial year, after the introduction of the first Appropriation Bill relating to that financial year, but on the day of the introduction of that Bill, lay before the House of Representatives a report on the Government's fiscal strategy.

(2) The fiscal strategy report shall include—

(a) An assessment of the extent to which the report containing an economic and fiscal update being laid before the House of Representatives under section 8 (1) of this Act is consistent with the intentions indicated under section 6 (3) (b) of this Act in the budget policy statement most recently published under section 6 (1) of this Act; and

(b) Where the economic and fiscal update departs from the intentions indicated under section 6 (3) (b) of this Act in that budget policy statement, an explanation of the reasons for the departure; and

(c) Where the Government's intentions under section 6 (3) (b) of this Act have changed from those indicated in that budget policy statement, an amended version of the intentions required by section 6 (3) (b) of this Act.

(3) The fiscal strategy report shall also include—

(a) Progress outlooks that—

(i) Include projections of trends in the variables specified in section 6 (2) of this Act, which projections shall illustrate, for stated significant assumptions, likely future progress towards achieving the longer-term fiscal strategy and objectives specified in the budget policy statement most recently published under section 6 (1) of this Act; and

(ii) Explain the reasons for any significant differences from previous progress outlooks; and

(b) An assessment of the consistency of the progress outlooks with the objectives specified under section 6 (2) of this Act in the budget policy statement most recently published under section 6 (1) of this Act; and

(c) Where the progress outlooks depart from the objectives specified under section 6 (2) of this Act in that budget policy statement, an explanation of the reasons for the departure; and

(d) Where the Government's objectives under section 6 (2) of this Act have changed from those specified in that budget policy statement, an amended version of the objectives required by section 6 (2) of this Act (which version shall accord with the principles of responsible fiscal management specified in section 4 (2) of this Act).

(4) The projections required by subsection (3) (a) (i) of this section shall relate to a period of 10 or more consecutive financial years commencing with the financial year to which the Appropriation Bill relates.

8. Economic and fiscal update—(1) The Minister shall for each financial year, after the introduction of the first Appropriation Bill relating to that financial year, but on the day of the introduction of that Bill, lay before the House of Representatives a report containing an economic and fiscal update prepared by the Treasury.

(2) The update shall contain economic and fiscal forecasts relating to the financial year to which the Appropriation Bill relates and to each of the following 2 financial years.

(3) The update shall contain a statement specifying the day on which the contents of the update were finalised, or the days on which the contents of different specified aspects of the update were finalised.

9. Economic forecasts—(1) The economic forecasts contained in the update shall, for each of the 3 financial years to which they relate, include forecasts of movements in New Zealand's—

(a) Gross domestic product, including the major components of gross domestic product:

(b) Consumer prices:

(c) Unemployment and employment:

(d) Current account position of the balance of payments.

(2) The economic forecasts shall also include a statement of all significant assumptions underlying them.

10. Fiscal forecasts—(1) The fiscal forecasts contained in the update shall, for each of the 3 financial years to which they relate, include forecast financial statements for the Crown.

(2) The forecast financial statements for trhe Crown shall include—

(a) A statement of the forecast financial position of the Crown at the balance date for each of those financial years:

(b) An operating statement reflecting the forecast revenue and expenses of the Crown for each of those financial years:

(c) A statement of the cash flows reflecting forecast cash flows of the Crown for each of those financial years:

(d) A statement of borrowings reflecting the forecast borrowing activities of the Crown for each of those financial years:

(e) Such other statements as are necessary to fairly reflect the forecast financial operations of the Crown for each of those financial years and its forecast financial position at the end of each of those financial years.

(3) The forecast financial statements for the Crown shall also include—

(a) A statement of commitments of the Crown as at the day on which the forecast financial statements are finalised (other than the commitments included in the statements prepared under subsection (2) of this section):

(b) A statement of specific fiscal risks of the Crown as at the day on which the forecast financial statements are finalised, being the fiscal risks in relation to—

(i) The Government decisions and other circumstances required by section 11 of this Act to be incorporated in the economic and fiscal update; and

(ii) Any other contingent liabilities of the Crown, including any guarantees or indemnities given under any Act:

(c) A statement of all significant accounting policies, including any changes from the accounting policies contained in the annual financial statements of the Crown most recently laid before the House of Representatives or published under section 31 of the Public Finance Act 1989:

(d) In relation to each statement required by paragraphs (a) to (d) of subsection (2) of this section and, where appropriate, in relation to any statement required by paragraph (3) of that subsection,—

(i) Comparative budgeted and estimated actual figures for the financial year immediately before the first of the financial years to which the fiscal forecasts relate; and

(ii) Comparative actual figures for the financial year 2 years before the first of the financial years to which the fiscal forecasts relate.

(4) The forecast financial statements for the Crown shall be for the same reporting entity as the annual financial statements for the Crown to be prepared under section 27 of the Public Finance Act 1989 for the first of the financial years to which the fiscal forecasts relate.

(5) The fiscal forecasts shall also include a statement of all significant assumptions underlying them.

11. Disclosure of policy decisions and other matters that may influence future fiscal situation—(1) Every economic and fiscal update prepared under section 8 (1) or section 13 (1) or section 14 (1) of this Act shall incorporate to the fullest extent possible consistent with subsection (4) of this section all Government decisions and all other circumstances that may have a material effect on the fiscal and economic outlook.

(2) Where the fiscal implications of Government decisions and other circumstances referred to in subsection (1) of this section can be quantified for particular years with reasonable certainty by the day on which the forecast financial statements for the Crown

are finalised, the quantified implications of those Government decisions and other circumstances shall be included in the forecast financial statements for the Crown.

(3) Where the fiscal implications of the Government decisions and other circumstances referred to in subsection (1) of this section cannot be quantified for or assigned to particular years with reasonable certainty by the day on which the forecast financial statements for the Crown are finalised, those Government decisions and other circumstances shall be disclosed in the statement of specific fiscal risks of the Crown required by section 10 (3) (b) of this Act.

(4) Subsection (1) of this section and section 10 (2) (e) of this Act shall not apply to a decision, circumstance, or statement where the Minister determines that—

(a) To incorporate that decision, circumstance, or statement in an economic and fiscal update is likely—

(i) To prejudice the substantial economic interests of New Zealand; or

(ii) To prejudice the security or defence of New Zealand or the international relations of the Government; or

(iii) To compromise the Crown in a material way in negotiation, litigation, or commercial activity; or

(iv) To result in material loss of value to the Crown; and

(b) There is no reasonable or prudent way the Government can avoid this prejudice, compromise, or material loss—

(i) In the case of a circumstance, by making a decision before the day on which the forecast financial statements for the Crown are finalised; or

(ii) In the case of a decision or circumstance, by incorporating in the update the fiscal implications of that decision or circumstance, or the nature of that decision or circumstance but without reference to its fiscal implications; or

(iii) In the case of a statement, by incorporating that statement in the update.

12. Statement of responsibility—Every economic and fiscal update prepared under section 8 (1) or section 13 (1) or section 14 (1) of this Act shall be accompanied by a statement of responsibility signed by the Minister and the Secretary and comprising—

(a) A statement by the Minister that all policy decisions with material economic or fiscal implications that the Government has made before the day on which the contents of the update or of the relevant aspect of the update were finalised, and all other circumstances with material economic or fiscal implications of which the Minister was aware before that day have been communicated to the Secretary; and

(b) A statement by the Secretary that the Treasury has supplied to the Minister, using its best professional judgment on the basis of economic and fiscal information available to it before the day on which the contents of the update or of the relevant aspect of the update were finalised, an economic and fiscal update incorporating the fiscal and economic implications of those decisions and circumstances, but not incorporating any decisions, circumstances, or statements that the Minister has determined under section 11 (4) of this Act should not be incorporated in that update; and

(c) A statement of the Minister's responsibility—

(i) For the integrity of the disclosures contained in the update; and

(ii) For the consistency with the requirements of this Act of the information contained in the update; and

(iii) For the omission from the update under section 11 (4) of this Act of any decision, circumstance, or statement.

13. Half-year economic and fiscal update—(1) Subject to subsection (3) of this section, the Minister shall, not earlier than the 1st day of December nor later than the 31st day of December in each financial year, cause to be published a report containing an economic and fiscal update prepared by the Treasury.

(2) The economic and fiscal update shall—

(a) Include the information required by sections 8 (2), 8 (3), 9, 10, and 11 of this Act, except that the reference to estimated actual figures in section 10 (3) (d) (i) of this Act shall be read as if it were a reference to actual figures, and the actual figures required by section 10 (3) (d) (ii) of this Act shall not be required; and

(b) Be accompanied by the statement of responsibility required under section 12 of this Act.

(3) The Minister shall not be required to cause a report to be published under subsection (1) of this section in any financial year if, in that part of that financial year beginning on the 1st day of October and ending with the 31st day of December, an economic and fiscal update—

(a) Has been published under section 14 of this Act; or

(b) Is required to be published under section 14 of this Act.

(4) The Minister shall, not later than 3 sitting days after the publication of a report under subsection (1) of this section, lay a copy of the report before the House of Representatives.

14. Pre-election economic and fiscal update—(1) The Minister shall, except as provided in subsection (4) of this section, cause to be published, not earlier than 42 days, nor later than 28 days, before the day appointed as polling day in relation to any general election of members of Parliament, a report containing an economic and fiscal update prepared by the Treasury.

(2) The economic and fiscal update shall,—

(a) Except as provided in subsection (3) of this section, include the information required by sections 8 (2), 8 (3), 9, 10, and 11 of this Act to be included in the economic and fiscal update prepared under section 8 (1) of this Act; and

(b) Be accompanied by the statement of responsibility required by section 12 of this Act.

(3) Where, before the day on which an economic and fiscal update is required to be published under this section, the annual financial statements of the Crown for the financial year immediately before the first of the financial years to which the fiscal forecasts relate have been laid before the House of Representatives or published under section 31 of the Public Finance Act 1989, the reference to estimated actual figures in section 10 (3) (d) (i) of this Act shall be read as if it were a reference to actual figures, and the actual figures required by section 10 (3) (d) (ii) of this Act shall not be required.

(4) Where the day of the dissolution of Parliament is less than 35 days before the day appointed as polling day in relation to the general election of members of the House of Representatives, the Minister shall cause the economic and fiscal update required to be published under this section to be published not later than 14 days after the day of the dissolution of Parliament.

(5) The Minister shall, not later than 3 sitting days after the first meeting of the new

Parliament, lay before the House of Representatives a copy of the report published under this section.

15. Current-year fiscal update—(1) The Minister shall, on the introduction of the first Appropriation Bill after the last day of March in each financial year, not being an Appropriation Bill that deals solely with matters relating to a previous financial year, lay before the House of Representatives a report containing a fiscal update for that financial year prepared by the Treasury.

(2) The update shall contain fiscal forecasts for that financial year and a statement of all significant assumptions underlying them.

(3) The fiscal forecast shall include forecast estimated actual financial statements for the Crown for that financial year including—

(a) A statement of the forecast estimated actual position of the Crown at the balance date:

(b) An operating statement reflecting the forecast estimated actual revenue and expenses of the Crown for that financial year:

(c) A statement of cash flows reflecting forecast estimated actual cash flows of the Crown for that financial year:

(d) A statement of borrowings reflecting the forecast borrowing activities of the Crown for that financial year:

(e) A statement of all significant accounting policies, including any changes from those contained in the annual financial statements of the Crown most recently laid before the House of Representatives or published under section 31 of the Public Finance Act 1989:

(f) Such other statements as are necessary to fairly reflect the forecast estimated actual financial operations of the Crown for that year and its forecast estimated actual financial position at the end of that financial year:

(g) In relation of each statement required by paragraphs (a) to (d) of this subsection and, where appropriate, by paragraph (f) of this subsection, comparative budgeted and actual figures for the previous financial year.

(4) The forecast financial statements for the Crown to be prepared under subsection (3) of this section shall be for the same reporting entity as the annual financial statements for the Crown to be prepared under section 27 of the Public Finance Act 1989 for the financial year to which the fiscal forecasts relate.

16. Referral to select committee—There shall stand referred to any committee of the House of Representatives responsible for the overall review of financial management in government departments and other public bodies—

(a) Every budget policy statement published under section 6 (1) of this Act:

(b) Every fiscal strategy report laid before the House of Representatives under section 7 (1) of this Act:

(c) Every report laid before the House of Representatives under section 8 (1) of this Act:

(d) Every report published under section 13 (1) or section 14 of this Act:

(e) Every report laid before the House of Representatives under section 15 (1) of this Act.

17. Publication, inspection, and purchase of statements and reports—(1) The

Minister shall, in respect of every statement or report referred to in section 16 of this Act, arrange for publication in the *Gazette* of a notice—

(a) Indicating, where the statement or report is published in advance of being laid before the House of Representatives, that the statement or report has been published; and

(b) Showing a place at which copies of the statement or report are available for inspection free of charge; and

(c) Showing a place at which copies of the statement or report are available for purchase.

(2) The Secretary shall, for at least 6 months after the date of the publication of the notice required by subsection (1) of this section, cause copies of the statement or report referred to in that notice to be available—

(a) For inspection by members of the public free of charge; and

(b) For purchase by members of the public.

18. Power of Secretary to obtain information—(1) The Secretary may from time to time request any department or any entity mentioned in section 27 (3) of the Public Finance Act 1989, or any entity that manages an asset or liability of the Crown, to supply to the Secretary such information as is necessary to enable the preparation of any of the fiscal forecasts referred to in sections 8, 10, 11, 13, 14, and 15 of this Act.

(2) Any request under subsection (1) of this section may specify the date by which and the manner in which the information requested is to be provided.

(3) Where a date is specified under subsection (2) of this section, that date shall be reasonable having regard to the time limits prescribed by this Act for the laying before the House of Representatives, or the publishing, of the report for which the information is being requested.

(4) Where any request under subsection (1) of this section is made to a department or entity, that request shall be in writing and that department or entity shall comply with that request.

19. Transitional provision—(1) The fiscal strategy report required to be laid before the House of Representatives under section 7 (1) of this Act for the financial year commencing on the 1st day of July 1994 shall include—

(a) The long-term objectives required by section 6 (2) of this Act and an explanation of how those long-term objectives accord with the principles of responsible fiscal management specified in section 4 (2) of this Act; and

(b) The intentions required by section 6 (3) (b) of this Act; and

(c) Progress outlooks that include projections of trends in the variables specified in section 6 (2) of this Act, which projections shall illustrate, for stated significant assumptions, likely future progress towards achieving the long-term objectives included under paragraph (a) of this subsection.

(2) Subsections (2) and (3) of section 7 of this Act shall not apply to the fiscal strategy report to which subsection (1) of this section applies.

(3) Subsection (4) of section 7 of this Act shall apply to the fiscal strategy report to which subsection (1) of this section applies as if the reference in section 7 (4) of this Act to subsection 3 (a) (i) of section 7 of this Act were a reference to subsection (1) (c) of this section.

This Act is administered in the Treasury.

INDEX